Lesson Planning for Elementary Physical Education

Meeting the National Standards & Grade-Level Outcomes

Shirley Holt/Hale

Tina Hall

SHAPE America | SOCIETY OF HEALTH AND PHYSICAL EDUCATORS®

health. moves. minds.

Human Kinetics

Library of Congress Cataloging-in-Publication Data

Names: Holt/Hale, Shirley Ann, author. | Hall, Tina J., author.
Title: Lesson planning for elementary physical education : meeting the
national standards & grade-level outcomes / Shirley Holt/Hale, PhD, Tina
Hall, PhD.
Description: Reston, VA : SHAPE, America Society of Health and Physical
Educators, [2016] | Includes bibliographical references.
Identifiers: LCCN 2015032747 | ISBN 9781492513780 (print)
Subjects: LCSH: Physical education and training--Study and teaching
(Elementary)--United States. | Physical education and
training--Curricula--United States. | Lesson planning.
Classification: LCC GV362 .H65 2016 | DDC 372.86--dc23 LC record available at http://lccn.loc.gov/2015032747

ISBN: 978-1-4925-1378-0 (print)

The authors wish to acknowledge Lynn MacDonald for contributing ideas for chapter 1 of this book.

Appendix A is reprinted, by permission, from SHAPE America, 2014, *National standards & grade-level outcomes for K-12 physical education* (Champaign, IL: Human Kinetics), 66-69.

The web addresses cited in this text were current as of September 15, 2015, unless otherwise noted.

Acquisitions Editor: Ray Vallese; **SHAPE America Editor:** Joe McGavin; **Senior Developmental Editor:** Bethany J. Bentley; **Copyeditor:** Bob Replinger; **Permissions Manager:** Dalene Reeder; **Senior Graphic Designer:** Joe Buck; **Cover Designer:** Keith Blomberg; **Photograph (cover):** © Human Kinetics; **Photographs (interior):** p. 14 © Human Kinetics; pp. 1, 3, 5, 11, 21, 47, 137 courtesy of Jim Davis; pp. 17, 19, 23, 73, 99 © Shirley Holt/Hale; **Photo Asset Manager:** Laura Fitch; **Photo Production Manager:** Jason Allen; **Senior Art Manager:** Kelly Hendren; **Associate Art Manager:** Alan L. Wilborn; **Illustrations:** © Human Kinetics; **Printer:** Total Printing Systems

SHAPE America – Society of Health and Physical Educators
1900 Association Drive
Reston, VA 20191
800-213-7193
www.shapeamerica.org

Printed in the United States of America   10 9 8 7 6 5 4

The paper in this book is certified under a sustainable forestry program.

Human Kinetics
1607 N. Market Street
Champaign, IL 61820
USA

United States and International
Website: **US.HumanKinetics.com**
Email: info@hkusa.com
Phone: 1-800-747-4457

Canada
Website: **Canada.HumanKinetics.com**
Email: info@hkcanada.com

E6625

Tell us what you think!
Human Kinetics would love to hear what we
can do to improve the customer experience.
Use this QR code to take our brief survey.

Contents

Kicking

Dribbling With Hands

Volleying

Striking With Short Implements

Striking With Long Implements

Jumping Rope

Preface

The purpose of this book is to provide physical educators at the elementary school level with guidance on designing lessons that are aligned with the National Standards for K–12 Physical Education and their accompanying Grade-Level Outcomes (SHAPE America, 2014) and that will steer students toward becoming physically literate individuals. The lesson plans contained in the book, along with the lesson-planning guidance, lay the foundation for middle and high school physical education, with full alignment to the National Standards and Grade-Level Outcomes.

ORGANIZATION

Lesson Planning for Elementary Physical Education: Meeting the National Standards & Grade-Level Outcomes is designed to assist you as a teacher of children in elementary physical education in meeting the Grade-Level Outcomes and, thus, the National Standards for Physical Education. Although teachers have a tendency to read quickly or even skip over the introductory chapters and move immediately to the lesson plans, the first three chapters of this book are important. These chapters set the foundation for a solid curriculum of physical education by exploring student learning, revisiting key concepts from the National Standards text, and providing assistance in teaching across the standards (i.e., embedding outcomes).

Chapter 1 presents an overview of the book, as well as guidance on how to use it for maximum efficiency and benefit in your teaching. Chapter 2 centers on the Grade-Level Outcomes for elementary physical education and the importance of assessment in physical education. Chapter 3 is written for a functional, working understanding of the concept of embedding skills within skills, concepts within concepts, and standards within standards.

Chapters 4 through 8 contain 65 lessons with 250 total learning experiences for teaching elementary physical education that align with the Grade-Level Outcomes. The lessons are designed to encompass the Grade-Level Outcomes for the foundational skills of physical education (Standard 1), movement concepts and the tactics and strategies applicable to elementary physical education (Standard 2), appropriate health-related fitness for children (Standard 3), and personal and social responsibility (Standard 4). The importance of recognizing the value of physical activity is addressed through Standard 5. The lesson plans are designed to move children from an introductory understanding of the skill or concept to a functional understanding of it so that they can demonstrate the concept or perform the skill successfully.

The lesson plans in chapters 4 through 8 are organized by the types of skills addressed. Chapter 4 addresses health-related fitness for children. Lessons explore the concept of fitness, the components of fitness, fitness assessment, nutrition, and physical activity. Chapter 5 focuses on movement concepts, including moving in self-space and general space, directions, pathways, levels, shapes, time, force, and flow. Chapter 6 centers on the locomotor skills of hopping, galloping, sliding, running, skipping, leaping, and jumping and landing. Chapter 7 relates to the nonlocomotor skills of balancing, transferring weight, and the actions of stretching, curling, and twisting. Chapter 8 covers the manipulative skills of throwing, catching, dribbling with hands and feet, kicking, volleying, striking with short and long implements, and jumping rope.

Appendix A contains a Scope and Sequence for K-12 Physical Education chart from *National Standards & Grade-Level Outcomes for K-12 Physical Education* (SHAPE America, 2014, p. 65). The chart provides a quick visual representation of skill progression: when to introduce the skills and concepts detailed in the Grade-Level Outcomes and when students might be expected to master the critical elements of the skills. *Emerging* indicates the grade levels when skills and knowledge should be introduced and practiced. *Maturing* indicates when students should be able to demonstrate the critical elements of the skills or expected knowledge while continuing to refine them. Finally, *applying* indicates the grade level at which students should be able to demonstrate the critical elements of the skills or expected knowledge in a variety of physical activity settings.

Lesson planning is the key to attaining the Grade-Level Outcomes; curriculum mapping, both vertical and horizontal, is the key to that planning. . Both vertical and horizontal planning are essential if your students are to meet the outcomes, which represent the benchmarks of physical education. The outcomes provide the vertical mapping for planning lessons across the grade levels, kindergarten through grade 5. Horizontal mapping provides the planning for the school year for each grade level. The number of times per week allotted for instructional physical education, and your students' needs and background experiences will affect your yearly planning and your students' attainment of the Grade-Level Outcomes. Appendix B provides a sample yearly plan to assist you with this critical component of teaching for student learning.

CONTENT OF THE LESSONS

The lesson plans in this book have been written by practitioners with a combined 55 years of teaching elementary physical education. The lessons center on one or more Grade-Level Outcomes, providing deliberate, progressive practice tasks; integrating appropriate assessments to evaluate and monitor student progress; and including resources, references, equipment lists, and student assignments, as appropriate.

Each lesson reflects best practices in instruction, providing you with the means to enhance your effectiveness in delivering lesson content. The focus is on you as an educator, not a manager of activity. In that role, you must be fully engaged in evaluating student learning and adjusting learning experiences to achieve desired outcomes. Instructional strategies may include pointers such as teaching for transfer, differentiating instruction for varying ability levels, and integrating conceptual material.

Although this book is intended to address a wide range of the elementary Grade-Level Outcomes, it does not cover every possible experience that you could use to achieve the outcomes. The sample lessons are not intended to be used as a complete curriculum; they are designed to be models that you may use as written or with some modification to fit the needs of your students and community. The lessons also provide a structure for you to follow in developing your own learning experiences and curricula.

WEB RESOURCE

This book features a web resource that includes all the lesson plans in PDF form, found at www.HumanKinetics.com/LessonPlanningForElementaryPhysical Education. The web resource allows you to access the lesson plans on a computer or mobile device while in class or download the files to your device in advance.

Additionally, you'll find a blank version of the lesson plan template that you can adapt to suit your own unique needs.

Helping students attain physical literacy requires high-quality lesson content, effective instruction, and maximized practice opportunities. This book provides you with the tools and resources you need to guide your students toward physical literacy and physically active lifestyles throughout their adult lives.

eBook
available at
HumanKinetics.com

OUR COMMITMENT: 50 MILLION STRONG BY 2029

Approximately 50 million students are currently enrolled in America's elementary and secondary schools (grades pre-K to 12). SHAPE America is leading the effort to ensure that by the time today's preschoolers graduate from high school in 2029, all of America's students will have developed the skills, knowledge and confidence to enjoy healthy, meaningful physical activity.

Foundations of Lesson Planning

CHAPTER 1

Planning Lessons for Student Learning

This book is designed to complement *National Standards & Grade-Level Out-comes for K-12 Physical Education* (SHAPE America, 2014) and help you develop and implement lesson plans that will lead your students to attain the Grade-Level Outcomes. The standards and outcomes are intended to culminate in physically literate individuals, that is, young adults who have "the knowledge, skills and confidence to enjoy a lifetime of healthful physical activity" (p. 11). As physical education teachers, we are ideally positioned to help students become physically literate. We can educate the whole person by providing learning experiences in the psychomotor, cognitive, and affective domains. We can provide high-quality physical education instruction, in which students demonstrate content mastery through formal assessment. The National Standards and Grade-Level Outcomes delineate the content that students should learn. Additionally, they provide a structure for developing learning experiences by describing what students should know and be able to do at the end of each grade level.

The lesson plans in this book are designed to align with the outcomes for elementary school (SHAPE America, 2014). Therefore, they present the founda-tional skills, knowledge, and values of physical education. You can implement the lesson plans in classes as they appear, or, more important, you can modify them to meet the unique needs of your students. Although the lesson plans in this text focus on the Grade-Level Outcomes for skills, knowledge, fitness, and so on, they are not, nor are they intended to be, a complete curriculum for everything to be taught. Instead, they serve as models for developing your lessons and learning experiences for your students, your school, and your community.

IMPORTANCE OF TEACHING FOR STUDENT LEARNING

National Standards & Grade-Level Outcomes for K-12 Physical Education (SHAPE America, 2014) provides important guidance for the teaching and learning process in physical education. The underlying premise of that document is that student learning is the essence of high-quality physical education. The standards and outcomes cannot be attained without student learning, and student learning cannot occur without effective lessons, learning experiences, and assessments.

As physical educators, we believe that physical education is a critical component of student development and the overall school curriculum. But we cannot support this position unless we take an education-centered approach, as opposed to a recreation- or public-health-centered approach, in our physical education programs. In an education-centered approach, student learning is the primary goal of instruction. Simply keeping students "busy, happy and good" (Placek, 1983) will not lead to physical literacy. Without instruction and learning, physical education diverges from the core mission of schools (Ennis, 2011) and is too easily marginalized. Physical education in elementary school has been marginalized by an increased focus on "core" academic subjects and the pressure to produce high scores on standardized tests. With ever-increasing accountability measures required in public education, physical educators must be prepared to both articulate and demonstrate what students have learned in physical education. Student learning is the essence of education; thus, student learning is the essence of physical education.

FACTORS INFLUENCING STUDENT LEARNING

Many factors influence student learning and the subsequent development of physical literacy. These elements include, but are not limited to, skill competency, student engagement, gender differences, and instructional environment (SHAPE America, 2014). Skilled children tend to be active children; skilled children tend to become physically active adults. Children as young as ages five and six who are proficient in motor skills are more physically active than their less-skilled peers (Kambas et al., 2012). Skilled middle school students are more active and more effective during game play than less-skilled students (Bernstein, Phillips, and Silverman, 2011). Fundamental motor skills and movement patterns form the foundation for physical activity. SHAPE America considers the development of motor skill competence to be the highest priority in its Grade-Level Outcomes (SHAPE America, 2014, p. 9). These skills require instruction from qualified teachers and practice under such teachers' direction (Strong et al., 2005, p. 736).

Motor skill competence is related to fitness in adolescence and adulthood (Barnett et al., 2008; Stodden, Langendorfer, and Roberton, 2009). Proficiency in motor skills leads to increased skillfulness in middle school, resulting in more options for physical activity participation and higher levels of health-related physical fitness and activity (Stodden et al., 2009, p. 228). Elementary physical educators play the most critical role in ensuring that all students develop motor skill competency through effective planning and teaching (lesson plans and instructional strategies).

Skill competency and perceived competency are both critical for student engagement and learning. When children believe that they have the skills to participate successfully in an activity, they approach it with more interest and confidence and are more willing to put effort into the task. When students do not believe that they have the skills to be successful, they are less likely to engage in the activity. Young children perceive themselves to be the fastest runners, the most skilled, and the best at every activity. In the later elementary years, interactions with peers, both cognitive and motor related, soon bring comparisons that can result in positive or negative perceptions of ability. Those social comparisons often occur in activities in which students perform individually while other students observe, as well as in competitive games or skill comparison situations. High-quality programs of elementary physical education, curriculum, and instruction develop skill competence for all students; and skill competence provides confidence, leading to healthful physical activity (i.e., physical literacy).

Elementary-age students observing an elimination game in physical education are not actively engaged in any kind of learning activity, nor are children standing in relay lines or waiting to be chosen for a team. Young children come to physical education eager to learn. Differenti-

Student growth and mastery are the results of deliberate practice.

ated instruction—matching the task to the ability of the learner—coupled with deliberate practice (Ericsson, Krampe, and Tesch-Romer 1993) focused on critical aspects of the skill, with congruent feedback, will result in total engagement in the learning. This deliberate practice sets the engagement aside from "mindless, routine performance and playful engagement" (Ericsson, 2006, p. 690).

Gender also plays a role in student learning. Male and female roles are defined early by societal factors, a situation that intensifies as students mature. Young girls' physical activity levels typically are lower than boys' are, and girls' activity levels drop off further in adolescence (Patnode et al., 2011). Traditional physical education, which has a focus on male-dominated sports, has not proven satisfactory for many adolescent females. Thus, it is important that you attend to gender differences and planning for positive learning experiences as early as the elementary school level. The foundational skills of elementary physical education and a maturing pattern of performance are the goals for all skills and for all students, male and female. The curriculum that you design must have the potential to engage all students, regardless of skill level or gender.

The challenge, then, is to create an instructional environment in physical education that maximizes student learning (i.e., skill development). A mastery-oriented instructional climate emphasizes skill acquisition and individual improvement over competition and comparison with others (Bevans et al., 2010; Gao, Lee, Ping, and Kosam, 2011). Mastery climates reflect effective teaching practices; progressive, sequential learning tasks are the core of the lesson plans. Teaching for a mastery climate requires you to maximize practice opportunities (deliberate and appropriate practice), adapt and modify instruction (differentiated instruction), and provide a positive, supportive environment for learning.

Implementing a mastery climate requires assessment. Both formal and informal assessments are necessary to measure student growth and mastery of the content. You should integrate assessment throughout the learning experiences to measure progress within and between lessons (formative) as well as cumulative learning at the end of the lesson series (summative). As the teacher, you are engaged in a cycle of assessing, analyzing the results, and applying your analysis through corrective feedback or modification of learning experiences. (For more information about assessments, see chapter 8 of *National Standards & Grade-Level Outcomes for K-12 Physical Education* (SHAPE America, 2014).

High-quality physical education is all about student learning; the teacher is the key to designing lessons and delivering the experiences that lead to that student learning. An effective learning environment does not just happen; you as a teacher must create the environment for that learning to occur. By using the National Standards and Grade-Level Outcomes as guideposts, you can help students become physically literate and physically active for a lifetime.

ORGANIZATION OF LESSON PLANS

The lesson plans presented in this book focus directly on the Grade-Level Outcomes within National Standards 1, 2, and 3. The outcomes for Standards 4 and 5 are embedded within the lesson plans. (See chapter 3 for the development of embedding outcomes in teaching children.) This format in no way diminishes the importance of Standards 4 and 5. Many physical educators and researchers in the field would remind us that without personal and social responsibility (Standard 4), teaching and learning are not possible. Without recognizing the value of physical activity (Standard 5), physical literacy and the enjoyment of healthful physical activity for a lifetime cannot be achieved.

Some Grade-Level Outcomes are presented as single lessons (e.g., the introduction of movement concepts), and some are presented as a portion of a lesson (e.g., the introduction of locomotor skills). Others, such as manipulative skills, are presented in a series of lessons either for a unit focus or for a single lesson as an emerging skill. The topics are revisited throughout the year. All Grade-Level Outcomes begin as emerging skills, and a progression toward a mature pattern of skill performance or a cognitive application of concepts follows.

Figure 1.1 presents the lesson plan format and is followed by a brief description of each of the lesson plan components.

FIGURE 1.1 Lesson Plan Format

Part 1

Focus

Subfocus

Appropriate grade level(s)

National Standard(s) addressed

Grade-Level Outcomes addressed

Lesson objectives

Part 2

Safety concerns

Materials and equipment

Organization and management

Part 3

Introduction

Learning experiences

Assessment

Closure

Part 4

Reflection

Part 1: Focus and Objectives

Part 1 of each lesson plan includes the lesson's focus, subfocus, appropriate grade levels, National Standard(s) addressed, Grade-Level Outcomes addressed, and lesson objectives. The focus for the lesson is the skill or concept that the teacher and students will concentrate on during the lesson. When a skill is being developed, a series of lessons may have the same focus.

The subfocus is the concept (or skill) that serves to enhance the focus. A subfocus has been taught earlier as a lesson. Students should have a cognitive understanding of the concept or prior experience with the skill before it is used as a subfocus. Sometimes, the subfocus includes more than one skill or concept.

The appropriate grade levels are included in the heading. When more than one grade level is listed, the lesson contains tasks that extend to the higher grade level.

The National Standards addressed and Grade-Level Outcomes addressed are included to help you align the focus of the lesson to the curriculum. The National Standards represent the framework for what students should know and be able to do as a result of high-quality planning and instruction in K-12 physical education. The Grade-Level Outcomes provide a scope and sequence of skill and knowledge acquisition that leads to attainment of the standards. Individual lessons are not designed to reach a grade-level outcome; the attainment of outcomes requires several lessons and prerequisite skills of previous grades and distributed practice throughout the year.

The lesson objectives are what most students can attain in one lesson. They identify what students should know or be able to do as a result of the lesson. For example, although throwing overhand, which demonstrates two of the five critical elements of a mature pattern, is an outcome for grade 3, the objective for one lesson is stepping forward on the opposite foot. This learning encompasses both cognitive and motor performance. The learner identifies which foot should be forward and can perform an emerging overhand throw pattern with the opposite foot forward. You should be able to assess the learning objective, including the student's performance and knowledge.

Part 2: Safety and Management

Part 2 addresses safety concerns and materials and equipment. When necessary, organization and management are listed or described. Safety concerns are included only in lesson plans that include tasks or organizational patterns that could present risks to students' well-being (e.g., sufficient space for jumping and landing, arrangement of mats to avoid collisions when transferring weight in gymnastics).

Materials and equipment include the items needed to teach the lesson. The amount of material will be based on the number of students in the class. Manipulative equipment should be available for each student. A lesson plan may need to be modified based on available equipment and indoor or outdoor facilities. The lesson plans provided are designed for an indoor facility unless otherwise noted, although they are suitable for teaching outdoors with minimal modification.

The organization and management section is included only as necessary for clarity or for suggestions to avoid long periods of inactivity. This section is not inclusive, because you might have established routines and management that work well in your learning environment. Diagrams for stations and some learning tasks are included within the lesson content.

Part 3: Lesson Content and Assessment

Part 3 focuses on lesson content: introduction, learning experiences, assessment examples, and lesson closure. The introduction begins the lesson content and includes a suggestion of what to say and do in the first two to three minutes of the lesson. The introduction is often scripted. This part of the lesson is critical, because it sets the tone for the class. Your introductory remarks should focus the children's attention, capture their imagination, and make them eager to participate in the lesson. During your introduction, tell students what the focus of the lesson is and why it is important. Relating the lesson to past and future lessons is also helpful. If you elect to begin your lesson with a warm-up or instant activity, the introduction of the lesson would follow.

Learning experiences begin after the introduction and are designed to develop the content, thus meeting the lesson objective. Select a review task from a previous lesson as an initial task; suggestions are offered in the lesson plans. During the initial task, observe the class as a whole to determine whether your students are ready to proceed with the learning experiences or whether you need to reteach certain skills from the previous lesson. You might have to adjust the learning experiences to match your students' needs. Continue with the remaining learning experiences if students appear to be succeeding but are challenged by the tasks. Adjust the learning experiences if the tasks are too difficult for the students, that is, if they are frustrated and have a low success rate. Reteach certain skills if you observe that most students are having difficulty with one part of the skill. Often, that includes refining a task by asking students to focus on a particular cue during practice.

Assessment examples follow the learning experiences in the lesson plan format, but they are designed to be part of the learning experiences, not separate. Students view them as an enjoyable activity, as a challenge. Examples include self-evaluation, peer observation, paper and pencil, digital video recordings, computer-generated presentations, group projects, and teacher observation of quality of movement. You will find that the assessments are practical, easy to administer, and readily adaptable for communicating with parents.

Closure is the final learning opportunity of the lesson. The lesson plan includes recommended closure questions to ask your students. During this two- or three-minute period, remind students of the lesson's objectives for the day. (They tend to remember only the activity, not the learning that occurred.) Begin closure by asking students, "What was the focus of our lesson today?" Probing questions will involve students in this learning process. You also might include a chance for students to demonstrate learning the skill one more time or to evaluate you performing the task, either correctly or incorrectly. Closure provides an opportunity to offer students hints of what is to come during the next class period as well as to encourage them to use the skill in other avenues of play.

Part 4: Reflection

In the reflection section, you have an opportunity to evaluate the teaching and learning process after the lesson is completed. The questions provided in the lesson plans guide your evaluation of how well the lesson attained its instructional objectives. Responses to the following reflection questions will provide additional guidance for planning the next lesson:

- Did this lesson meet the instructional objective?
- What tasks do I need to reteach?
- Was the lesson too easy or too difficult for this class or for certain students?
- What task will be the warm-up activity for the next lesson?
- Who needs extra help tomorrow or the next time we study this skill or concept?

THE ART OF TEACHING

Although the lesson plans in this book are written as single units progressing from introduction to closure, more than one day is often needed to complete the tasks and ensure student learning. The lesson plans presented here are designed for the flow of an idea to its conclusion. The length of your class periods and the skill level of your students will determine whether your class can complete a lesson plan in one day. Remember that mastering the skill or understanding the concept is the goal, not completing the lesson plan in 30 minutes. Reteach and provide appropriate practice (Silverman, 2011) as needed until you see evidence of skill mastery, as revealed in your responses to the reflection questions.

The lesson plans in this text are not arranged in a progression for fall-to-spring teaching. Concept and introductory lessons represent one lesson plan; skill development lessons are presented as a series of lessons focused on attaining the Grade-Level Outcome for that particular skill. Your selection of skills and concepts depends on your philosophy for the content areas of elementary physical education: dance, educational gymnastics, and the skills leading to sports and games. The extent of that selection is affected largely by the number of days per week that your school offers instructional physical education, your students' background experiences, and other related factors. The lesson plans in this text serve as a foundation for developing your physical education program, a program that will lead your students to a lifetime love of physical activity and the skills to be successful in that activity.

CHAPTER 2

Meeting the National Standards and Grade-Level Outcomes in Elementary School

We are teachers of children—children who have entered the world of elementary physical education in our gymnasiums, our multipurpose rooms, and our outdoor teaching environments. As teachers of elementary physical education, we are positioned at a unique place in the lives of our students where we are building the foundation for their physical literacy. In *National Standards & Grade-Level Outcomes for K-12 Physical Education* (SHAPE America, 2014, p. 4) physical literacy is defined as "the ability to move with competence and confidence in a wide variety of physical activities in multiple environments that benefit the healthy development of the whole person" (Mandigo, Francis, Lodewyk, and Lopez, 2012, p. 28; Whitehead, 2001). The physically literate individual has the knowledge, skills, and confidence to enjoy a lifetime of healthful physical activity (SHAPE America, 2014, p. 11).

Physical education is the foundation for physical literacy. During the elementary school years, children develop skills, gain confidence in themselves by achieving success, and acquire attitudes and habits. But in physical education during these years, skills are often neglected for participation-only activities, self-confidence is destroyed by inappropriate tasks and expectations, and negative attitudes toward physical activity are formed. The direction of skills, confidence, and dispositions is determined in large part by the teacher of elementary physical education—you, me, us. The choices of curriculum as well as selection of teaching strategies are primarily within the decision-making sphere of the elementary physical education teacher. *National Standards & Grade-Level Outcomes for K-12 Physical Education* (SHAPE America, 2014) provides the guidelines for both curriculum and teaching for elementary physical education.

CURRICULUM GUIDELINES

The guidelines for curriculum are explicit in the National Standards. The focus of elementary physical education is the acquisition of fundamental motor skills: locomotor, nonlocomotor, and manipulative. Locomotor skills include hopping, galloping, running, sliding, skipping, and leaping, as well as jumping and landing. Nonlocomotor skills are balancing, transferring weight, and the actions of stretching, curling, and twisting. Manipulative skills include throwing underhand and overhand, catching, kicking, dribbling with hands and with feet, volleying, striking with short and long implements, and jumping rope. The goal for each skill during the elementary school years is for the student to display a mature pattern of execution in a nondynamic environment and develop readiness for application in the dynamic environment of modified games and sports, educational gymnastics, and dance. Figure 2.1 provides an example for the development of a skill from kindergarten through grade 5.

The fundamental motor skills are presented in the Grade-Level Outcomes to develop maturing patterns and experiences in dance, educational gymnastics, and the skills leading to games and sports. The outcomes are based on motor development and motor-learning research and Piagetian theory of child development.

The lesson plans in this book, which are aligned with the Grade-Level Outcomes, are not a prescribed curriculum. The lessons reflect the philosophy of the authors (i.e., a balanced curriculum of dance, educational gymnastics, and the skills of games and sports). Your philosophy of physical education for children will determine the areas of curriculum emphasis for your program. Your students' attainment of the Grade-Level Outcomes will be affected by the number of days per week that they have physical education and the number of minutes per

FIGURE 2.1 Dribbling With Feet: Introduction to Application

Grade K: Student taps the ball with inside of feet, sending it forward.

Grade 1: Student dribbles the ball with inside of feet while walking in general space. (Student lacks control and must watch the ball.)

Grade 2: Student dribbles the ball while walking in general space with control of the ball and body. (Student still looks at the ball and its direction of travel.)

Grade 3: Student dribbles the ball in general space at a slow to moderate jogging pace with control of the ball and body. (Student still looks at the ball and its direction of travel.)

Grade 4: Student dribbles the ball in general space with control of the ball and body while increasing and decreasing speed of travel. (Demonstrates a maturing pattern.)

Grade 5: Student combines dribbling with other skills such as passing and shooting. (Maturing pattern transfers to application.)

class period. The lesson plans in this book were designed for students to attain the outcomes for each grade based on offering students physical education two or three times per week with classes lasting 30 to 45 minutes (30 minutes for students in kindergarten through grade 2, and 30 to 45 minutes for students in grades 3 through 5 (SHAPE America, 2010). If you see your students for physical education less often than twice per week, you will need to adjust the outcome expectations for them in the lesson plans that follow in this book and in the ones that you develop yourself. On the other hand, if you deliver instructional physical education to your students four or five days per week, you will be able to extend those expectations beyond those included in the lessons. But note that the key to those extensions is adding breadth to the children's experiences, not rushing ahead to meet outcomes that might not be developmentally appropriate for students at that grade level.

TEACHING FOR LEARNING

By using the lesson plans in the book, which are based on the Grade-Level Outcomes, to help your students attain competency in motor skills and movement patterns, the focus of your teaching will be on student learning. Each lesson planned and each experience for your students is designed with student learning as the objective of that experience, lesson, task, or activity. The critical elements that make up each fundamental motor skill and that accompany each lesson plan provide the breakdown of essentials for attaining a mature pattern of performance. Those critical elements provide the progressive composite for assessing student growth in acquiring skills. It is that focus on student learning that moves elementary physical education beyond "busy, happy, good" (Placek, 1983), into a recognized, respected discipline. The following story captures it best:

The fifth-grade class is walking toward the outdoor physical education area, where the students will participate in a skill assessment. Jared—a high-maintenance, high-energy student—is at the front of the line as the students walk. The student in line behind Jared is new to the school, and says, to no one in particular, "I wish I was still at my old school. We played lots of games in physical education; we didn't have to take tests." The line comes to an abrupt stop, as Jared turns and asks the student, "But what did you *learn?*"

Teaching for learning will necessitate planning—purposeful planning for student learning that reflects the Grade-Level Outcomes. Planning for physical education must be completed for each grade level, both across the grades and across the year. No longer can you plan the lesson for the day while driving to school or center it on a new piece of equipment or a fun activity captured at a recent conference. Planning reflects the objective for the lesson, and that objective is student learning. The Grade-Level Outcomes for elementary physical education provide the progression of skills, knowledge, and dispositions beginning in kindergarten and continuing through grade 5. Planning the curriculum throughout the school year (weeks 1-36), requires considerable time and concentrated effort. Refer to the sample yearly plans in appendix B for assistance.

Teaching for learning requires differentiated instruction, or instruction that meets the needs of each student. Within a single elementary physical education class, you might have several students who perform the overhand throw with all five of the critical elements of a mature pattern, one student who is struggling with the opposite-foot-forward element, and students at each stage of skill development, from emerging to applying. Children learn in different ways; they bring different levels of skill to physical education programs. The Grade-Level Outcomes are identical for each student in your class. Your challenge is to offer differentiated, often individualized, instruction to match the student, the task, and the expected learning outcome. Therefore, you need to alter tasks so that less-skilled students can experience success and higher-skilled children can face a challenge. Teaching elementary physical education takes more than one approach; you need to meet each student where he or she is to help the student grow in the skills, knowledge, and confidence that lead to physical literacy.

Differentiated instruction allows for all students to achieve success.

Teaching for learning in physical education requires deliberate practice of the skills specified in the lesson. Deliberate practice includes extending the tasks by varying and increasing the complexity of learning experiences with the primary purpose of "attaining and improving" skills (Ericsson et al., 1993). This deliberate practice for skill improvement is what separates focused practice for skill acquisition from "mindless, routine performance and playful engagement" (Ericsson, et al., 2006). Elementary-level physical educators have been guilty in the past of offering students limited or no skill practice before introducing game play and of engaging them in playful activities that include no focused outcomes. The lesson plans within this book include task extensions that vary and increase the complexity of the tasks and activities as the lesson progresses, thereby providing deliberate practice to improve skills. Figure 2.2 illustrates deliberate practice as compared with indiscreet practice for passing and receiving with feet for upper-elementary or early middle school students.

Within the framework of deliberate practice of specific skills comes teacher observation of critical elements; targeted, individual feedback; continued practice; and a repeat of the cycle. When the practice is focused on the quality of the skill and the feedback is targeted, students will be engaged both physically and cognitively, resulting in student success as well as confidence. That combination of success and confidence will lead, in turn, to intrinsic motivation and continued practice. The lesson plans within this text are designed to do just that—to provide students with developmentally appropriate tasks followed by focused practice on the skills of the lesson. Each lesson plan is designed to answer the question "What did you *learn* today?" as opposed to "What did you *do* today?"

Teaching for student learning necessitates assessment. You, as the teacher, must not assume that student learning, either cognitive or performance, has taken place. So, you must build assessment, both formative and summative, into your curriculum and into your purposeful planning. Therefore, you should weave into

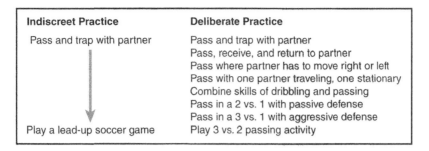

Indiscreet Practice	Deliberate Practice
Pass and trap with partner	Pass and trap with partner
	Pass, receive, and return to partner
	Pass where partner has to move right or left
	Pass with one partner traveling, one stationary
	Combine skills of dribbling and passing
	Pass in a 2 vs. 1 with passive defense
	Pass in a 3 vs. 1 with aggressive defense
Play a lead-up soccer game	Play 3 vs. 2 passing activity

FIGURE 2.2 Comparison of indiscreet practice with deliberate practice in soccer passing lessons.

your lessons formative assessments such as exit slips, peer and self-assessments, teacher observation, journals, and checks for understanding, as well as summative assessments such as student projects, teacher checklists, written tests, and so on. All assessments should align with lesson objectives. The lesson plans that appear in chapters 4 through 8 contain suggestions for both formative and summative assessment.

SKILL PROGRESSIONS, CRITICAL ELEMENTS, AND CUES

The scope and sequence chart in appendix A classifies the Grade-Level Outcomes as emerging, maturing, and applying. In the grade level at which the skill or concept is introduced and a student is first expected to display an outcome, the skill or concept is classified as emerging. These experiences in the skill and concept development continue until the outcome reaches the grade level for which students are expected to show a maturing pattern of performance or cognitive understanding by the end of that school year. Following the mature pattern of skill execution or functional understanding of the concept, the student enters the applying stage, in which he or she can begin to apply the skill in a variety of contexts, in combination with other skills and concepts, or in a dynamic environment of engagement.

The scope and sequence chart will help you plan your yearly curriculum and your weekly lessons and assist in identifying the grade-level expectations for your students. The lesson plans are written with both the classification of the skill—emerging, maturing, or applying—and the designated Grade-Level Outcome in mind.

Within the lesson plans for locomotor and manipulative skills is a listing of critical elements for the skill that is the focus of the lesson, the composite of which results in a mature pattern for that skill. Within the progression of Grade-Level Outcomes and the lesson plans is an expectation of "two of five," "three of five," and so on, eventually leading to the mature pattern (all the critical elements). Although students do not master the critical elements in a lock-step order (for example, a motor skill that has a sequential preparation, execution, and follow-through), many students will attain the critical elements in the order listed.

Suggested cues are also provided within some lesson plans. Cues are the two- or three-word phrases that teachers use as oral reminders to students to assist them in a correct performance of the skill, such as "Extend to target," "Ready hands," "Eyes forward," "Squash the bug," "Candy cane hand." Focusing on only

KEY POINT

The classification of skills and concepts in the National Standards and Grade-Level Outcomes are purposely written as gerunds ("ing" words) to portray student learning as a process, not as a beginning and ending. The learning is developmental, attained at different times for individual students, and ongoing.

one critical element and one cue at a time is beneficial; you provide the next after you observe functional understanding. Differentiated instruction will be evident as students advance at various rates toward mature patterns of skills.

Throughout the lesson plans, gymnastics sequences and dance ideas are woven into the movement experiences for K-5 students. You will find the lessons "Building a Gymnastics Sequence" and "Building a Dance," as well as numerous ideas for creative dance. If you use the National Standards and Grade-Level Outcomes as your guide to designing a program of physical education for your students, they will achieve an elementary school-age level of physical literacy.

CHAPTER 3

Making the Most of Every Lesson

The student who enters your physical education environment is not the child who his or her parents sent to school that morning, nor is he or she the student whom the classroom teacher sees each day. He is not the younger sibling with all the negative traits of the older brother or sister. She is not the child from that family that every teacher dreads. The student who enters your physical education class is a child unique to the world of physical education for that day. That child comes to physical education class with strengths and weaknesses. Some children are strong in the skills of physical education and struggle with the classroom curriculum; others excel in the areas of the classroom curriculum and must practice extra hard just to deliver average performance in the skills of physical education.

Each child who enters your physical education class brings the total package: mental, physical, emotional, and social. Physical skills and motor performance are not practiced in a vacuum without cognitive engagement. Physical and cognitive engagement in activities does not take place without the emotions and social interactions of present and past experiences. With that knowledge of child development and a belief in teaching the whole child, using embedded objectives is the natural avenue for teaching elementary school physical education. Although physical education has historically focused on the psychomotor domain of student learning, teachers must address the affective and cognitive domains as well. Elementary-age students, or anyone learning a new skill, must engage the cognitive domain for learning to take place. Students must know the critical elements that are to be the focus of their practice. Knowing the components of the skill (e.g., preparation, execution, follow-through) is key to reaching a mature pattern of development. The same is true for knowing the effects of changing the body's center of gravity and narrowing the bases of support while participating in educational gymnastics and for balance in dance and sports and games environments. The cognitive skills of concentration and engagement are crucial to student learning in the physical domain.

EMBEDDED OBJECTIVES

Embedded objectives are best described as secondary objectives that you place within the learning experience to maximize teaching effectiveness and student learning. These objectives are rooted in the learning or practice task by the very nature or challenge of the learning experience. You should not think of embedded objectives as by-products of or incidental to the primary objective or task, nor should you leave them to "teachable moments." You must plan for them within the lesson, embedding them as opportunities to meet more than one objective during the learning experience. They are teaching the whole child.

In elementary school, students' knowledge of the benefits of physical activity and fitness (National Standard 3) is a product of a high-quality physical education program of instruction and engagement. Most of the Grade-Level Outcomes for health-related fitness under Standard 3 for grades K-2 are cognitive (e.g., identifies active-play opportunities [Outcome S3.E1.K], discusses the benefits of being active and exercising or playing [Outcome S3.E1.1]) describes large-motor and/or manipulative physical activities for participation [Outcome S3.E2.1]), and they address students' awareness of opportunities to be physically active "outside of physical education class" (SHAPE America, 2014, p. 34). Students in grade 3 should be able to describe the concept of health-related fitness and provide examples of physical activity that enhances fitness (Outcome S3.E3.3). As students are introduced to health-related fitness assessment and progress toward designing a personal fitness plan in grades 4 and 5, fitness and nutrition knowledge should be embedded within your lessons throughout the year. Following is an example of an embedded objective:

Within a skill lesson (e.g., dribbling and traveling, chasing and fleeing, locomotors in combination with manipulatives), you might ask students to pause and count their pulse rates or simply "feel your heart beating."

You can embed an objective into that lesson by asking students: "While you're dribbling or chasing, are you getting your cardiorespiratory exercise for the day?"

The primary objective of the lesson is building the children's skills in dribbling, chasing, and so on. The embedded objective is to help students identify one component of health-related fitness (Outcome S3.E3.4) or recognize the difference between skill-related fitness (speed, balance, and agility required for dribbling) and health-related fitness (cardiorespiratory endurance) (Outcomes S3.E3.4 and 5) while they are actively involved in developing the skills targeted in the lesson's primary objective.

Accepting personal and social responsibility is a major emphasis of Standard 4, and opportunities for teaching respect for self and others are embedded within every lesson you teach.

The following examples are rich with opportunities for teaching respect and responsibility:

- Choosing partners and assigning groups
- Teaching and coaching peers
- Providing and accepting feedback

Physical education presents many opportunities for embedded objectives.

- Learning to help a teammate who performed poorly in a group situation, as opposed to placing blame on him or her
- Learning to control their frustration over a poor performance
- Learning to adjust their performance to accommodate less-skilled peers (e.g., reducing the force of a pass to someone who shows difficulty in catching)

Simple cognitive awareness of respect and personal responsibility are not enough; students must experience situations in which they demonstrate respect for self and others, and display personal and social responsibility. The opportunities to practice those skills exist within every practice task and every physical activity learning experience, but opportunities themselves do not guarantee positive student learning. You, as a teacher, play the major role in assuring a positive outcome. An example follows:

The fourth-grade students were outside, preparing for the distance run portion of their fitness test. Brett, a highly skilled student, stood beside his friend as the timed run began but soon sped far ahead as the timed run proceeded. But instead of maintaining his pace, Brett looked over his shoulder to see his friend lagging far behind. Brett stopped running and waited for his friend to catch up. The two friends finished the timed run together.

Although Brett's time in the distance run that day did not reflect his physical skill, it demonstrated his ability to "accept players of all skill levels into the physical activity," as prescribed in Outcome S4.E4.4b. Given the respect that Brett had shown for his friend, Brett's parents were content with his score on the timed run.

Students' ability to attain the Grade-Level Outcomes for Standard 5—The physically literate individual recognizes the value of physical activity for health, enjoyment, challenge, self-expression and/or social interaction—is ripe for development every time they attend your class. The ability of children to value physical education and physical activity is developed not by the cerebral, but by the affective—their feelings as they participate in physical education for the day.

Although older students and adults recognize the value of physical activity for health, children recognize success and enjoyment, and those two factors are major contributors to participation in physical activity for adolescents and adults (Corbin, 2001; Ennis, 2010; Silverman, 2011).

DESIGNING LESSONS FOR POSITIVE RESULTS

You must not assume that because you love physical activity and the challenges that physical education, dance, and gymnastics pose, all your students share that feeling. Your responsibility is to design developmentally appropriate physical education programs for skill development as well as success and enjoyment. It's also your responsibility to assess the affective domain to connect to children's feelings so that you can design lesson strategies for positive results. Simple measures such as discussions at the end of class, exit slips with a single question on feelings about the lesson and activities for the day, telling a friend, and writing in journals can provide you with the awareness you need to design such strategies.

Although the physical education curriculum emphasizes the physical and cognitive domains of learning (Standards 1 and 2), you must not ignore Standards 3, 4, and 5 or leave them for teachable moments. As you plan each lesson, ask yourself the following:

■ Where does fitness connect with this lesson? Which components of fitness are addressed within the flow of the lesson? (Standard 3)

■ Within this lesson, where are the opportunities for developing respect for self and others, and for demonstrating personal and social responsibility? (Standard 4) How can I structure my teaching to focus on the Grade-Level Outcomes in those areas?

■ What are my checks for understanding in the affective domain for my students following this lesson? (Standard 5)

Teaching elementary physical education is like a tapestry. Embedding objectives into your lessons is like weaving thread into cloth. Although the focus of the lesson is performance in the physical domain, you must weave the threads of cognitive and affective learning throughout the lesson. You might even say that physical learning cannot take place without the affective and cognitive learning domains. The threads woven together create the tapestry, and that tapestry is physical literacy.

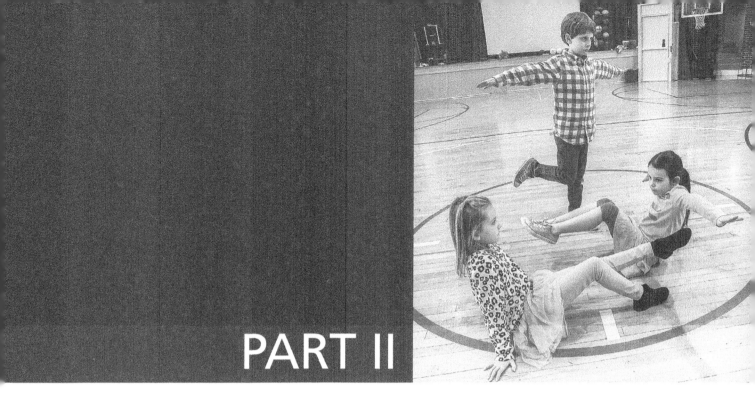

PART II

Lesson Plans

CHAPTER 4

Teaching for Competency in Health-Related Fitness

Fitness for young children is a product of their living a physically active, healthy lifestyle. Vigorous outdoor play, recess, outdoor activities after school, and high-quality physical education all contribute to a physically active lifestyle and therefore to children's fitness. Physically active children tend to be physically active adults; inactive children tend to be inactive adults and therefore suffer myriad health issues related directly to inactivity.

Fitness for children is a product of a high-quality physical education program. It is not calisthenics in large groups or coerced running for exercise. Fitness for young children is being actively engaged in physical education and having a basic understanding of the importance of activity, of the heart as a muscle strengthened by activity, and of the combination of good nutrition and activity (Graham, Holt/Hale, and Parker, 2013). These concepts for children, kindergarten through grade 2, are embedded within lessons of high-quality physical education.

Young children are naturally active; they love running, jumping, and sliding. But their physical activity decreases as they approach adolescence, slowing as they progress from primary to upper-elementary and middle school. For that reason, among others, it is important to instill fitness knowledge in children in the upper-elementary grades (3-5), just as their level of physical activity is beginning to decrease. That's where you come in. Through your physical education curriculum, you must provide students with the knowledge and enjoyment of movement that will help form the foundation for their pursuit of daily physical activity.

Students in grades 3 through 5 can acquire such fitness competency through a series of focused lessons distributed throughout the year, as well as fitness components within physical education lessons. The lessons in this chapter introduce students to the concept of fitness, the components of health-related fitness, the health benefits of participating in various physical activities, the role that nutrition plays in fitness, and fitness assessment.

Teaching for daily fitness and increased physical activity levels includes

- planning all lessons for maximum active participation,
- providing differentiated instruction for skill acquisition and enjoyment,
- planning and providing opportunities for physical activity beyond the instructional physical education program, and
- providing individual assistance to those youngsters whose fitness levels are below those needed for good health and wellness.

The fitness lessons that follow are not designed to be taught as a unit; they are to be distributed throughout the school year within the curriculum. Some are designed with activities for a full 30 minutes. Some are to be taught in collaboration with the classroom teacher. Others are minilessons to be incorporated within your physical education lessons.

CONCEPT OF PHYSICAL FITNESS
Grades 3, 4

The physically literate individual demonstrates the knowledge and skills to achieve and maintain a health-enhancing level of physical activity and fitness.

Grade-Level Outcomes

- Describes the concept of fitness and provides examples of physical activity to enhance fitness (S3.E3.3)
- Recognizes the importance of warm-up and cool-down relative to vigorous physical activity (S3.E4.3)
- Identifies physical activity as a way to become healthier (S3.E1.3b)
- Identifies the components of health-related fitness (S3.E2.4)

Lesson Objectives

The learner will:

- Name four of the components of fitness
- Demonstrate at least two activities used in each of these four components of fitness
- Discuss the effects of these four components of fitness
- Describe a physically fit person in relation to the components of fitness

Materials and Equipment

- Pencil and rubber band for demonstration of flexibility
- Student journal and pencil for each student

Introduction

Who likes to play? Did you know that playing makes you healthy? We are going to learn a part of being healthy today called physical fitness. Who has heard of this before? What do you think being physically fit means? Today, we will learn about four parts, or components, of physical fitness.

LEARNING EXPERIENCE: CARDIORESPIRATORY OR AEROBIC ENDURANCE— INCREASING THE HEART RATE

Can you hear your heart beating? When the room is very quiet, just before you go to sleep at night, you can "hear" your heart beating. Another way to "listen" to your heart is by counting your pulse. Let's count our pulse while we are seated in our resting position. First, how many seconds are in a minute?

- Allow students enough time to find their pulse. Tell them to practice counting to themselves. On the signal "Go," allow them six seconds to count. Now, ask them to multiply the number of pulse beats they count by 10.

That's how many times your heart beats in one minute when you are resting.

- Repeat once for practice.

(Don't worry if the pulse count is not accurate. The increase of the pulse during activity is the focus, and that increase will be obvious to the children.)

What do you think will happen to your heart rate when you walk?

- Have students walk in general space for about 30 seconds and then stop and find their pulse. Repeat the 6-second count.

Raise your hand if the number was higher this time.

What do you think will happen to your heart rate when you jog or run, or jump rope?

- Standing in self-space, students perform magic jump rope (jumping without a rope) for 30 seconds. Students jump up and down on two feet and turn the pretend rope until you give the signal to stop. On your signal, they stop and position their fingers ready to count their pulse.
- Students find their pulse and repeat the 6-second count.

What happened to your pulse? Why does your heart beat faster when you are active? Activities that make your heart beat faster are called aerobic activities. Aerobic activities help you build cardiorespiratory endurance, which helps your heart (cardio) and lungs deliver oxygen to your muscles through your blood. Cardiorespiratory endurance is one component, or part, of fitness.

Note: A number of terms (e.g., cardiorespiratory endurance, cardiorespiratory fitness, cardiovascular fitness, aerobic fitness, aerobic capacity) are used to describe this component of health-related fitness. These terms describe the ability of the heart and lungs to circulate oxygen-rich blood to the exercising tissues, the ability of the muscle cells to use the oxygen for energy production, and the ability of the circulatory system to return blood to the heart (Ayers & Sariscsany, 2011). We recommend using the term *cardiorespiratory endurance* with elementary school students because it "reflects the ability of a person to perform functional fitness activities of daily life associated with the three principal systems supporting performance (cardiovascular, respiratory, muscular)" (Corbin et al., 2014). Also, many elementary students understand that *cardio* refers to the heart. Students will learn about aerobic fitness in middle school when the FITT principle is introduced.

LEARNING EXPERIENCE: MUSCULAR STRENGTH AND ENDURANCE

Muscular strength and muscular endurance are other important components of fitness. Strength is how much you can move or hold with your muscles, and endurance is how long you can do it. Who is the strongest person you know? What makes him or her strong? We build a strong heart muscle by exercising the heart by running, swimming, or jumping rope. We also build strong leg muscles when we run and jump. We build strong abdominal muscles (point to the abs) when we do curl-ups. How can we build strong arm muscles? What type of things do you do when you play that build strong muscles? Today we are going to learn other exercises that help you build muscular strength and muscular endurance.

Push-Ups

- Demonstrate a correct 90-degree push-up. Emphasize a straight body and arms bent to a 90-degree angle before returning to starting position. Provide an example of poor technique (buttocks in the air, belly swaying toward the floor, arms remaining straight). Have students try proper technique for about 30 seconds.
- Modified push-up. Demonstrate the modified push-up with weight on the knees. Have students try for about 30 seconds.
- Inverted push-up. Demonstrate a "belly-up" push-up. Have students try for about 30 seconds.

Crab Walk and Kicks

- Demonstrate the crab walk and have students travel without touching others for about 30 seconds.
- Have students, in self-space, alternate the right and left legs for crab kicks. They should hold each kick for 5 seconds.

If you were able to do most of those tasks, you demonstrated muscular strength. If you did not get tired doing those tasks for 30 seconds, you demonstrated muscular endurance. Think of a long-distance runner. He or she has more endurance than runners who go a short distance as fast as they can. The short-distance runner is called a sprinter and needs muscular strength to go fast. Remember: How much you can move or hold—in this case, your own weight—is muscular strength. How many you can do or how long you can do it is muscular endurance.

LEARNING EXPERIENCE: FLEXIBILITY

Another component of fitness introduces another new word: flexibility. What do you think flexibility means? (Demonstrate with a rubber band and a pencil.) Can a rubber band stretch and bend? How about the pencil? Which one is flexible? Flexibility is the ability to stretch and bend. Who can tell me the sports or physical activities in which flexibility is important? Do we need to be flexible for good health and wellness? Why?

V-Seat Stretch

- Demonstrate the V-position by stretching gently toward the toes and then holding for five seconds. Have students try the V-stretch. Inform them that not everyone can stretch the same distance.
- Seated in the V-position, students place their fingers on their knees and "walk" their fingers forward to see how close they can get to their socks. They hold for five seconds. Then, ask whether they can walk fingers forward to touch the shoelaces. They hold for five seconds. Last, if successful with the shoelaces, they walk their fingers forward to their toes and beyond.

Isn't it easier when we approach with a gentle stretch?

Side Stretches

Lead students in side stretches by placing one hand on the waist and stretching the opposite hand above the head and across the body. Hold for five seconds. Alternate sides and repeat three to five times.

Shoulder Stretch

- Demonstrate from a back view by extending your right hand upward and reaching behind your back to touch your left hand (FitnessGram). Have students attempt the stretch and hold for five seconds. Repeat with the left hand upward and reaching.

Discuss briefly the importance of stretching: Warming up muscles prevents injury and enhances performance. Warming up and cooling down is important with vigorous physical activity. Share that it is best to stretch after a few minutes of moderate activity. Discuss the importance of flexibility in each of these areas.

Assessment

Students write two or three sentences in their journals describing a physically fit person. Prompt: What does it mean to be physically fit?

Closure

Today, we talked about fitness in several areas. We performed activities in each of the areas. Raise your hand if you can name one of the components of fitness that we introduced today.

- How do we improve fitness? Name two activities that are good for improving fitness.
- How do we make our muscles stronger?
- How do we become more flexible?
- Why is stretching important before physical activity? Why is cooling down important after physical activity?
- Can you tell by looking at a person that he or she is physically fit? How do you know? (This might open up an opportunity to teach students that not all thin people are fit and that heavy people might be fit in some components.)

Reflection

- Can students identify four of the components of fitness?
- Can they define and discuss the components introduced today?
- Can they make the connection between a physically fit person and those components of fitness?

CARDIORESPIRATORY ENDURANCE

Grades 3, 4

Standard 3 The physically literate individual demonstrates the knowledge and skills to achieve and maintain a health-enhancing level of physical activity and fitness.

Grade-Level Outcomes

- Identifies the heart as a muscle that grows stronger with exercise, play, and physical activity (S3.E3.1 review)
- Identifies physical activity as a way to become healthier (S3.E1.3b)
- Analyzes opportunities for participating in physical activity outside physical education class (S3.E1.4)

Lesson Objectives

The learner will:

- Define cardiorespiratory endurance
- Recognize that different activities contribute differently to cardiorespiratory endurance
- Identify an exercise or physical activity that improves cardiorespiratory endurance
- Analyze physical activity options for their contribution to cardiorespiratory endurance (grade 4)

Materials and Equipment

- Valentine heart
- Model or picture of the human heart
- Playground balls (one per student)
- Jump ropes (one per student)

Introduction

Earlier in the year, we discussed the concept of fitness and the importance of fitness to good health. Who can tell me what physical fitness means? Today, we are going to focus on one component of fitness—cardiorespiratory endurance. Cardiorespiratory is a really big word for the heart and lungs. Does the human heart look like this? (Show valentine heart.) *No, the human heart is a muscle that looks like this.* (Show model.) *Like all muscles, it becomes stronger by exercise and physical activity. Today, we will analyze various activities to determine whether they are good for the heart.*

LEARNING EXPERIENCE: PULSE RATE

When we had our earlier lesson on fitness, you learned to count your pulse. Let's practice counting our pulse for a few seconds. Remember to listen for the beat.

- Allow students enough time to find their pulse. Remind them to count to themselves. On your signal "Go," allow them six seconds to count. Then ask them to multiply by 10.
- Repeat for another count.

(Don't be concerned if students' count of the pulse rate is not accurate; the number will increase with the exercise or activity. The goal is to have children learn the level of activity needed to increase the pulse rate.)

LEARNING EXPERIENCE: INCREASING CARDIORESPIRATORY ENDURANCE

Let's do various activities and see whether our pulse rate increases, decreases, or stays about the same.

Sticky Popcorn

Have students stand in self-space. On your signal, they begin jumping up and down in that self-space (30 seconds). On your next signal, each student jumps carefully toward another person, touching shoulders with that person and continuing to jump up and down (30 seconds). On your next signal, the two partners jump carefully to "stick" with two other persons; now, four are jumping together (30 seconds). On your next signal, the four jump to "stick" with another four, forming a group of eight. The group continues jumping until you give the signal to stop. (Jumping alone, with a partner, with a group of four, with a group of eight—30 seconds four times.)

Have students stop and quickly position their fingers for a pulse count. They check their pulse for six seconds and multiply by 10.

Sit and Reach

- Have students sit in self-space with their legs in a V, a comfortable distance apart. While keeping their legs flat on the floor, students walk their fingers from the knees to their socks, shoelaces, or toes, stretching gently as far as they can reach. They hold for four counts.
- Instruct students to move their legs closer together and repeat.
- Have students move their legs together and bend one leg upward with the foot flat on the floor and the ankle close to the knee. Then have them walk their fingers up the extended leg. They repeat with the other leg extended.
- Have students check their pulse rate. Ask whether their pulse rate is faster or slower than it was when they were jumping.

Dribbling in Self-Space

- Have students select a playground ball for dribbling and stand in self-space. On your signal, they begin dribbling the ball in self-space, using either the preferred or alternate hand. They move from self-space only if they lose control of the ball. They continue dribbling in self-space for two minutes; on your signal, students place the ball between their feet for safekeeping and are ready for your signal to check their pulse rate.
- Have students check their pulse rate.

Dribbling and Traveling

- Instruct students to dribble while traveling in general space, either walking briskly or jogging. Students continue dribbling and traveling for two minutes; on your signal, they place the ball between their feet for safekeeping and are ready for your signal to check their pulse rate.
- Challenge students to travel as fast as they can while controlling the ball and the body (grade 4). (Monitor students for fatigue; reduce the number of minutes for the activity if you see students stopping to rest or walking slowly.)
- Have students check their pulse rate.

Jumping Rope

- Have each student select a jump rope. Instruct them to stand in self-space with enough room for safe jumping. On your signal, they begin jumping rope. Remind them that the type of jump is not important; they should just continue jumping until they hear your signal. They continue jumping for one minute, stop, and get ready for the pulse count.
- Challenge students to jump as fast as they can without losing their balance (grade 4). (Students who have difficulty jumping can use "magic rope" (invisible rope) or place the rope on the ground and jump continuously forward and backward (grade 4, really fast).
- Have students check their pulse rate.

Assessment

Grade 3

Ask students to rank the activities from the lesson on their contribution to cardiorespiratory endurance, with 5 being the highest and 1 the lowest, and discuss the reasons for their rankings.

Grade 4

Ask students to list opportunities for physical activity outside the school day. Write them on the whiteboard or chart. Have students score each activity on a scale of 1 to 3, with 3 contributing the most to cardiorespiratory endurance, 2 somewhat, and 1 none or limited cardio. Have them compare and discuss the results in small groups.

Closure

Discuss the various activities that the class did and the way that each affected their pulse rates.

- What was the focus of our lesson today?
- Tell your neighbor what "cardiorespiratory" means.
- What does pulse rate mean? How is it measured?
- Which activities caused the pulse rate to increase?
- What type of activity is necessary to increase pulse rate?
- How does that help us build cardiorespiratory endurance?
- What does this tell us about exercising for a healthy heart?

Recess

Ask students to participate in at least one activity to improve cardiorespiratory endurance during recess. For example, they could run a lap around the track, jump rope, or play a game of tag with their friends.

Homework

Challenge students to participate in at least 30 minutes of physical activity each day that increases their heart rate. Better yet, have them include their families in 30 minutes of physical activity outside and teach everyone how to check pulse rate.

Reflection

- Can students discuss the link between cardiorespiratory fitness and good health?
- Can they identify activities that contribute to cardiorespiratory endurance, as well as those that do not?

HEALTH-RELATED FITNESS ASSESSMENT

Grade 3

The physically literate individual demonstrates the knowledge and skills to achieve and maintain a health-enhancing level of physical activity and fitness.

This lesson is valuable as an introduction to the fitness components in midfall, while the upper grades are in the midst of their fitness assessment. A repeat of the lesson in midwinter or early spring provides an excellent review of the fitness components, as well as an informal assessment of students' progress. You will be pleasantly surprised at how well students remember their scores and their personal improvements. Journaling will give them a reference to the previous experience.

Grade-Level Outcome

Demonstrates, with teacher direction, the health-related fitness components (S3.E5.3)

Lesson Objective

The learner will demonstrate three of the components of fitness while performing tasks from a fitness assessment.

Materials and Equipment

- Individual mats for curl-ups (enough so that all students at the station can practice)
- Bench for practice of sit and reach
- Recording of cadence for pacer

Organization and Management

1. Set up four stations (curl-ups, sit and reach, 90-degree push-ups, and shoulder stretch) around the perimeter of the gymnasium, each representing one of the fitness components.
2. Use the center of the gym for the aerobic activities.
3. Refer to *FitnessGram Test Administration Manual* for charts and descriptions.
4. At each station, hang posters on the wall that illustrate the correct exercise.
5. Use the center of the work space for the aerobic activities (e.g., magic jump rope, running in place, pacer with recorded cadence).
6. Divide the class into five groups for the stations, preferably with equal numbers in each group for ease of selecting partners.

Note: Correct form is critical for the fitness assessment. Demonstrate each of the assessment items while giving the cues for correct execution. As students participate at each of the stations, walk among them observing to ensure correct execution and to offer assistance.

Introduction

Earlier in the year, we talked about fitness, the meaning of being physically fit, and the various components of fitness. Who can tell me what it means to be physically fit? Let's see whether we can remember the components of fitness. As you name them, I will write each one on the whiteboard, and we will then define each one.

Allow time for brief discussion and definition of each of the components.

Today we will practice each of the components in a slightly different way. We will still be experiencing the components of health-related fitness, but we'll use the activities that are part of the FitnessGram test. You might have heard the fourth- and fifth-grade students talking about the test. They take the test to measure their personal fitness. We will do the FitnessGram test activities as practice for the health-related fitness test that you will take in fourth grade.

LEARNING EXPERIENCE: CURL-UPS

The first station today is for curl-ups. Who can tell me what curl-ups measure?

Demonstrate a correct curl-up, emphasizing the following keys to success:

- Feet are on the floor with no one holding them.
- Knees are bent at a comfortable distance from the buttocks.
- Fingers "walk" forward only 3 to 4 inches (7.5 to 10 cm), touching the floor at all times.
- The head drops to the floor after each curl-up. Tell students that if they forget this one, they will have a stiff or sore neck when they come to school tomorrow.

If space or number of mats is limited, position partners so that you can watch for correct technique and provide needed cues.

LEARNING EXPERIENCE: SIT AND REACH

The second station is for the sit and reach. This activity is a measure of flexibility. Who can tell me why flexibility is important?

Demonstrate the correct technique for the sit and reach while reminding students of the following keys to success:

- Stretch forward gently with no one pushing on your back.
- The leg touching the bench is extended and remains straight; no bending of the knee.
- Fingers are on top of the bench reaching forward.
- Gentle stretching; no bouncing. Hold for five seconds and try to reach farther than the last time.

Have students practice at either end of a bench. Students waiting can practice stretching with legs in a V or practice by "walking" the fingers from the socks to the shoelaces to the toes.

LEARNING EXPERIENCE: PUSH-UPS

In an earlier lesson, we discussed muscle strength and muscle endurance. Today we will test the muscle strength of the upper arms. The third station is for push-ups. We will practice a 90-degree push-up. No longer do we want to lower our faces to the floor; too many collapsed arms and smashed faces!

Demonstrate a correct 90-degree push-up, starting with arms straight and lowering the body only until the arms bend at a 90-degree angle. Remind students of the following keys to success:

- Body is straight like a plank; no bananas and no tummy touches on the mats.
- Arms bend at only a 90-degree angle and then push back up to straight position.

Have students begin with just one push-up and then try for two or three. Ask partners to monitor the 90-degree stopping point.

LEARNING EXPERIENCE: SHOULDER STRETCH

We did this exercise earlier in the year when we discussed the concept of fitness. Who can tell me what fitness component the shoulder stretch measures?

Demonstrate the shoulder stretch while emphasizing the following keys to success:

- Gently stretch to bring the upper arm toward the center of the back.
- Gently stretch to bring the lower arm upward toward the center of the back.
- Partners do not try to push or pull the arms.

LEARNING EXPERIENCE: CARDIORESPIRATORY ENDURANCE

The last station is in the center of the gymnasium. We will do some activities that we have done before to increase our cardiorespiratory endurance.

Have students at this station stand in self-space in the center of the work area so that they can see the clock on the wall. Have them watch the clock and jump magic rope or run in place for 1 minute. Let them rest for 30 seconds and then try to jump or run for 2 minutes.

Remember when we learned to take our pulse? Count your pulse after 1 minute of activity. Count after 2 minutes. Is there a difference? We hope so!

Time permitting, allow students to enjoy learning about the pacer with the recorded cadence. The idea of pacing is important but difficult for students to do when they begin endurance running. This practice will be a separate activity after students have completed all stations.

Assessment

No formal assessment. Have students write in their journals about the areas in which they felt most competent and the areas in which they know they need more practice.

Closure

Today, you did a fitness assessment. What does that mean? You probably can name the area of fitness that was the most difficult for you and the one that was the easiest. Let's name each of the fitness areas from today and discuss ways to improve each one. I will record the ways you have suggested to improve specific areas of fitness.

Reflection

- In what areas of health-related fitness, if any, is the class as a whole in need of remediation or focused teaching?
- Which students struggled with all or almost all of the fitness components today?
- How can I help those students improve in overall fitness?

HEALTH-RELATED FITNESS ASSESSMENT

Grades 4, 5

The physically literate individual demonstrates the knowledge and skills to achieve and maintain a health-enhancing level of physical activity and fitness.

Grade-Level Outcomes

- Identifies the components of health-related fitness (S3.E3.4)
- Completes fitness assessments (pre and post) (S3.E5.4a)
- Identifies areas of needed remediation from personal test and, with teacher assistance, identifies strategies for progress in those areas (S3.E5.4b)
- Analyzes results of fitness assessment (pre and post), comparing results to fitness components for good health (S3.E5.5a)
- Designs a fitness plan to address ways to use physical activity to enhance fitness (S3.E5.5b)

Lesson Objectives

The learner will:

- Complete both a fall and spring health-related fitness assessment (FitnessGram)
- Identify areas that need remediation after completion of the fitness assessment
- Identify two strategies (exercise or physical activity) for addressing each area of remediation

Materials and Equipment

- Refer to *FitnessGram Test Administration Manual* for equipment needed for assessment
- Either paper or digital equipment for recording of assessment scores
- Student journals and pencils

Learning Experiences

Typically, the first official assessment of students' fitness occurs in grade 4. The assessment should be a positive learning experience for students, not a period of testing to be dreaded. The following keys to success adapted from *FitnessGram Test Administration Manual* will help you create a positive atmosphere for fitness testing:

- Be aware of any potential health problems among your students; read the cumulative folders and check with the school nurse in advance.
- Students should have adequate conditioning and practice of each test item before taking the official test. The purpose is an assessment of practiced fitness protocol, not a surprise testing.
- Prepare students for each test component, including advance notice, practice of the test item, and cues on proper attire. Share with students "the secret" to success for each test item.
- Test results are confidential. Assure all students that scores will be kept private.
- Administer only one test per day. Test administration should leave time for practice for the next day or a return to the focused lesson for the day.
- Administer the test in such a way that students are never sitting and waiting, either before or after their assessment.

After the Test

FitnessGram provides a computerized summary of fitness scores as well as strategies for improving scores. But students gain much more by being involved in the recording of scores than by receiving the computerized summary. Figure 4.1 is one example of a bar graph summary report of the health-related fitness assessment with student involvement.

The discussion of the fitness assessment after the test is just as critical for students' self-esteem as the manner in which the test is given. Just as the assessment results are confidential, so is the development of the summary report. Provide adequate personal space for each student. Quietly tell scores that could be of a concern to the student or have scores already recorded on the student's summary report.

Resources

For free downloads of selected chapters from *FitnessGram Test Administration Manual,* visit the Presidential Youth Fitness Program at www.pyfp.org.

Assessment

Grade 4

Have students record in their journals responses to the following questions:

- In what areas of fitness, if any, do I need to improve?
- What activities will help me improve each of those areas?
- What is my goal for the spring fitness assessment?

Reading students' responses to those questions is important. Children often have unrealistic expectations or goals for themselves; they also can be extremely hard on themselves in terms of achievement. Students value teacher interaction in the journal.

Grade 5

Have students design a personal fitness plan to address areas in which they need remediation. The preceding questions will guide their thinking as they begin to design the plan.

Closure

- What was your favorite component of the fitness assessment?
- What was the most difficult? The easiest? Why?
- Why do you think assessing fitness is necessary?

Reflection

- Did some students experience great difficulty with the fitness assessment? How can I best help them?
- In what areas, if any, did most of the class have difficulty?
- What adjustments must I make in my teaching based on the results of the fitness assessment?

If the fitness assessment is given in the fall and the spring, a midyear check of personal improvements can be conducted with a station format. Following the completion of the stations, students can then read their journal entries from the fall and respond to each with a progress statement.

FIGURE 4.1 Health-Related Fitness Profile

Name: _____ Homeroom: _____

Key:

HR = health risk (Seek help to develop a plan to improve this component.)

MP = making progress (Keep working and playing hard.)

HF = healthy fitness zone (Way to go; keep being active.)

EHF = exceeds healthy fitness zone (You rock!)

Based on students' scores, check the appropriate box for overall fitness.

Fitness Component

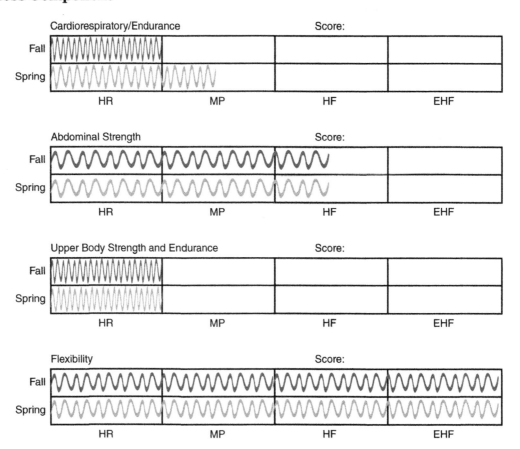

Approaching healthy and fit: achieves healthy fitness zone in three areas

Healthy and fit: achieves healthy fitness zone in all four areas

Super healthy: exceeds healthy fitness zone in all four areas

Note: Test item measure and score will be added by teacher or students, as in the following example:

- Cardiorespiratory: pacer test, mile run
- Abdominal strength and endurance: curl-ups
- Upper-body strength and endurance: push-ups, modified pull-ups, pull-ups, flexed arm hang
- Flexibility: sit-and-reach, trunk lift, shoulder stretch
- Body composition should not be reported on a child's fitness profile.

NUTRITION AND PHYSICAL ACTIVITY

Grades 1-3

This lesson is meant to be done in collaboration with the classroom teacher.

The physically literate individual demonstrates the knowledge and skills to achieve and maintain a health-enhancing level of physical activity and fitness.

Grade-Level Outcomes

- Differentiates between healthy and unhealthy foods (S3.E6.1)
- Recognizes the "good health balance" of nutrition and physical activity (S3.E6.2)
- Identifies foods that are beneficial before and after physical activity (S3.E6.3)

Lesson Objectives

The learner will:

- Discuss good nutrition as a component of health and wellness
- Categorize food according to MyPlate

Materials and Equipment

- 3-by-5-inch (7.5 by 12.5 cm) index cards cut in quarters
- Math cubes (four colors)
- White paper plates, one per child
- Student journals, pencils
- Crayons or markers

Introduction

Remind students of earlier discussions of the "good health balance," eating healthy foods for good performance, and the importance of eating well before and after activity embedded in past lessons.

Can you remember what you ate for dinner last evening? How about snacks? Did you have a snack before bedtime? Today we are going to look at the foods we have eaten in a one-day period. We will then compare our eating with MyPlate to see whether we have a balanced food intake in one day.

LEARNING EXPERIENCE: FOOD LOGS

- On a selected day, have students list their responses to the following: What did you eat for dinner last night? For breakfast this morning? For lunch today or yesterday? Snacks?
- Allow time for students to record their listing for each in their journals.

Record Food Items

Prepare quarter-size index cards by cutting 3-by-5-inch (7.5 by 12.5 cm) index cards into four equal pieces. Have enough for each child to record all the foods eaten in response to the preceding questions.

Have students record each food item, one per square on the quarter index cards, listing only one food item per square. Some children may need assistance in breaking down certain items, such as a sandwich, into the components—lettuce, mayo, meat, and so on.

LEARNING EXPERIENCE: BUILD A PLATE

You are going to "build a plate" by using the squares of your food choices—breads, cereals, and pastas together; fruits; vegetables; dairy products; meats, beans, and eggs together; and all sweets together.

- Have students divide their plates into four parts by drawing with a crayon or marker. They are to place the squares that represent the foods on the section of the plate that matches the category: fruit, vegetable, grain, protein. All the squares for dairy are to be placed beside the plate, as if there is a separate small plate to hold the dairy squares.

Recommended portions of MyPlate are not divided equally into four measures, but the division of the plate into quarters will give students the general idea. You can make the exact divisions in advance if you so desire.

- Instruct students to place all the sweets that they have eaten on the other side of their plates, opposite the dairy squares.

If you have colored cubes that represent the food categories, give each child the number needed— one color cube per food square. Students then place the cubes on the plate to match the appropriate food category.

Compare the Plates

Using MyPlate as a model, students compare their completed plates with the model recommended for good health. Discuss nutrition and its relationship to good health and wellness. Talk about foods that should make up a lesser or greater amount of the daily intake.

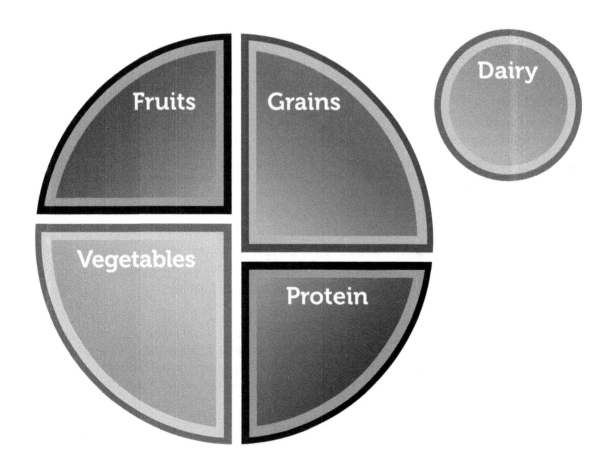

Assessment

Have students write a personal goal for nutrition in their journals. Remind them that foods are not good or bad; balance is the key.

Closure

- Were you surprised at the types of food you ate during a single day?
- Was your plate balanced with all four categories plus dairy?
- Why is good nutrition important when you are young?

Reflection

- Do students understand the role of nutrition in good health?
- Can they analyze their food intake in relation to MyPlate?

NUTRITION AND PHYSICAL ACTIVITY

Grades 4, 5

This series of minilessons can be incorporated within physical education. Each lesson focuses on one of the essential nutrients.

Standard 3 The physically literate individual demonstrates the knowledge and skills to achieve and maintain a health-enhancing level of physical activity and fitness.

Grade-Level Outcomes

- Identifies foods that are beneficial for before and after physical activity (S3.E6.3)
- Discusses the importance of hydration and hydration choices relative to physical activities (S3.E6.4)
- Analyzes the impact of food choices relative to physical activity, youth sports and personal health (S3.E6.5)

Lesson Objectives

The learner will:

- Identify the importance of food for energy and energy for good performance in physical activity
- Discuss the relationship between nutrition and good performance in sports and physical activities
- Discuss the need for water in relation to physical activity

Materials and Equipment

MyPlate chart

Introduction

Would you like to be able to run faster, be stronger, or be a better athlete? One of the key ingredients to being a good athlete is good health; one of the keys to good health is good nutrition. People who participate in sports, gymnastics, and dance need a special focus on protein, carbohydrate, fat, and water. Each of these is important for work in sports and physical fitness.

Link each minilesson to the importance of nutrition and physical activity. Select one of the essential nutrients for the focus of each minilesson.

LEARNING EXPERIENCE: ESSENTIAL NUTRIENTS

Carbohydrate is the main fuel source for muscles. It supplies energy to muscles during exercise. Do you eat toast for breakfast? How many eat cereal? What is your favorite fruit? Name one vegetable that you like. All these foods supply us with carbohydrate to give our muscles energy during physical activity.

- Have students name the food categories that provide carbohydrate: breads, cereals, fruits, vegetables.

Protein provides the building blocks of body tissues. It forms the important parts of muscles, bones, and blood. It helps in tissue repair. How many of you had some protein in your diet yesterday?

- Discuss the foods that provide protein—meat, fish, poultry, eggs, milk products, and dried beans. Have students name the foods they ate that provided protein.

Fat supplies energy and insulates and cushions organs. Yes, we all need some fat! Why?

(To cushion organs, to keep us warm, and to supply energy.)

Water is the coolant for the body. It helps maintain adequate blood volume, lubricates joints, and maximizes muscle strength.

- Discuss the following questions:
  - Why do you get thirsty when you exercise vigorously?
  - How much water do you need each day?
  - Do you need more water when you exercise and play a sport? Why?
  - Should you drink water before, during, and after activity?
  - Is drinking a soda the same as drinking water?

LEARNING EXPERIENCE: MYPLATE DISCUSSION

- Remind students of their earlier discussion of MyPlate. Allow time for discussion of the following questions:
  - Which category of foods should we partake of the most in a given day?
  - What category should we eat the least of?
  - Are all the categories needed to ensure good health and to be physically active?
- With students in grade 5, brainstorm a typical day. Ask students what foods they normally eat. List them on the board (flipchart). Compare the listing of foods with MyPlate and with the essential nutrients needed for good health and energy for physical activity and sports.
  Keep the responses general to avoid embarrassing a student who has poor eating habits.

Assessment

Grade 4

Provide the students with activity, food, and water intake daily journals from three imaginary students. Have them evaluate each imaginary student for areas of deficiency.

Grade 5

Provide the students with activity, food, and water intake daily journals from three imaginary students. Have them evaluate each imaginary student and provide suggestions for improvement. Allow time for students to discuss their evaluations and suggestions for improvement.

Closure

- Why is good nutrition important for athletes?
- Why do you need to drink lots of water when you play in a soccer game, play chase with friends, or ride a bike?
- Does it matter what foods you eat?
- How can nutrition help you be a better athlete?

Reflection

- Can the students discuss the relationship between nutrition and good performance in physical activities?
- Can they identify the food groups important for good health and performance in physical activity?

FOCUS▸   PHYSICAL ACTIVITY

Grades K-3

The physically literate individual demonstrates the knowledge and skills to achieve and maintain a health-enhancing level of physical activity and fitness.

Grade-Level Outcomes

- Identifies active-play opportunities outside physical education class (S3.E1.K)
- Discusses the benefits of being active and/or exercising or playing (S3.E1.1)
- Describes large-motor and/or manipulative physical activities for participation outside physical education class (S3.E1.2)
- Charts participation in physical activities outside physical education class (S3.E1.3a)

Lesson Objectives

The learner will:

- Recognize the connection between being healthy and participating in regular physical activity
- Identify active-play opportunities outside physical education class
- Discuss the positive benefits of regular physical activity

Materials and Equipment

- Paper and crayons (grade 2)
- Student journals, pencils (grade 3)
- Whiteboard or flipchart

Introduction

What's the first thing you do when you go home after school—videogames, snacks, homework, outdoor play? How many of you play outdoors after school every day? What types of activities?

- Allow several minutes of responses from students.

Today we will look at the activities you do at home after school and during playtime.

LEARNING EXPERIENCE: OPPORTUNITIES FOR ACTIVITY

Have the students share opportunities to be physically active outside physical education class:

- Recess
- At home
- In before- or after-school care

Grade 1

- Continue the lesson by discussing the health benefits of engaging in various forms of play.

Grade 2

- Discuss when, where, and with whom students can find opportunities for play. Have them illustrate their favorite form of play that uses equipment (playground activities or manipulatives such as jump rope, balls, and so on).
- Discuss the health benefits of engaging in various forms of play.

Grade 3

- Have the students take a few minutes to list in their journals the activities they do when they go home after school—riding their bikes, playing in a soccer league, walking the dog, playing outside with friends, playing video games, using the computer, and so on.
- List on the board (flipchart) the various activities named.
- Have them share how various forms of physical activity make them feel.
- Discuss the health benefits of various forms of play.

LEARNING EXPERIENCE: GOOD HEALTH BALANCE

Remember, physical activity and good nutrition work together as a team for good health and well-being. We call this the "good health balance team."

- For students in grades 1 and 2, compare the "good health balance team" with learning to walk a balance beam and reaching the arms out for good balance; the arms represent good nutrition and physical activity. Emphasize to the students, "We need both!"
- For students in grade 3, compare with learning to skate, skateboard, or snowboard.

A combination of physical activity and good nutrition every day provides the body with what it needs to be physically fit, to be healthy, and to perform well in school and at play.

Closure

- What did we learn about physical activity and health today?
- Tell your neighbor two reasons why physical activity is important.
- Did you know that physical activity every day is just like brushing your teeth?

Reflection

- Are the children making the connection between their play and health?
- Does it appear the children are physically active outside PE class?
- Would it be beneficial to post physical activity ideas on the website or in the monthly newsletter?

PHYSICAL ACTIVITY

Grades 4, 5

Standard 3 The physically literate individual demonstrates the knowledge and skills to achieve and maintain a health-enhancing level of physical activity and fitness.

Grade-Level Outcomes

- Analyzes opportunities for participation in physical activity outside physical education class (S3.E1.4)
- Charts and analyzes activity outside physical education class for fitness benefits of activities (S3.E1.5)

Lesson Objectives

The learner will:

- Identify and analyze opportunities for physical activity
- Connect physical activity opportunities with specific health and fitness benefits
- List four components of health-related physical fitness
- Identify the components of good health balance

Materials and Equipment

- Student journals
- Pencils

Introduction

Link this lesson to the previous lessons on fitness by reviewing what it means to be physically fit, the components of fitness, and good nutrition.

What's the first thing you do when you go home after school—video games, snacks, homework, outdoor play? How many of you play outdoors after school every day? What types of activities? Today we are going to look at the various activities we do at home, in our recreational time, and when we play. Do they all provide the same benefit for physical fitness and good health? Do they all strengthen the heart? Why is daily physical activity important?

LEARNING EXPERIENCE: AFTER-SCHOOL EXPERIENCES

Have the students take a few minutes to write in their journals about the activities they do when they go home after school or in after-school care—riding their bikes, playing in a soccer league, walking the dog, playing outside with friends, playing video games, using the computer, and so on.

- Ask them to add to the list what they typically do at recess.
- List on the board (flipchart) some of the activities named.
- Have students rank the activities from highest to lowest for physical activity.
- Have students rank the physical activities for enjoyment of participation.

Grade 4

- Ask the students where they can find opportunities for play after school.
- Search for opportunities for physical activity in your school's community during the school year and during summer vacation. Then, assign the search to students and have them report their findings in the next class period.
- Have the students rank the physical activities for enjoyment of participation.

Grade 5

- Have the students keep a record of their physical activity for one week—sports practice, walking the family dog, playing video games, and so on—by recording the activity and the amount of time spent in that activity. Don't forget recess and physical education.
- Have the students rank their individual activities from highest to lowest for physical activity.

LEARNING EXPERIENCE: SIXTY MINUTES PER DAY

Do you know that for good health you should be physically active at least 60 minutes a day? In that 60 minutes of daily activity, most of your play should be at a moderate or vigorous intensity level.

Grade 5

- As a class activity, discuss and categorize the intensity level of each activity listed on the flipchart, given by the students—V for vigorous, M for moderate, and L for low.

Look at your list of physical activity options. Are most of your favorite activities moderate or vigorous, or are they low? Do not ask students to give responses aloud.

- Introduce the 60-minutes-per-day guideline for physical activity. Discuss with the class the benefits for good health and the reasons for daily activity.
- Have each student total the number of minutes spent in physical activity for each day of the week.
- Have the students code the activities they recorded in their journals according to the previously described intensity levels.

LEARNING EXPERIENCE: TOTAL FITNESS

Cardiorespiratory fitness is not the only component of fitness. What were the other components that we learned? Right, muscular strength and endurance and flexibility.

- Create two columns and list on the whiteboard (flipchart) activities that help build muscular strength and endurance and activities that increase flexibility. Share examples such as climbing, hanging, swinging, jumping, running, doing cartwheels, and so on. Have the students extend the list. Guide the discussion beyond just push-ups, curl-ups, and stretching.
- Have students write in their journals two goals for increasing the quantity or quality of their physical activity.

LEARNING EXPERIENCE: GOOD HEALTH BALANCE

Remember, physical activity and good nutrition work together as a team for good health and well-being. We call this the "good health balance team." We need both! Think about the balance you need when learning to skate, skateboard, or snowboard. A combination of physical activity and good nutrition every day provides the body with what it needs to be physically fit, to be healthy, and to perform well in school and at play.

- Am I in balance if I exercise every day but eat only sweets and drink soda with heavy sugar content?
- Am I in balance if I eat the right foods every day but never exercise or play?
- So what is the good health balance? Why is it called that?

LEARNING EXPERIENCE: BODY COMPOSITION

This balance of activity and good eating habits also plays an important role in another component of fitness that we haven't discussed yet—body composition. What could those words possibly mean? Body composition is the balance of lean tissue and fat within the body. We talked earlier about the role of fat in protecting the body from injury and supplying energy. Yes, we all need some fat; we also need lean tissue. Being physically active every day and practicing good nutrition will give us the balance of fat and lean tissue needed for good health and good performance in activity.

- Can you tell whether a person is physically fit by his or her size?
- How do you know whether a person is physically fit?

Closure

- What did we learn about physical activity and fitness today? Is physical activity important only for fitness?
- Tell your neighbor two reasons why physical activity is important.
- What is the minimum amount of time you should be physically active each day? What intensity levels are best?
- What are the components of physical fitness? Is a person physically fit if he or she is very strong but not flexible? How about a person who is able to run very fast but has little muscular strength? What was the new component of fitness we learned today? What was our original definition of fitness? Why does it take all the components of fitness to be truly fit?
- What is the "good health balance team"? Why are both parts important for good health?

Remember to do physical activity every day, just like brushing your teeth!

Reflection

What do the children's journal entries tell me about their fitness, their activity levels, their self-concepts, and their personal concerns?

CHAPTER 5

Teaching for Competency in Movement Concepts

Movement concepts for the motor skills of physical education include but are not limited to personal and general space; pathways, shapes, levels, and directions; time, force, and flow; and working alone, with partners, and in a group. These concepts define how and where the body moves as well as the quality of the action. The use of movement concepts allows you to provide richness to movement tasks, versatility to skills, and breadth and depth to the application of the skills. The difference between a bunt and a home run is the concept of force. Zigzag pathways create open spaces for sending and receiving passes. Dribbling becomes a games skill when moving in general space. Pathways, shapes, and levels add excitement and individual creativity to gymnastics sequences and dance routines.

When first introduced to elementary students, movement concepts are the focus of the physical education lesson. After students gain mastery of the movement concept, that is, after they achieve understanding in a movement context, the concept is used in collaboration with motor skills and in combination with other concepts. The movement concept is then no longer the central focus; it becomes a modifier used to extend the fundamental motor skill.

This chapter contains lesson plans designed for the introduction and mastery of the movement concepts for grades K-2 and a review for students in grade 3. The lesson plans are designed for the younger students of elementary physical education, matching the Grade-Level Outcomes for those early years. When students demonstrate functional understanding (cognitive and performance) of the movement concepts, they have mastered the Grade-Level Outcome. You can then proceed with the skill lessons; the movement concepts are embedded within these lessons.

SELF-SPACE AND GENERAL SPACE
Grades K-3

Standard 2 The physically literate individual applies knowledge of concepts, principles, strategies and tactics related to movement and performance.

Grade-Level Outcomes

- Differentiates between movement in personal (self-space) and general space (S2.E1.Ka)
- Moves in self-space and general space in response to designated beats/rhythms (S2.E1.1)
- Combines locomotor skills in general space to a rhythm (S2.E1.2)

Lesson Objectives

The learner will:

- Respond correctly with self-space and general space movements (K)
- Move in self-space and general space with teacher designated beats or rhythm (grade 1)
- Travel in general space with a combination of locomotor movements (grade 2)
- Recognize and travel to open spaces in relation to others (grade 3)

Materials and Equipment

- Drum
- Music (optional for locomotor movements)

For younger students who are experiencing difficulty establishing self-space, use poly spots or similar props to designate each student's personal space. Remove the props when students demonstrate understanding of the concept.

Introduction

Today we are going to learn about self-space and general space. Both are important as you move in relation to others in games and dance and in relation to equipment in gymnastics. Self-space is the amount of space you occupy when not traveling. General space is the entire work area—gymnasium, outdoor play space, classroom.

Relate to students the importance of space when walking with a tray in the cafeteria, stopping without bumping into others in a basketball game, walking in a crowded mall, and so on.

LEARNING EXPERIENCE: SELF-SPACE

Locate a space where you can stretch, bend, twist, and move in all directions without touching another person, as if you have a bubble surrounding you. That is your personal space, your self-space.

- Have the students explore self-space while seated by extending their arms and legs as far as possible.
- Remind them to move their arms and legs in all the spaces around them: high, low, in front, in back, and to the sides.
- Have students repeat the task by standing in their personal space. Remind them to keep one foot stationary and not to travel.
- Have students reach as high as they can to define their personal space. To increase the height of their personal space, have them jump.
- Repeat the task asking them to stretch as wide as they can, thus defining the width of their personal space.
- Repeat with students curling in a ball while lying on the floor to add awareness of how small their personal space can be.

The Amoebae

After the students have explored self-space, have them try The Amoebae, a favorite creative dance activity. The amoebae (children) begin as blobs curled on the floor in self-space. On your signal, they begin to move by stretching, twisting, and extending, always remaining in self-space. The dance is greatly enhanced by the use of body sacks (commercially purchased or oversized pillowcases made by stitching together old sheets) that cover each child but allow full range of movement in self-space.

LEARNING EXPERIENCE: GENERAL SPACE

Stand in your self-space. On my signal, begin traveling in the open spaces of the room; this is general space. When you hear the drumbeat, stop wherever you are.

- On your signal, have students check their personal space by moving their arms and stretching wide to be sure they are not able to reach others. (They may need a few trials to understand the idea of "taking personal space with you" as they travel in general space.)

Establish the boundaries of the work space before children begin traveling. Lines on the floor and permanent or environmental structures outdoors can define the boundaries of general space.

Travel throughout general space without bumping into others; avoid their bubbles.

- Ask students to walk very quickly, without bumping into others, and to stop on your signal.
- Have students travel with various locomotor actions, traveling without bumping others and stopping in a balanced position without falling down.
  - Introduce hopping, jumping, galloping, sliding, and skipping, with the emphasis on moving in a variety of ways. Provide the beat of the locomotor movement with a handclap, drum, or percussive instrument.
- Have students travel in general space with each of the locomotor movements.
- Have students travel in general space with their favorite movements; remember that they may crawl, slither, do cartwheels, or perform actions just for fun.

LEARNING EXPERIENCE: CROWDED STREETS, BUSY TRAFFIC

Designate the boundaries for travel in general space. Have students travel in that space without colliding with others. On your signal, you reduce the amount of general space by shrinking the boundaries. (You can easily do this by walking forward while facing the class, thus reducing the boundary for that side of the work area.)

- Remind students to travel without bumping into others as the space becomes more confined.
- Continue to reduce the amount of general space, thus increasing the challenge to travel in general space with no collisions.
- Just for fun: Declare rush hour traffic when everyone moves very quickly in general space.

Grade 1

Children's literature, teacher-designed dances, and developmentally appropriate cultural and folk dance provide excellent resources for students to move in self-space and general space with combinations of locomotors and actions in self-space.

Grade 2

Look for open spaces as you travel. Travel quickly to that open space, pause briefly to look for another open space, and move to that space. Remember, if someone else arrives at a space first, it is no longer open.

- Challenge students to travel to all the open spaces within the work area without ever bumping another person.
- Have students vary the speed of travel and change pathways and directions to arrive at open spaces.

LEARNING EXPERIENCE: A DANCE OF LOCOMOTORS I

In combination with Standard 1, students have been practicing and maturing in hopping, jumping, galloping, sliding, and skipping. A Dance of Locomotors brings together movement in general space with these locomotors.

- Divide the class into groups of four. (Small-group work provides excellent opportunities for embedded teaching of Standard 4, working cooperatively with others and acceptance of others.)
- Review with the class the locomotor skills that have been practiced: walking, hopping, jumping, galloping, sliding, and skipping.

Today, you are going to create a Dance of Locomotors. The dance will include four locomotor skills from the list you just stated. Each person in your group will be the leader for one of the locomotors. I will provide the signal for switching the leader and locomotor skill.

Give the class adequate time to make group decisions and to practice
- the locomotor that each leader will use,
- the order of the locomotor skills, and
- a beginning and an ending shape.

If the class has experienced directions, pathways, and shapes, those can also be part of the dance.

Grades 3-5

Spatial concepts will be embedded within skill lessons, small-sided practice tasks, gymnastics, and dance.

Assessment

No formal assessment of self-space and general space.

Closure

- What was the focus of our lesson today?
- Why is traveling in general space without bumping others important?
- How would you describe self-space?
- Name a game or sport in which the concept of open spaces is important. Describe the situation within the game or sport.

Reflection

- Do the students have a cognitive understanding of self-space and general space?
- Can they move in general space without bumping others?
- Can they stop on your signal in a balanced position?

DIRECTIONS
Grades K-2

Standard 2 The physically literate individual applies knowledge of concepts, principles, strategies and tactics related to movement and performance.

Grade-Level Outcome

This lesson introduces the concept of directions, which will apply in grade 5 to outcomes regarding applying strategies and tactics in chasing activities (S2.E5.3a), fleeing activities (S2.E5.3b) and invasion game practice tasks (S2.E5.5a).

Lesson Objectives

The learner will:

- Name the six directions of movement
- Identify the directions when demonstrated by others
- Move in the direction designated by the teacher

Materials and Equipment

Drum

Introduction

All movement takes place in a given direction. When I wiggle my nose (model), it moves from side to side or left to right. When I blink my eyes, they move up and down. Our lesson today is about directions—movement directions.

Link your introduction to the importance of movement directions to games and sports skills as well as to safety, such as walking with a full tray in the cafeteria.

Grade 2

We will try to remember them as "6 + 2." Let's see how many we can name. The "+ 2" are more difficult to guess. We will discuss these as we move.

LEARNING EXPERIENCE: EXPLORATION OF DIRECTIONS

Explore your self-space by making your body parts move in as many different directions as you possibly can.

- Designate the body part that is to lead the action—arm, leg, foot, elbow, shoulder, even the nose—in as many different directions as possible.

As you move in self-space, you are changing directions.

LEARNING EXPERIENCE: FORWARD

Stand in your self-space. On my signal, begin walking in general space in the direction you are facing; this is forward direction. Forward direction is the way each of us is facing. You will be traveling in what seems like many different directions, yet everyone is moving forward.

- Allow sufficient time for students to practice moving forward with various locomotors. (Young children like the imagery of marching like a robot, galloping like a horse, jumping like a kangaroo, hopping and skipping just for fun.)

LEARNING EXPERIENCE: BACKWARD

What is the opposite of forward? Walk backward in general space, looking over your shoulder to avoid colliding with others who are also walking backward.

- Challenge the students to gallop backward—just for fun.

Safety Check: *Jogging or running backward is not recommended for young children.*

What are the first two directions you have learned?

LEARNING EXPERIENCE: SIDE TO SIDE, RIGHT AND LEFT

Now move side to side, like ice skaters, remembering to move your entire body side to side, not just your feet.

- Demonstrate a slide step across the work area, traveling to the right, extending the right arm in the direction of the travel. Ask, "What locomotor action is this? Correct, a slide." (Review from locomotors (see chapter 6) the different types of sliding actions: like a basketball player slides side to side, a baseball player slides to the base, a dancer slides to one side with the body briefly airborne, and arms leading the action.)

Today we're going to slide like an ice skater.

- Have students slide step to the right with the right arm extended and to the left with the left arm extended.
- Challenge students to weave in and out around others as they travel to the right and to the left.

Now you have traveled in four directions. Tell a friend the four directions we have traveled thus far.

LEARNING EXPERIENCE: UP AND DOWN

Assume a position in your self-space like a jack-in-the-box (curled position, close to the floor, on your feet). On my signal, pop up out of your box and extend your body upward (model). Get back in your box. Close the lid. Ready? Pop! What directions did we just move? Up and down.

- Have students travel throughout general space with the up-and-down movements. Imagery: pogo sticks, kangaroos. Remind them to take small jumps; the action is up and down with little forward movement.

Assessment

Have students stand beside a partner (Outcome S4.E4, working with others). Partner A tells his or her partner which direction he or she is going to move and then travels in that direction. Partner B gives a thumbs-up if the action matched the verbal. Repeat with partner B traveling. Allow sufficient time for the students to complete all six directions (forward, backward, right, left, up, down). (Remember, the emphasis is on the direction, not the correct execution of the locomotor.)

Grade 2

Changes in direction: On your signal, have students change directions as they travel in general space. (Link changing directions as a tactic in chasing and fleeing games, and offensive strategies in sports.)

LEARNING EXPERIENCE: CLOCKWISE AND COUNTERCLOCKWISE

Grade 2

At the beginning of class we said that the movement directions were "6 + 2." We are now ready for the "+ 2." The words are big—clockwise and counterclockwise—but the movements are not difficult. Stand in self-space. Spin around, leading with your right shoulder. This is clockwise—the direction that the hands move on an old-fashioned clock.

Following the clockwise movement, have students spin to the left as you label this movement counterclockwise. (Link this action to ice skaters, gymnasts, platform divers, football and basketball players performing an evasive tactic.)

You have moved in "6 + 2" different directions today: forward, backward, left, right, up, and down, plus clockwise and counterclockwise. Travel in any direction you choose, but keep going in the same direction until you hear the signal to stop. I will observe to see whether I can correctly name the direction you are traveling. Ready? Begin.

Assessment

Name the direction in which you want the students to move. Cue them to stop when they hear the signal and to listen for the next direction for their movement. These types of informal observation assessments provide valuable feedback of class or group understanding of the concept and areas where reteaching is needed.

Directions: A Dance Malfunction in the Toy Shop (Grades 1 and 2)

The master craftsman has just created a new supply of toy soldiers and robots. He knows they look good, but can they move? You may choose to be a robot or a toy soldier; your stance and movements will be as such. The first test is traveling forward. On my signal, begin to move in a forward direction.

Give students the following instructions:

- Make your movements jerky, like a robot or wooden soldier.
- Make sharp turns as you travel. Good, now let's see if the robots and toy soldiers can move backward.
- Remember to move like a robot by using small steps and almost rigid leg actions.
- These are special toys; they can extend an arm to the right or left and move in that direction.
- The robots and toy soldiers cannot move their total bodies from high to low, but they can move body parts. Test the arms—up and down. Bend at the waist—down and up.
- Oh, no, something seems to be wrong. There are short circuits in the robots. The toy soldiers are confused. They are all moving in circles clockwise. Now they are moving counterclockwise. Quick, turn off the power. Short circuit: Collapse in self-space!

Assessment

Assessment opportunities for both peer and teacher observation are provided within the learning experiences.

Closure

- What was the focus of our lesson today?
- Let's name the directions. I call them "6 + 2." Who can name them?
- I will write the name of a direction on the whiteboard. Tell your partner a game or sport in which you might see that direction of movement (grade 2).

Reflection

- Can students move in the designated directions?
- Can they identify the directions when demonstrated by another student or you?

PATHWAYS
Grades K-2

Standard 2 The physically literate individual applies knowledge of concepts, principles, strategies and tactics related to movement and performance.

Grade-Level Outcomes

- Travels in three different pathways (S2.E2.K)
- Combines shapes, levels, and pathways into simple travel, dance, and gymnastics sequences (S2.E2.2)

Lesson Objectives

The learner will:

- Identify the three pathways: straight, curved, zigzag
- Move in each of the designated pathways

Materials and Equipment

- Drum
- Scarves or streamers (optional)
- Music for locomotors (optional)
- Obstacle course materials: props for straight, curved, and zigzag (wands, jump ropes, and so on)

Introduction

Today, we are going to learn the three movement pathways and move in each of them. These pathways will be used later to create offensive and defensive strategies for games and sports, to add excitement in gymnastics floor patterns, and to express ideas in creative dance.

Link pathways to students' everyday experiences, such as going home to share exciting news versus going home with a not-so-good note from the teacher or walking home when a favorite friend or relative is waiting versus walking home with nothing to do.

LEARNING EXPERIENCE: PATHWAYS IN SELF-SPACE

With students seated in self-space, have them move in the following pathways as you model the action:

Straight

- Move hands in straight pathways up and down.
- Move hands side to side.
- Make straight pathways in the air with feet and legs while resting on bottoms and hands; move feet and legs in straight pathways up and down.

Curved

- Move hands in curved pathways—up, down, all around—making smooth curves.
- Make curved pathways in the air with feet and legs—up, down, all around.

Zigzag

- Zigzag hands side to side in the air. Zigzag them up and down.
- Zigzag feet and legs while resting on bottoms and hands in self-space.

Children enjoy exploring pathways in self-space with streamers or scarves.

Assessment

Tell a partner the three pathways you have moved today.

LEARNING EXPERIENCE: PATHWAYS IN GENERAL SPACE

With students standing in their personal spaces (check the "bubbles"), allow sufficient time for them to explore pathways while traveling in general space.

Straight

Walk in a straight pathway in general space. What will you do when you come to the boundary of our work space or when you meet another person?

(For example, backward walking, tunnel for partner to go through or over and under)

- Straight pathways, forward travel only. Boundary or person, jump and turn to continue straight pathway forward.
- Straight pathways forward. On the signal, pause, do a one-quarter turn and continue in a straight pathway forward. (This one is great fun for students as the frequency of the signal increases.)

Curved

Move in general space, making curved pathways with your feet, not your arms.

Make large, curved pathways and small, curved pathways.

- Move in curved pathways with the body stretched high in the air.
- Move in curved pathways with the body close to the floor.
- Move your arms as if you are a glider plane or a soaring bird.

Remember that your feet make the pathway on the floor as you travel.

What pathway would you make if the curve stayed in one direction (to your right) only? Make a circle pathway as you travel.

Zigzag

Move in general space making a zigzag pathway as you travel.

(The letter Z on the floor)

- Jump like a rabbit, side to side; glide like an ice skater. (Emphasize the sharpness of the corners for the zigzag.)
- Zigzag backward—zag then zig!

LEARNING EXPERIENCE: MY PERSONAL PATHWAY (GRADES K, 1)

The letters of the alphabet (capital letters) are formed with combinations of straight, curved, and zigzag pathways. Have students travel the pathways throughout general space from one side of the work space to the opposite side. (Ask the classroom teacher what letters kindergarteners are studying.)

Assessment

You have moved in three different pathways: straight, curved, zigzag. When I name a pathway, show me that pathway as you travel in general space. When you hear the signal, stop and listen for the next pathway for your movement.

LEARNING EXPERIENCE: PATHWAYS WITH ROPES

Give each student a jump rope, preferably a cloth one. Have students place the rope on the floor in a straight, curved, or zigzag pathway.

- Have students walk beside their rope, matching the pathway created.
- As a class, decide what locomotor movement will match each pathway, such as hopping for straight, galloping for curved, and jumping for zigzag. Challenge students to travel their jump rope with the chosen locomotor.
- Just for fun, have students create new locomotors for the pathway, such as slithering, crawling, or doing cartwheels.

Grade 1

Students travel in general space, matching locomotors to pathways for all the jump ropes on the floor.

LEARNING EXPERIENCE: OBSTACLE PATHWAYS (GRADE 2)

With the equipment provided for pathways (jump ropes, wands, and so on), have students select two or three pieces of equipment to create a pathway of their choice on the floor. Have each student connect his or her series of pathways with another student's pathways to form an obstacle course.

As a class, decide the locomotor actions to be used for travel through the obstacle course, such as walk the straight pathways, hop the curved pathways, and jump over the zigzag pathways (S4.E6, embedded teaching with the use of equipment and necessary safety).

LEARNING EXPERIENCE: PATHWAY SEQUENCE (GRADE 2)

Have students select a partner (S4.E4). Each partner creates a pathway sequence consisting of the three pathways studied in the lesson; each student decides the order of the pathways for his or her travel. Partner A performs his or her sequence, and partner B observes for correct demonstration of the pathways as well as correct order of the sequence.

- Following completion of the sequence, the partner observing provides feedback on correct execution as well as memorization of the sequence. The students repeat the sequence for partner B.
- Challenge the observer to replicate the partner's sequence after he or she observes and gives feedback. (Increase the complexity of the sequence by adding concepts, such as directions and levels, a focus on locomotors, and a beginning and ending shape.)

Assessment

Assessment opportunities for both peer and teacher observation are provided within the learning experiences. Pathway Sequence, grade 2, is an informal peer assessment. It can easily become a formal assessment with the addition of paper and pencil recording of the sequence and established criteria.

Closure

- What was the focus of our lesson today?
- What are the three pathways of movement?
- Where in the room (outdoor area) do you see straight pathways, curved, zigzag?

Grade 2

- Why are pathways important in games and sports?
- What pathway does a basketball player use to dribble to the basket if no defenders are between the player and the basket?
- What pathway does a football player use to avoid a tackle?
- What pathway does a soccer player use when dribbling the soccer ball through the defense?

Reflection

- Do the students have a cognitive understanding of the various pathways?
- Were they able to move in each of the designated pathways?

Link to the Classroom

Show the class posters that illustrate pathways and the letters of the alphabet. Ask individual students to find the pathway on the poster that you name. Ask individual students to find the capital letter of their first name; ask the student what pathway the letter represents. Choose different letters to illustrate the three pathways and combinations of pathways.

LEVELS

Grades K-2

| **Standard 2** | The physically literate individual applies knowledge of concepts, principles, strategies and tactics related to movement and performance. |

Grade-Level Outcomes

- Travels demonstrating low, middle and high levels (S2.E2.1)
- Combines shapes, levels, and pathways into simple travel, dance, and gymnastics sequences (S2.E2.2)

Lesson Objectives

The learner will:

- Identify the three levels of movement
- Travel in general space at the designated level
- Demonstrate changes in levels in a simple sequence of movement

Materials and Equipment

- Drum
- Deflated balloon

Introduction

Identify for the students the three levels of movement:

- High level is above the shoulders, higher than the head.
- Low level is below the knees, close to the floor.
- Middle level is between the two, the space from the knees to the shoulders.

Provide examples of each level within a movement context, such as jumping in the air to catch a ball, executing a gymnastics roll on a mat, and spinning a hoop around the waist.

Levels of movement will be important later in our games, gymnastics, and dance work in physical education.

LEARNING EXPERIENCE: LEVELS IN SELF-SPACE

With students standing in self-space, have them explore the three levels of movement.

- High level: Extend arms in all directions above the head—forward, backward, and to the sides.
- Low level: Explore the space at low level, close to the ground or floor. (Imagery: searching for lost coins in muddy water.)
- Middle level: Explore middle level space with eyes closed. (Imagery: in a very dark room, unsure of surroundings.)

LEARNING EXPERIENCE: LEVELS IN GENERAL SPACE

Provide sufficient time for students to explore traveling in general space at the three levels.

- High level (as many body parts as possible at high level): Traveling throughout general space with the trunk stretched and the head high. (Imagery: like a tall giraffe with its head in the clouds.)
- Low level (all body parts at or below knee level): Traveling at low level in many different ways. (Imagery: A snake slithers, a duck waddles, and a turtle crawls.)
- Middle level (as many body parts as possible between high and low levels): Traveling to open spaces in the room—quickly, slowly, quietly. (Imagery: almost invisible.)

LEARNING EXPERIENCE: CHANGING LEVELS

With Designated Beat

Have the students assume a low-level balance, such as jack-in-the box position. On your signal, they rise slowly to middle level and then continue to a high-level balanced position.

- Challenge students to move in response to the designated beat, such as four counts to middle level, pause, four counts to high level, and then reverse from high to low with eight counts.

The gradual rising and sinking movement is difficult for young children; allow several repetitions for practice of a controlled movement.

- Repeat with six beats, four beats, and two beats of the drum. Finally, have students start in a squat position at low level. On your signal (one beat), they jump to a high level and freeze.

With Changes in Tempo

Using a deflated balloon as the visual prop, ask students to assume a position at low level, explaining that their changes in levels will be in response to the inflating and deflating of the balloon.

- Slowly inflate the balloon to half size. Students respond by rising to middle level (continue inflating the balloon) and then rising from middle to high level.
- Vary the tempo of the action—rising and sinking, changing levels quickly, slowly, and in combination of quick and slow.
- Challenge students with combinations of rising and sinking with complete stillness. Thus, they must be able to freeze at any moment in the action.
- As you inflate the balloon to its fullest, students rise to high level.

What will happen if I release the balloon? At what level will it travel? In what pathway? Will it travel quickly or slowly?

Release the balloon as the students travel quickly in general space, with zigzag pathways, collapsing to low level as the balloon descends.

No collisions should occur as students travel; they should use self-space to collapse.

Note: When movement concepts are first introduced, they are the central focus of the lesson. All tasks are centered on helping students understand, in both cognition and performance, the meaning of the concept. In subsequent years, the movement concept is reviewed with a series of tasks and then followed with a developmentally appropriate challenge.

LEARNING EXPERIENCE: SEQUENCE OF LOCOMOTORS AND LEVELS (GRADE 2)

Have students travel in general space performing a variety of locomotor movements and demonstrating the three levels as they travel. (The selection of the following tasks depends on the concepts studied by the students before this lesson, that is, pathways and shapes.)

- Students combine locomotors with shapes by traveling in general space with a selected locomotor skill, stopping to create a wide shape (then narrow, curled, twisted) in balance, and then traveling with a different locomotor skill.
- Challenge students with balances at different levels.
- Students explore locomotors, pathways, and levels for travel in general space.

Allow sufficient time for students to create a sequence of locomotors and levels, demonstrating each of the levels in either travel or balances. (Enhance the complexity of the sequence with pathways, shapes, levels, and locomotors, as well as a beginning and ending shape.)

Assessment

Kindergarten

Show students a drawing with hands at high level, medium level, and low level; have them circle a figure in response to your directions.

Grade 1

Select photos from sports magazines showing the various levels; have students match the photo and the designated level.

Grade 2

The sequence of locomotors and levels easily becomes an assessment by having the students record the sequence, memorize it, and perform it.

Closure

- What movement concept did we study today?
- Name the three levels. Define each level.
- Kindergarten: Is a tall basketball player the only person who can reach to high level?
- Grade 2: How are levels used in gymnastics? Name a sport in which levels are important. Why are levels important in that sport?

Reflection

- Do students understand that everyone has a high, middle, and low level regardless of how tall they are?
- Can the children position body parts at different levels?
- Can they travel at each designated level?

FOCUS ►

SHAPES
Grades K, 1

The physically literate individual applies knowledge of concepts, principles, strategies and tactics related to movement and performance.

Grade-Level Outcome
Forms wide, narrow, curled, and twisted body shapes (S1.E7.Kb)

Lesson Objectives
The learner will:

- Identify the basic shapes of wide, narrow, curled, and twisted
- Make the shapes with the body and body parts

Introduction

In the classroom, your teacher talks about the shapes of circles, squares, and triangles in mathematics. Your mom and dad talk about getting in shape for fitness. Our lesson today is about shapes in physical education, shapes that the body makes. There are four shapes: wide, narrow, curled, and twisted.

Grade 1: Relate to dance, gymnastics, and sports for children.

LEARNING EXPERIENCE: NARROW SHAPES

In self-space, students make narrow shapes, long and thin, stretching to be really narrow.

Cue: *Legs and arms close to the body or close together.*

- Narrow shapes with the body in various positions: sitting, lying on the floor, standing
- Narrow shapes at different levels: low, medium, high (Imagery: like a piece of spaghetti)

LEARNING EXPERIENCE: WIDE SHAPES

In self-space, students make wide shapes by extending their arms and legs far to the sides.

Cue: *Legs and arms extended away from the body.*

- Wide shapes with the body in various positions
- Wide shapes at different levels (Imagery: like an open umbrella or a really big yawn.)

LEARNING EXPERIENCE: CURLED SHAPES

In self-space, students make curled or round shapes by curling the spine forward.

Cue: *Curling the spine.*

- Curled shapes with the body in various positions
- Curled shapes at different levels (Imagery: like a ball or the letter C)

LEARNING EXPERIENCE: TWISTED SHAPES

In self-space, students make twisted shapes by rotating a body part around a stationary axis. (Model the twisting action as opposed to crossing legs and arms).

Cue: *Rotate the arms, the legs, and the trunk.*

- Twisting of arms inward, outward
- Twisting the legs inward, outward

- Twisting the trunk clockwise, counterclockwise (Imagery: like a pretzel or a shoestring in a knot)
- How many body parts can you twist?

LEARNING EXPERIENCE: COMBINING SHAPES AND ACTIONS: TRANSFORMERS

We are going to combine body shapes and actions in an activity called Transformers. The word transform means to change from one thing to another—thus the name of the activity. You are going to be a transformer that changes shape four times. Your shapes will be wide, narrow, curled, and twisted. I will give the signal for changing shapes.

- Have the students make a wide shape in self-space—standing, sitting, or lying on the floor.
- Provide an eight-count signal for slowly changing from the wide shape to a narrow shape.
- Have students continue the shape and action sequence for all four shapes, emphasizing the slowness of the change and clear distinction of the shapes.

Grade 1

Students choose the order of the shapes.

Just for fun, name the transformer you created.

LEARNING EXPERIENCE: SHAPE STATUES

Divide the students into groups of four. Each person in the group makes one of the shapes. Students in each group touch to form a group statue that demonstrates each of the shapes.

Connect the shapes to form a single statue by having each person touching one other person in the group.

Grade 2

Challenge students to travel in their group statue while maintaining shapes and connections.

Assessment

Have students respond by creating the body shape you name. You can also assess cognitive understanding by students' spoken responses to these questions:

- What body parts create narrow shapes?
- Wide shapes?
- Curled shapes?
- What is the key to creating a twisted shape?

Closure

- We had fun today being transformers (Shape Statues), but what were we studying? What was the objective of our lesson?
- What are the four body shapes?

Show the children pictures of the various body shapes in sports or physical activity contexts. (Watch for photos of local athletes in the newspaper.) Have the children identify the body shape shown in the action photo.

Grade 1

- Which of the shapes does a basketball player use in a defensive guarding position?
- Which shape does the gymnast use for forward and backward rolls?

Reflection

- Can the children use their whole bodies and body parts to make each of the shapes?
- Can they identify each of the shapes when demonstrated or when seen in photos of athletes in sports, gymnastics, or dance?

FOCUS >

TIME

Grades K-2

Standard 2 The physically literate individual applies knowledge of concepts, principles, strategies and tactics related to movement and performance.

Grade-Level Outcomes

- Travels in general space with different speeds (S2.E3.K)
- Differentiates between fast and slow speeds (S2.E3.1a)
- Varies time and force with gradual increases and decreases (S2.E3.2)

Lesson Objectives

The learner will:

- Move body parts slowly and quickly
- Move in general space at slow and fast rates of speed
- Move in general space gradually increasing and decreasing speed

Materials and Equipment

Drum

Introduction

When you are moving through the hallway at school, does the teacher want you to move very, very fast? When you hit the ball in a T-ball game, should you run slowly to first base or as fast as you can?

(Use examples that relate to the students in your class, linking the lesson to everyday activities, sports, gymnastics, and dance as appropriate.)

Sometimes moving as fast as possible is important; sometimes we should move more slowly. That is the focus of our lesson today: time and speed—the difference between moving slowly and moving quickly.

LEARNING EXPERIENCE: CONTRASTS IN TIME

In self-space, students move their hands slowly toward each other and then quickly apart. (Imagery: slowly as if about to capture an insect and then realizing at the last moment that the insect is a bee.)

- Students move their hands quickly toward each other, stop at the last second, and then move them slowly apart.
- Repeat contrasts several times, observing for students' ability to develop contrast.

Have students travel in general space with chosen locomotor movement.

- They travel slowly with the same locomotor movement.
- They travel fast with the same locomotor movement.

Safety Check: *Ensure that students do not collide with one another or lose their balance.*

Have students travel in general space with their favorite locomotor movement. On your signal, they change the speed from slow to fast or fast to slow.

Imagery for Contrasts in Time

Use these scenarios to provide imagery for students:

- Pretend you are walking through a dark alley at night; move very slowly. On the signal, run quickly in the opposite direction as if a mouse has suddenly frightened you.

- Begin traveling slowly in a large circle as if you are a lion stalking your prey. Make the circle smaller as you sneak up on your prey. Quickly pounce on the target you are stalking.
- Rise slowly from low to high as if you are stiff and unsure of every movement. On the signal, collapse quickly to the low-level position.
- Travel as if you are a balloon floating slowly through space. On the signal, explode as if you were pricked with a pin. Travel erratically and very quickly for a few seconds and then sink slowly to the floor.
- Run quickly in general space as if you are a distance runner on top of the world. Decrease your speed as if you are on your last legs, moving slowly uphill. Increase your speed as if you have a burst of energy. Slow to a steady pace and then walk.
- Run as if you are a sprinter in the last leg of the relay; run as if you are on mile 20 of the 26-mile marathon.

LEARNING EXPERIENCE: ACTION WORDS FOR TIME

Brainstorm with students action words that describe moving quickly and slowly. Record them on the whiteboard. Here are some examples:

Fast	Slow
Pounce	Creep
Run	Crawl
Collapse	Sneak

- Allow sufficient time for students to explore each of the action words with appropriate movement speed.

LEARNING EXPERIENCE: TIME SEQUENCE

Select three words with contrasts in time to form a time sequence. Review the use of a comma and a period in a sentence; they indicate pause and stop. On your signal, students begin the first movement and continue that action until the next signal. They pause and then begin the second movement. They continue until the signal, when they pause and begin the third movement. On your signal, they stop. Example: slow, creep, pounce. The student moves slowly as if stalking prey in the jungle, pauses, then creeps slower, pauses, then pounces quickly on the prey.

Grade 1

Have the students design their personal time sequences by choosing three action words. (Remind the students that the sequence is to show contrasts in time and variations in speed.) Sequences can be shown to a partner or recorded on paper.

LEARNING EXPERIENCE: INCREASING AND DECREASING SPEED (GRADES 1 AND 2)

Students travel in general space at a moderate speed, gradually increasing and decreasing speed. (Imagery: A car starts moving slowly and gradually gains speed. It then experiences engine trouble and slows almost to a stop, regains speed, and moves quickly again.)

- Challenge students to travel in general space with the beat of the drum. Maintain a steady, moderate beat until the class is responding correctly (moderate speed).
- Then increase and decrease the beat of the drum for increases and decreases in travel speed. (Gradual increases and decreases in speed are challenging for young children; they tend to travel either as fast as possible or extremely slowly.)

Grade 2: Slow-Motion Sports

Have students think of a favorite sports action, such as a jump for a rebound in a basketball game, the punt in a football game, the swing of a bat, or a strikeout pitch in a baseball game. Have them focus on only one action, performing the movement as if it is a video of the action. (This will require several minutes of practice.)

- Have the students perform the action as if the camera is set on slow motion, repeating the movement sequence three times.
- They perform the action as if the camera is switched to fast speed, repeating the movement sequence three times.

Remember, the action is the same; only the speed has changed.

Assessment

Time sequences become informal assessments with students' recording of sequences on paper and established criteria, followed by teacher or partner observation. (Focus of assessments—both cognitive and performance understanding—is on contrasts in speed. Increasing and decreasing speed is introduced and practiced. Mastery of increasing and decreasing speed specific to games, gymnastics, and dance occurs at a later grade level.)

Closure

- What was the focus of our lesson today?
- Tell your neighbor the two contrasts in time and speed we studied.
- Do you think you are in more control when traveling slowly or very quickly? Why?

Grade 2

- Describe a situation when you need to move slowly while playing on the outdoor equipment at recess. Describe a situation when you need to move quickly.
- Describe a situation in games or sports when you need to move quickly. Describe a situation when you need to move slowly.

Reflection

- Can students move body parts and the whole body both slowly and quickly?
- Can they move fast or slow in response to descriptive words of time?
- Can they run at a moderate to fast speed with body control, stop on your signal, and have no collisions?

FORCE
Grades K-2

Standard 2 The physically literate individual applies knowledge of concepts, principles, strategies and tactics related to movement and performance.

Grade-Level Outcomes

- Differentiates between strong and light force (S2.E3.1b)
- Varies time and force with gradual increases and decreases (S2.E3.2)

Lesson Objectives

The learner will:

- Demonstrate strong and light force with body shapes
- Travel with light and strong movements
- Contrast strong and light body actions

Materials and Equipment

- Pictures illustrating strong and light force
- Balloons, eight
- Small balls for throwing, eight
- Kicking balls, slightly deflated, eight
- Hoops, two

Introduction

Show students pictures that illustrate strong force, such as a weightlifter with muscles displayed or an ant carrying an object twice its size. Ask students what the two have in common.

Do the same with pictures that illustrate light force, such as a single snowflake and a cartoon elephant in a tutu. (The purpose of the contrasts is to demonstrate that strong force and light force are not dictated by size.)

The focus of our lesson today is force—the contrasts between strong and light. Knowing when to use strong force and when to use light force is important in throwing, kicking, and striking as well as in dance and gymnastics.

LEARNING EXPERIENCE: CONTRASTS IN FORCE

In self-space, have students pose as statues that demonstrate strong force. Repeat several times, exploring different shapes and designs for strong force.

Repeat the statue, tightening every muscle in your body (S2.E4).

Observe the class for differences in shapes that demonstrate the concept of strong force, remembering to highlight several.

- Repeat the task for statues that demonstrate light force.

Think of yourself as so light that a puff of wind would blow you away—a ghost, a leaf in the wind. You have no tension, no tightness.

- Students travel in general space using strong and light movements. (This one is challenging for young children because they equate heavy with strong; spoken cues will be helpful as they are moving with strong force.)

Imagery

- A single snowflake that becomes a large snowball.
- A gentle raindrop that becomes a fierce thunderstorm.

LEARNING EXPERIENCE: ACTION WORDS FOR FORCE

Brainstorm with students action words that describe strong and light force. Allow several minutes for the class to experience moving in response to each. Here are some examples:

- Punch in the air as if boxing a heavyweight opponent.
- Flick in the air as if dusting a speck on a cobweb.
- Glide across the room like a skilled ice skater.
- Stomp on the floor as if getting mud off of your shoes.

LEARNING EXPERIENCE: PRACTICE STATIONS FOR FORCE

- Station 1: Punching or striking a balloon in the air with strong movements, striking a balloon with light movements

I should be able to identify the action as strong or light by watching you hit the balloon.

- Station 2: Kicking a ball so that it travels completely across the general space area, kicking a ball so that it travels only to the target zone halfway across the

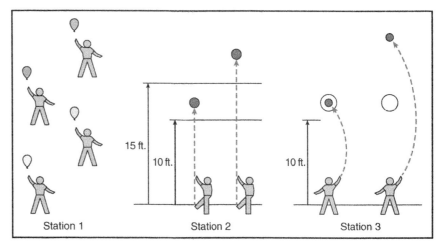

general space area (gymnasium, blacktop, playground area)

- Station 3: Throwing a ball so that it travels as far as possible, throwing the ball with lighter force so that it lands in or near a hoop

Assessment

Practice stations provide an excellent venue for formative assessment of performance understanding of the concept. Position yourself at one station and inform students of the observation focus.

Closure

- What was the focus of our lesson today?
- Tell your neighbor an example of light force and an example of strong force.
- Why do you need to be able to use different amounts of force in physical education activities?

Reflection

- Can students identify strong and light movements?
- Can they move with strong and light force?
- Can they kick, throw, and strike with a contrast between strong and light force?

FOCUS›

FLOW
Grades 2, 3

Standard 2 The physically literate individual applies knowledge of concepts, principles, strategies and tactics related to movement and performance.

Grade-Level Outcomes

This lesson is a prerequisite to the following outcomes:

- Combines locomotor skills and movement concepts (levels, shapes, extensions, pathways, force, time, flow) to create and perform a dance (S1.E11.3)
- Combines locomotor skills and movement concepts (levels, shapes, extensions, pathways, force, time, flow) to create and perform a dance with a partner (S1.E11.4)
- Combines locomotor skills and movement concepts (levels, shapes, extensions, pathways, force, time, flow) to create and perform a dance with a group (S1.E11.5)

Lesson Objective

The learner will demonstrate the contrast in bound-flow and free-flow movements.

Materials and Equipment

- Drum
- Music that depicts flow, music that depicts start and stop rhythm (jerky)
- Cardboard pizza circles, one per student (available at local pizza restaurant)

Introduction

Today, we introduce a movement concept called flow. When we think of the word flow, we usually think of free-flowing water. Actually, there are two types of flow in movement—bound and free. A movement that is stoppable at any point is bound. A baseball or softball player executing a bunt checks his or her swing for the soft tap. A movement that is unstoppable is an example of free flow. The swing of the baseball or softball player with full power is not stoppable at will; the swing continues until it is completed. There are times in games, gymnastics, and dance when we need bound-flow movements and instances when we need a free-flow movement. The combination of bound-flow and free-flow movements adds excitement to gymnastic routines and heightens the expressiveness of creative dance.

LEARNING EXPERIENCE: IN SELF-SPACE

Contrast free flow and bound flow with movements such as raising one arm high in the air and lowering it with the designated count 1, 2, 3, 4, and then raising the arm high in the air and letting it drop. Discuss with students the difference in the two actions: one is stoppable; the other is not.

- Allow several minutes for students to explore bound-flow movements within self-space, emphasizing the stoppable action with the arms, legs, and total body.
- Allow similar time for exploration of free-flow movements within self-space, emphasizing the concept of being unstoppable.

LEARNING EXPERIENCE: TRAVELING WITH CONTRASTS

- Have students walk in general space as if carrying a bowl of soup that is too full; have them travel like a cloud or a balloon floating, or like an eagle soaring in the sky.
  - Focus the travel on bound flow; students are able to stop at any moment.
  - Focus the travel on free flow; students are seemingly unable to stop at any moment, yet the travel action is under control.

- Have the students travel in a zigzag pathway, making exaggerated sharp and quick cuts, depicting bound flow. Contrast with free-flowing curving pathways. Use music that contrasts the bound flow and free flow; students move accordingly.

LEARNING EXPERIENCE: PURPOSEFUL CONTRASTS

- Drop a feather or light scarf to the ground and then drop a ball, allowing students to observe the difference in free-flow and bound-flow movement of an object.
- With students standing in self-space and each student holding a pizza circle flat on the palm, have them explore moving the cardboard circles in various ways around the body—high to low, side to side, around the body, varying speeds and positions to determine bound flow and free flow in the actions.

Is it possible to move the circle from high to low level with it flat on your palm? Is it possible to have the circle flat on your palm, yet turned sideways, and not allow it to fall to the floor?

- Explore the actions for the free flow.

Purposely move the circle very slowly, stoppable at any moment. Where in space can you now move the circle? In what positions around the body? Explore this bound flow.

Grade 3: Pizza Circle Dances

Combine free-flow and bound-flow movements into a sequence:

1. Beginning and ending shape
2. Combination of bound-flow and free-flow actions
3. Minimum travel from self-space

(Use soft background music to establish length of sequence, about 60 to 90 seconds.)

Assessment

Observe for student cognitive understanding of bound flow and free flow.

Closure

- What was the focus of our lesson today?
- What are the two types of flow? How do they differ?

Grade 2

I will name an action from a sport, gymnastics stunt, or dance. You will then classify the action as bound flow or free flow.

Examples: jumping to catch a ball, forward roll, headstand, defense posture in basketball

Grade 3

Name an example of bound flow and free flow in a favorite game, gymnastics, or dance activity.

Reflection

- Can students demonstrate both bound-flow and free-flow movements?
- Can they identify both when you demonstrate the movements?

REVIEW OF MOVEMENT CONCEPTS

Grade 3

The physically literate individual applies knowledge of concepts, principles, strategies and tactics related to movement and performance.

Grade-Level Outcomes

- Combines movement concepts (direction, levels, force, time) with skills as directed by the teacher (S2.E3.3)
- Employs the concept of alignment in gymnastics and dance (S2.E4.3a)

Lesson Objectives

The learner will:

- Apply movement concepts in a teacher-designed movement sequence
- Choreograph and perform a movement sequence

Materials and Equipment

- Music
- Streamers or scarves
- Whiteboard
- Paper, pencils for recording sequences

Introduction

In second grade, you learned about the concept of time (speed), force, and flow. What are the different speeds we travel? Can someone explain force and give an example? Who else can contrast the idea of light and strong force that relates to sports? Our last one today is flow. Spread your arms into a wide shape. Show me how you can bring your hands together using bound and jerky movements. Right, the movement stops and starts. Now contrast that with free-flow movements. Today, we are going to review these concepts with a fun movement sequence. Then you will be able to create your own sequence.

LEARNING EXPERIENCE: MOVEMENT SEQUENCE

Movement sequences are like sentences. They have a beginning and an ending.

Write the following sentence on the whiteboard: Walk four steps, turn, stretch into a wide shape, collapse to the floor, and rise to standing.

What do commas and periods mean in a sentence? The same is true for a movement sequence: A comma means pause, and a period means stop.

- Allow time for students to practice the sequence from the whiteboard until it they seem to have it memorized.
- For each of the following movement concepts, have the students perform the sequence several times before you present the next concept. (The sequence remains the same; the movement concepts change.)
  - Change the sequence to slow motion.
  - Change the sequence to fast motion.
  - Make the movements as small as possible and travel with light force.
  - Make the movements as large as possible and travel with strong force.

- Use bound and jerky movements.
- Use free-flowing movements.
- Add streamers or scarves and repeat bound flow and free flow.
- Add music and ask students to perform movements based on feel or rhythm of the music. (Several different creative music pieces work best here.)

LEARNING EXPERIENCE: CHOREOGRAPH A SEQUENCE

Have each student create a sequence to include the following: one shape, one locomotor skill, one nonlocomotor action (stretch, bend, twist), a turn, and one vibratory (shaking) movement. The sequence should include a variation of time, force, and flow. Write the requirements or criteria for the sequence on the board, informing students that the order of the components is their decision. (You should select the music in the early stages of the sequence and routine design; choose one piece of music for everyone to use.)

- Allow students ample time to create and practice their sequences. Have them illustrate or write their sequences.
- Ask them to perform their sequences in general space (all at the same time) three consecutive times and then freeze.
- With partners, students teach each other the sequence.
- Partners work cooperatively (S4.E4.3a) and combine the two sequences in an ABAB choreography. Allow sufficient time for partners to learn and practice the two sequences.
- Partners perform the sequence for another group. (Encourage students to accept and give praise [S4.E4.3b] for the sequences.)

Choreography is a challenging yet enjoyable process for children and one that should not be rushed. You should expect this lesson to take more than one class period.

Assessment

- Observe both cognitive and performance understanding of the concepts of time, force, and flow.
- Teaching the movement sequence can become an informal assessment with partner or teacher observation.

Closure

- What was the focus of our lesson today?
- Share with your neighbor a way that time, force, or flow could be used in a specific gymnastic movement. Explain why the one you shared is important to the quality of that movement.
- Using your favorite music, create your own movement sequences at home; have your friends or family join you.

Reflection

- Do students clearly differentiate the concepts of time, force, and flow?
- Do they work well together in the partner activity and praise each other in the small-group performance?

CHAPTER 6

Teaching for Competency in Locomotor Skills

Locomotor skills are the foundation for all movement. From the crawling action of a baby, to the first steps of a toddler, to the combination of skills used by professional athletes in dance, sports, and gymnastics, locomotor movements provide our daily functional movements as well as our recreational and aesthetic enjoyment of physical activity. We are reminded by Gallahue et al. (2012) that these are not naturally occurring skills. Although many youngsters develop a rudimentary form of running, skipping, jumping, and so on, the maturing pattern for successful participation and physical literacy requires instruction.

All too often, teachers of elementary physical education present the locomotor skills with a single lesson for the introduction and practice of each and then assume that the students have mastered the skill. This assumption results in one of two situations: an absence of any further practice of the locomotor skill until it is needed for an activity or an immediate application of the skill in an activity.

Locomotor skills, like nonlocomotor and manipulative skills, are not mastered in a single lesson. They require repetitive, deliberate practice of the focused skill over time. Hopping, galloping, jogging, and sliding are mature pattern benchmarks for the end of first grade. Skipping is a Grade-Level Outcome for second grade. Running and leaping with mature patterns are expectations by the end of third grade. Placing students in activities that require the application of these skills in the early years of elementary school is comparable with having youngsters participate in competitive sports before they develop the necessary skills. Chasing, fleeing, and tag games do not benefit students' emerging skills; application activities are appropriate only after mature patterns have been attained.

The introductory tasks in the first lesson plan of this chapter can easily be used for distributed practice throughout the year. They are examples of appropriate, targeted tasks to develop emerging locomotor skills; you will be able to design many more as you observe your students and reflect on their progress. The revisitation of locomotor skills adds breadth to the students' experiences with the addition of movement concepts, such as directions and pathways. As with the introductory lessons, locomotors can be practiced for a few minutes in the early review and warm-up stages of the lesson or before introduction of the nonlocomotor or manipulative lesson for the day. This brief but important time provides you the opportunity to observe the class, as well as individual students, for feedback on critical elements of the locomotor skills. The difference between the average student and those who excel is often the fine-tuning of the skill. Locomotors are no exception; mature patterns are important.

LOCOMOTOR SKILLS

Space Awarenes

Grades K-3

Standard 1 The physically literate individual demonstrates competency in a variety of motor skills and movement patterns.

Grade-Level Outcomes

- Performs locomotor skills (hopping, galloping, running, sliding, skipping) while maintaining balance (S1.E1.K)
- Performs jumping and landing actions with balance (S1.E3.K)

Lesson Objectives

The learner will:

- Travel in general space without bumping others or falling down
- Travel in general space with a variety of locomotor skills
- Identify the basic locomotor skills (hopping, galloping, running, sliding, skipping, leaping) when they are demonstrated correctly by the teacher or another student

Note: Although locomotors are critical to the foundational skills of physical education, they are rarely the focus of an entire 30-minute lesson for young children. The following guidelines will help in planning for their mastery at the designated grade level:

- At the kindergarten level, students are encouraged to travel safely in general space; locomotors are introduced without expectation of mastery.
- Demonstration and lots of repetition are often the best ways for young children to learn the proper execution of a locomotor skill.
- For most students the progression for mastering locomotors is hopping, galloping, sliding, skipping, and leaping. Running is a naturally occurring skill for young children, but a mature pattern of running develops with appropriate teacher-guided practice and a focus on critical elements.

The following lessons are designed for 8 to 10 minutes at the beginning of the 30- minute physical education lesson for the introduction and practice of locomotors. The remainder of the lesson is focused on another skill category, such as manipulatives or nonlocomotors.

HOPPING

Materials and Equipment

- Drum for signal
- Whiteboard or flipchart for recording

Introduction

If I watched your class during recess outside, how many different ways to move would I see? (List students' answers on the board: running, walking, jumping, hopping, and so on.) These ways to travel are called locomotor movements; they are used in games, dance, and gymnastics.

Focus on the locomotor movement to be introduced today with links to games that students play at recess, in sports, and in dance and gymnastics when applicable.

The locomotor for today is hopping: up and down, same foot, one to one.

Critical Elements for Hopping

- Take off on one foot and land on the same foot.
- Upward push and absorption of landing shock is accomplished by the ankle.
- Arms push up and down (to lift and for balance).
- Knee seldom straightens fully.

LEARNING EXPERIENCE: HOPPING IN SELF-SPACE

Hopping up and down in self-space, landing on the same foot each time

- Five times on the preferred foot, five times on other foot
- Hopping on one foot until the drum signal and then hopping on the other foot. (Remind the children to switch to the other leg for hopping when tired.)

LEARNING EXPERIENCE: HOPPING IN GENERAL SPACE

Traveling in general space by hopping.

Safety Check: Hop in a forward direction only.

- Hope five times preferred foot, five times other.
- Hop on one foot until signal for switching to other foot.

Assessment

Observe students who have difficulty lifting the foot from the floor or maintaining movement on the same foot, or who lose balance.

Closure

- What locomotor movement did we introduce today?
- Do rabbits hop? Kangaroos? They actually jump—they use two feet and legs to rise up off the ground, not one, as in hopping—even though the books we read call what rabbits and kangaroos do hopping. How is hopping different from jumping?

Reflection

- Can students hop in self-space without losing balance?
- Can they travel forward, hopping in general space while maintaining their balance?
- Can they maintain the hopping action on both the preferred and the nonpreferred foot for three or more hops?

FOCUS▶   JUMPING

Materials and Equipment

Drum for signal

Introduction

What do a grasshopper, Tigger the Tiger, and a basketball player have in common? They jump. We can jump forward, backward, high in the air, across rain puddles. Always when we jump we need to land with good balance, bending our knees for a soft, balanced landing.

Review from the hopping lesson the difference between hopping and jumping.

There are two kinds of jumping. One is a locomotor skill that moves us through general space. The other jumping is a nonlocomotor skill; it moves us only up and down in self-space. Our focus today will be on landing softly when we jump.

Critical Elements for Landing

- Hips, knees, and ankles bend on landing.
- Shoulders, knees, and ankles align for balance after landing.

LEARNING EXPERIENCE: JUMPING IN SELF-SPACE

- Jumping in self-space—repetitive jumps with little height
  - Landing with good balance, that is, not falling down
  - Landing with bent knees ready to spring back for the next jump
- Jumping forward from self-space position
  - Landing with good balance
  - Landing with bent knees to absorb the force

Safety Check: Check for sufficient room so that students can jump forward with no collisions.

LEARNING EXPERIENCE: JUMPING IN GENERAL SPACE

Jumping to travel in general space—repetitive jumps with very little height or distance

- Landing with good balance, that is, not falling down
- Landing with knees bent, ready to spring back for the next jump

Assessment

Observe students for balanced landings, that is, not falling down.

Closure

- What was our new locomotor skill today?
- How many feet are used for jumping? How many are used for hopping?

Reflection

- Do students land with good balance when jumping forward and upward?
- Do they land on two feet simultaneously?
- Do certain students need extra help with the skill?

FOCUS ▶   <u>GALLOPING</u>

Materials and Equipment

Drum for signal

Introduction

Last time, we worked on hopping on both the right foot and left foot. Complete this sentence for your neighbor: Hopping is on _____ foot; jumping is on _____ feet. The locomotor for today is galloping. What animal do you think of when I say, "Galloping"?

Critical Elements for Galloping

- Trunk faces in forward direction.
- Lead leg lifts and moves forward to support weight.
- Rear foot closes quickly to supporting foot.
- Lead leg lifts to repeat action.
- Arms are in front, bent slightly.

LEARNING EXPERIENCE: REVIEW OF LOCOMOTORS

Review locomotors introduced thus far, offer cues for proper execution, and have students practice in general space.

LEARNING EXPERIENCE: GALLOPING

- With students scattered throughout general space, demonstrate the correct gallop, emphasizing leading with the same foot throughout the action.
- Have students stand with the lead foot in front, ready for the gallop. On your signal, they gallop in general space with no collisions and no loss of balance.
- Have students change the lead foot and continue the gallop in general space.
- Just for fun, have them gallop like a cowgirl, like a cowboy riding a horse, and backward.

Look over your shoulder to avoid collisions with others. Lower your body slightly to help with balance going backward.

Assessment

Observe students who are having difficulty keeping the lead foot in front throughout the action or having difficulty maintaining balance.

Closure

What locomotor did we introduce today?

Reflection

- Can students gallop in general space while maintaining their balance?
- Can they gallop with both the preferred and the nonpreferred foot leading the action?

FOCUS▸

SLIDING

Subfocus▸

Pathways

Materials and Equipment

Drum for signal

Introduction

What first comes to your mind when I say, "Sliding"? Baseball players slide to avoid being tagged out at the base. We slide on ice in the winter. Basketball players slide as they move quickly side to side. There are many types of sliding movements.

Introduce the sliding movement as a locomotor skill—a gallop to the side with the side of the body and foot leading, with the airborne lift of a dancer. Contrast the movement with gliding on the feet forward pretending to ice skate.

Critical Elements for Sliding

- Trunk faces in forward direction; head is turned sideways in direction of travel.
- Lead leg lifts and moves sideways to support weight.
- Rear foot closes quickly to supporting foot.
- Body is momentarily airborne.
- Arms are lifted, extended to the sides.

LEARNING EXPERIENCE: SLIDING

Review the critical elements for galloping. Note the similarities and differences between galloping and sliding. Demonstrate the slide with verbal cues of sideward direction, head turned, and body airborne. With students scattered throughout general space, have them slide in their preferred sideward direction.

- Sliding to the right, looking in that direction
- Sliding to the left, looking to the left
- Sliding in preferred direction, changing the direction on your signal
- Sliding with zigzag and curved pathways, avoiding collisions (movement concept lesson as prerequisite)

Assessment

Observe students having difficulty achieving the airborne lift of the body or maintaining balance.

Closure

- What locomotor movement did we introduce today?
- What is the difference between a gallop and a slide?
- In sports we have three kinds of slides: basketball player, baseball player, skater. Which slide did we practice today?

Reflection

- Can students travel in general space with the sliding action, maintaining their balance?
- Can they slide to both the right and the left?

FOCUS▸

Subfocus▸

RUNNING

Time

Introduction

Have students name their favorite ways to travel in general space. Remind them that a repeat is OK because each person is naming his or her favorite way to move.

Thus far in our lessons we have worked on hopping, jumping, galloping, and sliding. Today, we will travel with what is probably your favorite—running. We are going to focus on a certain kind of running—jogging. Who can tell me what jogging is? Jogging is running at a slower speed. You often see people jogging on the track or in your neighborhood. We will use jogging indoors and save our fast running for outdoors where we have more space.

Critical Elements for Running

- Arm–leg opposition throughout action.
- Toes point forward.
- Foot lands heel to toe.
- Arms swing forward and backward—no crossing of midline.
- Trunk leans slightly forward.

LEARNING EXPERIENCE: JOGGING

- Have students run in general space with no collisions with others; they stop on your signal without falling down.
    - Slow the speed of the travel to what the students think is jogging. (Demonstrate the difference between running for speed and jogging.)
    - Allow several 30-second practices of jogging and stopping on your signal.
- Demonstrate exaggerated slowness to show that jogging is not walking; jogging is running at a slower pace.
- Have students jog at medium speed, as if running a marathon.

Assessment

Observe students for common errors: running on toes, extreme crossing of the midline.

LEARNING EXPERIENCE: TRAVELING WITH VARIOUS LOCOMOTORS

Review locomotors by having students travel with the designated locomotor, not colliding with others, and switching to the next locomotor without losing balance.

- Have students hop, gallop, slide, and jog.
- Have students explore various combinations of locomotors while you observe cognitive understanding and emerging skills.
- Have students change locomotors. Students now decide the order of the four locomotors—hopping, galloping, sliding, and jogging. On your signal, they begin the first locomotor and change the locomotor action with each signal.

Assessment

Partner assessment of locomotors: Have each student stand beside a partner. Partner A tells partner B which locomotor he or she is going to use for traveling. After partner A demonstrates the chosen locomotor, partner B gives a thumbs-up if the demonstration was of the chosen locomotor.

Closure

- What locomotor movement did we add today?
- Watch as I travel across the work area; tell your neighbor the name of the locomotor movement I am using for my travel. (Repeat for each of the locomotors introduced thus far.)

Reflection

- Can students run in general space without bumping others and while maintaining their balance?
- Can they differentiate between jogging and running for speed?

Note: Students will not develop the mature pattern of running easily, if at all, by jogging indoors in the confined space of a gymnasium. You need to design lessons that include enjoyable running outdoors, with sufficient space for increasing speed and sufficient space for all students to run simultaneously without fear of collisions.

SKIPPING

Skipping is one of the more difficult locomotor skills for children to master. The progression is normally from a gallop to a skip action on every other foot to a full skipping action.

We have found it best not to overanalyze the skipping action, not to break it down as a step-hop-step-hop; this approach often results in a stiff step-hop action, not a fluid motion. A demonstration by you, repetitive experiences, skipping with music, and skipping with a partner has proved successful in teaching the skill.

Kindergarten and first-grade students should not feel pressure to skip correctly; a mature pattern as a Grade-Level Outcome is appropriate for second grade.

Critical Elements for Skipping

- Step and hop on one foot and then on the other foot.
- Arms move in opposition to feet.
- Arm and leg lift on hopping action.
- Feet alternate lead.

LEARNING EXPERIENCE: PARTNER PRACTICE

- Have students travel through general space by skipping with a chosen partner.
- Have students keep a side-by-side relationship with the partner as they skip. (Kindergarteners may choose to gallop or skip.)
- Challenge students to adjust speed to maintain the side-to-side relationship as they travel with a partner.

LEARNING EXPERIENCE: FOLLOW THE LEADER

- Have students travel through general space with a chosen partner with one partner as the leader and the other partner as the follower. First graders skip as they travel; kindergarteners may choose to skip or gallop. On your signal, partners switch the leader by turning and traveling in the opposite direction.

LEARNING EXPERIENCE: COPY CAT

- Partner A travels by hopping, jumping, jogging, galloping, sliding, or skipping to a new location in general space. Partner B copies the locomotor movement to travel to the same location. Partner B then becomes the leader and chooses a new locomotor and a new location.

(This copycat action can easily become a dance for children by adding a beginning and ending shape; music is an option.)

Assessment

No assessment of skipping until second grade. Teacher observation and encouragement only for grades K and 1.

LEAPING

Grades 2, 3

Leaping is the last of the locomotor skills for young children to master. Therefore, it is introduced in grade 2, and performance in a mature pattern is a Grade-Level Outcome for grade 3.

Materials and Equipment

Jump ropes, one per student

Introduction

Thus far in our study of locomotor movements, you have traveled with hopping, jumping, galloping, sliding, running, and skipping. Today, we will add the last of our locomotors—leaping. What do you think of when I say, "Leaping"? (Possible responses include leap frog, ballet dancers, basketball players, acrobatics, and maybe over a creek or mud puddle.)

Introduce leaping as a locomotor skill, a form of jumping—taking off on one foot and landing on the other foot. Demonstrate the skill of leaping, emphasizing the flight phase of leaping: extension of the legs, extension and lift of the arms, and forward motion of the body while in the air. Leaping is an extension of a run or jog.

Critical Elements for Leaping

* Takeoff is on one foot, and landing is on opposite foot.
* Legs extend for height and distance.
* Arms extend and lift for airborne time.
* Knee bends to absorb force on landing.

LEARNING EXPERIENCE: TRAVEL BY LEAPING

Have the students travel throughout general space with a combination of running and leaping: run, run, run, leap; run, run, run, leap; emphasizing taking off on one foot, landing on the other foot, and continuing with the run.

* Have students practice the running and leaping movement pattern, emphasizing the extension of the legs in flight for distance while airborne, as in leaping over puddles in the rain.
* Some puddles are small; some are large. Students should vary the distance of the leap.
* Allow sufficient practice time for students to establish their own rhythms for running and leaping, such as how many steps to take before the leap and which foot to use for the takeoff.

Challenge yourself to extend your arms and legs and lift your body for increased hang time as if suspended in midair when you leap. Pretend that you are Peter Pan flying for just one second. Extend your arms sideways and legs forward and backward.

Grade 3

* Have students position jump ropes in a straight line in their personal space, then practice leaping over their ropes in personal space.
* Challenge students to travel through general space, leaping over the scattered ropes.

Safety Check: Alert students to check for open space before leaping.

Assessment

* Conduct informal observation of students in grade 2, because this is for practice only.
* Observe critical elements for students in grade 3.

Closure

- What locomotor skill did you practice today?
- What makes the leap more difficult than other locomotor skills?
- Describe a time in dance, gymnastics, or sports when you have seen the performer leaping.

Reflection

Grade 2

- Are the students able to take off on one foot and land on the other foot in a leaping action?
- Does the leaping action move them horizontally through the air rather than vertically?

Grade 3

- Are the students demonstrating the critical elements of a mature pattern for the leaping action?
- Are they using extension to stay airborne with extensions and using a strong push-off of the body for flight?

REVIEW OF LOCOMOTORS

Movement Concepts

Grades 1, 2

Standard 1 The physically literate individual demonstrates competency in a variety of motor skills and movement patterns.

Grade-Level Outcomes

- Performs locomotor skills while maintaining balance (S1.E1.k)
- Hops, gallops, jogs, and slides using a mature pattern (S1.E1.1)
- Skips using a mature pattern (S1.E1.2)

Lesson Objectives

The learner will:

- Travel in general space with mature patterns of hopping, galloping, sliding, and jogging (grade 1)
- Travel in general space with a mature pattern of skipping (grade 2)
- Identify the basic locomotor movements when they are correctly demonstrated by the teacher or another student
- Combine locomotors into a sequence

Note: A mature pattern of skill execution is the expectation at the end of the year—grade 1, grade 2. Lessons of practice before the summative assessment should focus on progress and demonstration of critical elements.

Materials and Equipment

- Drum
- Music (optional)
- Whiteboard for recording movement sequences, pencil and paper for student recordings

Introduction

Earlier in the year, we focused on moving without bumping into others and stopping on signal without falling down. You have traveled in general space by walking, hopping, jumping, galloping, sliding, jogging, and skipping. What is the name for these movements? Today, we will review the locomotor movements as we travel in general space.

LEARNING EXPERIENCE: LOCOMOTORS IN GENERAL SPACE

- Traveling in general space with the various locomotors, teacher directed
- Traveling in general space, changing to a different locomotor on signal
- Traveling with a favorite locomotor
- Traveling in a new way, creating a new locomotor action, with pathways, directions, levels added for the new locomotor

LEARNING EXPERIENCE: CORNER-TO-CORNER LOCOMOTORS

- Divide the class into four groups, positioning each group in one corner of the work area. Number the groups 1, 2, 3, and 4.

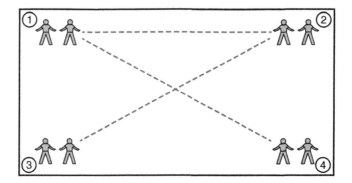

- Call two numbers and the name of a locomotor movement, such as 1 and 4, jogging. In response, groups 1 and 4 exchange places, traveling corner to corner by jogging.
  - Practice with different combinations of numbers and different locomotors
  - Free travel, traveling with personal choice of locomotor movement
  - All groups, everyone exchanging corners (offers an excellent opportunity for observation of travel without collisions)

Note: Include skipping in the corner-to-corner exchange only after sufficient practice and after observing that the children are comfortable with the skill; first graders may skip or gallop.

LEARNING EXPERIENCE: COMBINING LOCOMOTOR MOVEMENTS INTO SEQUENCES: MOVEMENT SENTENCES

Let's put together some of the locomotor movements we have practiced by making a movement sentence. I will write the first one, and then we will write one together. Walk, hop, gallop. What does a comma mean when you are reading? Right, it means to pause. The drum will be our signal to pause. Ready? Walk . . . hop . . . gallop.

- Exploration of various body shapes for sentence endings: question mark, exclamation mark, period
- Group sentences composed by students
- Individual sentences composed by each person in class, recorded on paper, and shown to a partner, you, or the class

Assessment

Observe locomotors during practice, during sequences, and during corner-to-corner exchanges. These formative assessments provide valuable information regarding individual performances as well as total class performance of the benchmark skill.

On a checklist (electronic or paper and pencil) list the basic locomotor movements, as well as the critical elements for each skill. Observe students periodically as they perform the locomotor movements, coding the checklist when they demonstrate mastery of the critical elements as well as mastery of a mature pattern of overall skill execution. Checklists can be rather simple, using a "+" for mastery, or they can be more complex, including the date of mastery. You should assess skills more than once. Remember that young children often can perform skills correctly but not consistently.

Closure

List on the whiteboard the locomotors as students name them. For each locomotor listed, have students describe a game, gymnastics, or dance action in which the locomotor is used.

Reflection

- Are the students ready for summative evaluation of each of the locomotors?
- Which students, which classes, need concentrated practice on specific locomotors?

REVIEW OF LOCOMOTORS

Directions, Pathways

Grade 3

tandard 1 The physically literate individual demonstrates competency in a variety of motor skills and movement patterns.

Grade-Level Outcome

Performs a sequence of locomotor skills, transitioning from one skill to another smoothly and without hesitation (S1.E6.3)

Lesson Objectives

The learner will:

- Travel in general space with mature patterns of hopping, galloping, sliding, jogging, skipping, and leaping*
- Combine locomotors into a sequence with smooth transitions
- Have a clear beginning and ending for the sequence

*A mature pattern of leaping is the expectation at the end of grade 3.

Materials and Equipment

- Drum
- Whiteboard
- Pencil and paper for student recordings

Introduction

If I asked you to name your favorite sport, what would that be? Let's analyze the sport of _____ to see whether we can name all the ways to move, all the locomotor skills we see in that sport.

Brainstorm with the class all the locomotor movements observed in the sport.

When we look at the list on the board, we see the locomotors you learned in kindergarten, grade 1, and grade 2. What about dance and gymnastics? What locomotors would they add to our list?

LEARNING EXPERIENCE: LOCOMOTORS IN GENERAL SPACE

Traveling in general space with the various locomotors, teacher directed

- Traveling in general space, changing to a different locomotor on your signal
- Traveling with a favorite locomotor
- Traveling in a new way, creating a new locomotor action

Allow several minutes for practice and review of all the locomotors—general space, corner to corner.

LEARNING EXPERIENCE: LOCOMOTOR SEQUENCES

Have students create a sequence of locomotor movements by combining locomotors, changes in direction, and pathways into three-part sequences. Each student designs a personal sequence of his or her three favorite locomotor movements.

- The sequence must have a clear beginning and ending shape.
- Your signal provides the change in locomotors.

- Students decide directions and pathways of the movements.
- The sequence should be fluid and have smooth transitions from locomotor to locomotor, from beginning shape to ending shape.

LEARNING EXPERIENCE: DANCE OF LOCOMOTORS II

Divide the class into groups of four. The group assignment is the creation of a dance that demonstrates locomotors. The dance must include four different locomotor movements. Each person in the group chooses a locomotor for which he or she will be the leader. The group leader is the leader for only the first locomotor movement; each subsequent locomotor has a new leader. That person moves to the lead position for his or her chosen locomotor.

Reminders for the Class

- Changes in direction and pathways create interesting floor patterns.
- The signal for changing leaders is created by the group—a sound, a count, a shape, a location.
- The sequence begins with a stillness shape before movement.
- The sequence may end with a shape or with a nonlocomotor action, such as collapse, sink, crumble, or freeze.

Each group records its dance on paper, indicating leaders, locomotors, and floor pattern. Following sufficient practice for memorization, the dances may be (1) shown to you, (2) shown to the class, or (3) kept as a digital recording.

Assessment

You or peers can assess the dance performance using criteria established by and shared with the class.

Closure

- What was the focus of our lesson today?
- Why is it important to be able to hop, jump, gallop, slide, skip, and leap?
- Name a sport, gymnastics event, or dance that uses each locomotor.

Reflection

- Do the students have a mature pattern of the locomotors when they use them in practice?
- Do they demonstrate a mature pattern of the locomotors when they use them in a creative dance?
- Are certain students still struggling with a specific locomotor?
- How will I address their needs?

Children's Example: Dance of Locomotors

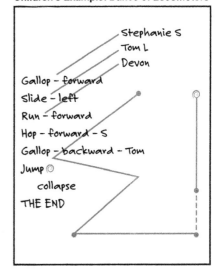

JUMPING AND LANDING: DISTANCE

Partner Relationships (Standard 4)

Grades 1, 2

Standard 1 The physically literate individual demonstrates competency in a variety of motor skills and movement patterns.

Standard 4 The physically literate individual exhibits responsible personal and social behavior that respects self and others.

Grade-Level Outcomes

- Demonstrates 2 of the 5 critical elements for jumping and landing in a horizontal plane using two-foot takeoffs and landings (S1.E3.1)
- Demonstrates 4 of the 5 critical elements for jumping and landing in a horizontal plane using a variety of one- and two-foot takeoffs and landings (S1.E3.2)

Lesson Objectives

The learner will:

- Bend the knees and swing the arms in preparation for jumping
- Travel in a forward direction while airborne
- Land in a balanced position with bent hips, knees, and ankles

Critical Elements for Jumping and Landing (Horizontal Plane)

- Arms, back, and knees bend in preparation for jumping action.
- Arms extend forward as body propels forward.
- Body extends and stretches slightly upward while in flight.
- Hips, knees, and ankles bend on landing.
- Shoulders, knees, and ankles align for balance after landing.

Materials and Equipment

- Large mat with tape line each 6 inches (15 cm)
- Measuring stick or tape measure
- Individual jump ropes, one per student

Organization and Management

Sufficient space for students to jump and land safely with no collisions is critical for this lesson. When first introduced, jumping for distance is best practiced with students all facing the same direction in one or two lines with sufficient space between students for distance and landings.

Introduction

You did jumping as a locomotor skill in kindergarten. Tell your neighbor the difference between jumping and hopping. There are different types of jumps; there are jumps for different skills in sports, gymnastics, and dance. Today, we are going to practice jumping for distance—jumping forward. Jumping is a two-sided coin; we cannot practice jumping without also practicing landing. So although our emphasis today is on jumping, we will also practice landing correctly.

Review landing correctly from kindergarten lessons.

LEARNING EXPERIENCE: SWING, SPRING, AND JUMP

- Have students stand in self-space, sufficiently spaced for safe jumping forward.
  - Arms: They practice swinging the arms forward and backward.
  - Legs: They add bending of the hips, knees, and ankles as the arms swing forward and backward (model).
  - Jump: They add the jumping action. Demonstrate: "Swing and spring, swing and spring, swing and spring . . . jump." Have them practice several jumps, observing for safe landings.

When I observe your first jumps, I noticed that some of you are doing a stepping action, leading with one foot. Let's see whether we can take off on two feet and land on two feet.

- Have students repeat practice as you say, "Swing and spring, swing and spring; swing and spring … jump." Observe for students using two feet for takeoff and landing.
- Challenge students to jump farther each time. Have them explore swinging the arms gently and vigorously to determine the impact of the arm swing on the distance of the jump.

Common Errors

- Stepping action
- Arms at sides, no swing
- Stiff legs before jumping action
- Stiff legs on landing

Assessment

Allow several minutes of guided practice, observing for the following:

- Two feet for takeoff and landing
- Swinging of the arms in preparation for the jump
- Bending of the knees on landing

LEARNING EXPERIENCE: VARYING THE DISTANCE

Have each student select a jump rope and place it in a "V" on the floor.
Note: Teach the students to do a safety check when you call the signal. When you give the oral signal for a safety check, all students stop activity and observe their work area for sufficient space for the activity and safety in performing the tasks. They need sufficient space between ropes for safe jumping and landing with no collisions.

   Standing at the smallest space behind the rope, students jump over the rope as you observe for safe landings.

- Students practice jumping over the rope at the midsection and then at the widest section.
- Students may adjust the rope to be wider or narrower to guarantee success at the widest section of the rope.

(Observe for correct jumping action, soft landings, and two-foot takeoffs. You may need to remind the class that jumping is from a stationary position, not a running approach.)

LEARNING EXPERIENCE: MY HEIGHT, MY DISTANCE

Working with a partner (one rope for each set of partners), partner A places the jump ropes in a straight line on the floor. Partner B then stretches the rope to be as tall as the partner is when he or she lies beside the rope on the floor. The challenge is then to jump the distance of your height. Reverse the role and begin anew. When one partner jumps, the other partner observes for a soft landing.

Note: When children are trying for maximum distance, they can easily forget the critical elements of the jumping action. Observe and provide individual or class cues as needed. Reinforce that students should have no crash landings.

LEARNING EXPERIENCE: STATIONS FOR PRACTICE

- Station 1: Jumping the "V." The focus is on two-feet takeoffs and two-feet landings.
- Station 2: Jumping for distance. Standing on the mat, students jump forward for distance. Tape marks provide easy measurement of distances. The focus is on balanced landings.
- Station 3: Record students' jumps in feet and inches (centimeters). (You record.) The focus is on critical elements. (This station serves as your observation of the critical elements for each student.)
- Station 4: Jumping your height. The focus is on swinging the arms for maximum distance.

Note: Students thoroughly enjoy trying to better their individual scores when the skill is revisited and seeing their progress from one year to the next. The one-on-one situation at station 3 also provides time for individual evaluation of the jumping pattern and correction of critical elements.

Assessment

- Observe throughout the lesson.
- Record critical elements during station practice.
- Conduct formal assessment of mature pattern in grade 3.

Closure

- What skill were we improving today?
- What should you remember about your arms in preparation for jumping? Your legs?
- What should the knees do to ensure a good landing? Why is a soft landing important when jumping?

Reflection

- Do students swing their arms back and forth in preparation for jumping?
- Do they land with knees bent to absorb force?
- Are they beginning to demonstrate airborne qualities during the jump?

JUMPING AND LANDING: HEIGHT

Grades 1, 2

Standard 1 The physically literate individual demonstrates competency in a variety of motor skills and movement patterns.

Grade-Level Outcomes

- Demonstrates 2 of the 5 critical elements for jumping and landing in a vertical plane (S1.E4.1)
- Demonstrates 4 of the 5 critical elements for jumping and landing in a vertical plane (S1.E4.2)

Lesson Objectives

The learner will:

- Bend the knees and swing the arms in preparation for jumping
- Swing arms upward when jumping
- Land in a balanced position with bent hips, knees, and ankles

Critical Elements for Jumping and Landing (Vertical Plane)

- Hips, knees, and ankles bend in preparation for jumping action.
- Arms extend upward as body propels upward.
- Body extends and stretches upward while in flight.
- Hips, knees, and ankles bend on landing.
- Shoulders, knees, and ankles align for balance after landing.

Materials and Equipment

- Large mat, milk crate (box filled with large empty cans from cafeteria or packed with newspaper), or 12-inch (30 cm) platform structure
- Stretch rope with balloons suspended
- Colored 1-inch (2.5 cm) tape
- Masking tape

Introduction

During our last lesson on jumping, you practiced jumping for distance. You learned that the arms swing back and forth and the knees bend in preparation for jumping. We also talked about the importance of bending the knees when landing to absorb the force. Today, you are going to jump for height. Your arms still swing back and forth in preparation; the knees still need to bend when landing. So, what is different about jumping for height? The arms now swing upward as you jump high in the air, and you now land in your same space. Ask your neighbor, "What is the same when jumping for distance and when jumping for height? What is different?"

LEARNING EXPERIENCE: REVIEW OF JUMPING ACTION

Safety Check: Check for sufficient space for jumping forward.

With students scattered in general space, allow several minutes of jumping forward with practice review of the swing and spring action of the arms and legs. Students should bend the hips, knees, and ankles for soft landings.

Assessment

Initiate peer assessment of critical elements of arms, legs, and landings. Students should try to achieve a score of 3 for all three critical elements. The student does three jumps, and the peer focuses on one at a time—preparation, body airborne, and landing.

LEARNING EXPERIENCE: VERTICAL JUMPING

- Students jump for height in self-space with swing and spring, coupled with soft landings.
- Arms extend upward for height.
- Challenge the students to jump really high by stretching the body upward and reaching toward the ceiling or sky. Imagery: jumping high to receive a ball in basketball, football, or baseball.

Note: Emphasize the need for soft landings as the height of the jump increases. A soft landing is crucial when jumping for height; the student is looking upward.

- Continue practice of vertical jumping for several minutes, observing the class as a whole and individual students for critical elements (extension upward, soft landings with knees bent) and providing individual assistance as needed.

LEARNING EXPERIENCE: STATIONS FOR PRACTICE

Jumping for height, jumping for maximum distance, and jumping personal height

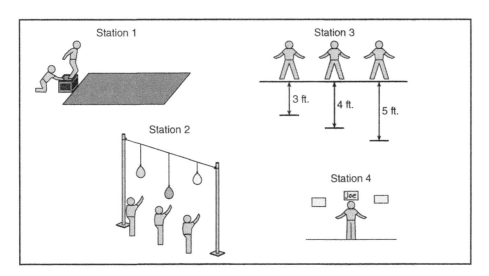

Jumping for Height

Station 1: Jumping off a Crate or Box

The focus is on jumping upward, not forward.

The temptation is just to step off the crate. Jump high in the air as you take off from the crate. Don't jump for distance. Focus on a good landing by bending the knees to absorb the force.

Stand beside the crate with one hand extended at a height that will challenge students to extend really high on the jump; adjust the hand placement to provide a challenge to each student.

Safety Check: Students may not jump off the crate unless another student is holding the crate to prevent slipping.

Station 2: Jumping to Tap a Balloon

Suspend balloons at various heights. Students jump to tap the balloon of their choice. The focus is on two-feet takeoffs and two-feet landings.

Balloons suspended in this manner have a built-in increased challenge. As the student taps the balloon, the string holding it wraps around the rope, raising the balloon. Each successful jump creates a higher one. The stretch rope can also be angled higher or lower by adjusting one end of the rope where it is attached to the pole, enabling individual challenge to the student.

Station 3: Jumping for Distance

Standing behind the starting line, students jump for distance—3 feet, 4 feet, 5 feet (90, 120, 150 cm). The focus is on balanced landings.

Safety Check: Always position students with their backs to the wall so that they are jumping away from the wall.

Station 4: Jumping Your Height

Place pieces of masking tape on the wall. Students work with partners. Partner A lies on the floor with heels at the starting line; partner B places a piece of tape on the floor just above partner A's head. The challenge is to jump your own height in distance; the reward is to write your name on the piece of tape that indicates your height. ("Jump Jim Joe," a folk dance, is an excellent revisitation practice for jumping.)

Assessment

- Teacher observation at station 1
- Peer assessment during lesson
- Formal assessment of mature pattern in grade 3

Closure

- What was the focus of our lesson today? What kind of jump did you perform? (Stand with your feet together, legs straight, arms at sides. Model as you ask the following questions and as students give their responses.)
- Am I ready to jump? What do I need to do with my arms? My knees? What will I need to remember when I land?
- What is different with my arms when I jump for height as compared with when I jump for distance?
- Is jumping upward needed in gymnastics, dance, or games and sports? How? Why?

Reflection

- Do students swing their arms back and forth in preparation for the jump and then upward for height as they jump?
- Do they land with knees bent to absorb the force?
- Do the students achieve vertical projection, not horizontal, on the vertical jump?
- Do they achieve horizontal airborne time, not vertical, on the jump for distance?

JUMPING AND LANDING

Grade 3

Standard 1 The physically literate individual demonstrates competency in a variety of motor skills and movement patterns.

Grade-Level Outcome

Jumps and lands in the horizontal and vertical planes using a mature pattern (S1.E3.3)

This lesson is a prerequisite to the following:

- Uses spring-and-step takeoffs and landings specific to gymnastics (S1.E3.4)
- Combines jumping and landing patterns with locomotors and manipulative skills in dance, gymnastics and small-sided practice tasks in games environments (S1.E3.5)

Lesson Objectives

The learner will:

- Identify the five different types of jumps
- Jump with each of the designated take-offs and landings
- Bend knees to absorb force when landing

Materials and Equipment

Ropes or tape lines on the floor (number of ropes or tape lines determined by space)

Introduction

In kindergarten, first grade, and second grade, you practiced jumping and landing: jumping for height, jumping for distance, and landing without losing balance. You have practiced the critical elements of the jumping action as well as the landing, making progress toward a mature pattern in each of the jumps. The first part of our lesson today will be to practice those jumps and review the critical elements of each.

LEARNING EXPERIENCE: REVIEW OF JUMPING AND LANDING

With students scattered in general space, have them practice jumping for height and jumping for distance. Observe for maturing jumps; provide individual cues as needed. Repeat tasks from second grade as needed for students to establish mature jumping patterns (all critical elements).

LEARNING EXPERIENCE: TAKEOFFS AND LANDINGS

After observing jumping patterns that are approaching mature patterns, introduce the class to various types of takeoff actions and landings. Relate each of the jumping actions to specifics in games and sports, gymnastics, and dance, such as one foot to two feet for a jump stop in basketball or split stop in tennis, takeoffs and landings in gymnastics and dance.

- Arrange a series of ropes or tape lines on the floor approximately 4 feet (120 cm) apart (see diagram for placement). Divide the class into equal groups based on the number of ropes or tape line series. Maximum use of space means fewer students per line and more practice of skills.

Position each group of students behind the first rope (or tape line) for their series of ropes. Partner 1 travels forward, jumps over each rope in the series, and returns to the starting line after jumping over the last rope. Each person begins when the person in front of him or her has jumped over the third rope.

Two Feet to Two Feet

The first jump is the one you learned in kindergarten and first grade—taking off on two feet and landing on two feet. When you approach the jumping line, pause, and then jump over the line two feet to two feet. Make each jump perfect—don't rush the action. Stop in a balanced position before you continue to the next rope.

One Foot to the Same Foot

This is the easy one. What is it called when you take off on one foot and land on the same foot? A hop. Hop over each rope (tape line).

Two Feet to One Foot

Approach the jumping line as before, take off on two feet, and land on only one foot. Keep your balance when you land.

One Foot to Two Feet

Approach the jumping line, do not pause, take off on one foot, and land with a balanced stop on two feet. (Imagery: approach on the diving board.)

One Foot to the Other Foot

This is the difficult one—taking off on one foot and landing on the other foot. This is the leap. It works best with a running approach: run, run, run, leap. We did this one with your work on locomotors. Extend the legs and arms for height and distance. (Imagery: leaping over a large puddle of water.)

LEARNING EXPERIENCE: PEER AS COACH

Before students begin their series of jumps, have each student tell the person behind him or her which jump he or she is going to perform. After completion of the jumping series, the "coach" tells the performer one critical element that was performed correctly and gives feedback to correct one missing or incorrect critical element. Encourage the "coach" to be specific in the praise as well as the remediation (Standard 4).

LEARNING EXPERIENCE: JUMPING SEQUENCE

Have each student create a sequence with a combination of any three jumps. Students can show the sequence to you, a partner, or the small group, or can record it on paper.

Criteria

- Sequence must have a beginning shape and an ending shape.
- Sequence must have three different jumps.
- Jumps should be performed with mature patterns.
- Sequence may include floor pattern, changes in direction, and pathways.

Assessment

Peers assess different types of jumps.

Closure

- What was the focus of the lesson today?
- How were these jumps different from those you learned in first and second grades?
- Now for the difficult question: Let's see whether we can name the game or sport, gymnastics stunt, or dance step in which each of the jumps is used. (Recall each of the five jumps and discussion of when each is used in games, gymnastics, or dance. Relate each to a skill that students will use in fourth- and fifth-grade physical education.)

Reflection

- Can students jump and land safely without falling down and with bent knees?
- Are they making progress in the performance of the various types of jumps?

BUILDING A DANCE

Grades K-5

To very young children, movement is life. They move when they are happy; they move when they are sad. They move just for the joy of moving. Dance is movement, and many childhood movements are dance-like. The *Peanuts* comic strip by Charles Schultz portrays it best with the caption for Snoopy, "To Dance Is to Live." Movement for young children is purposeful to accomplish a task in work or play; movement is used to express emotions; movement provides a creative outlet.

Dance is important in elementary physical education as evidenced with outcomes at each grade level in the National Standards. Throughout the lesson plans of this text, dance "stems" are included. A dance stem is an idea from which a dance grows—locomotor and nonlocomotor skills; stretching, curling, and twisting actions; and movement concepts linked to the Grade-Level Outcomes. Dance can be used to express emotions, to tell a story, to study the elements of movement, or just to feel the joy of movement. For students in kindergarten through grade 2, dance is movement and the joy of moving, and the teacher often guides the structure of the dance.

For students in grades 3 through 5, dance becomes a summative project to express understanding of the combination of movement concepts with the locomotor and nonlocomotor actions as well as to communicate or exhibit forms of self-expression.

The quality of the movements is important; the choice of movements and use of concepts is determined by the student. Dance for these students is purposeful, and they select movements to fulfill that purpose. Whereas dance for younger students is "free," dance for the upper-elementary students is repeatable—this is, choreographed and recorded. Movements selected are purposeful. They can be slow or fast, smooth or jerky, confined or extended, free or bound. Body shapes, actions of the total body and body parts, beginning and ending shapes, music or no music—all are chosen to create and convey a culminating dance action or performance.

Within the lesson plans for locomotors, nonlocomotors, and movement concepts, you will find the following dance stems:

- Dance of Locomotors I, II
- Dance Malfunction in the Toy Shop
- Transformers
- Action Words
- Slow-Motion Sports
- Pizza Circle Dance

- The Amoebae
- Balances and Actions
- Colors
- Contrasts in Time
- Copy Cat
- Movement Sentences

Creative, expressive dance is the dance of physical education for young children. Developmental and grade-appropriate folk or cultural dance is an excellent environment for the reinforcement of locomotor skills combined with pathways, directions, spatial awareness, and partner and group relationships. Children's literature is rich in opportunities for expressive dance for young children. You should talk frequently with kindergarten and first-grade teachers about the children's favorite books in the classroom.

For students in upper-elementary physical education, cultural dance and developmentally and grade-appropriate popular dances broaden the dance curriculum. Once learned, many dances for older children provide enjoyable physical activity that enhances fitness and promotes positive social interaction. Dance is an important part of the curriculum, but it is often slighted because of teacher inhibitions. Just as motor skill ability enhances confidence to participate in sports, dance skills provide another option for a physically active future.

CHAPTER 7

Teaching for Competency in Nonlocomotor Skills

The nonlocomotor skills of balancing and transferring weight are central to the study of gymnastics for children. Educational gymnastics focuses on the skills of balance and weight transfer with differentiated instruction and student-centered problem solving as compared with the predetermined skills of traditional, Olympic-style gymnastics. The lesson plans presented in this chapter focus on the skills and concepts of educational gymnastics:

Skills	Concepts
Balance	Body shapes
Weight transfer	Levels
Stretching, curling, twisting actions	Muscular tension
Jumping and landing	Alignment
Traveling	Extensions

Lesson plans are presented in a progression from beginning skills to the advanced work of sequences on equipment and apparatus. The progression of lesson plans is purposely designed for students' growth in the skills of gymnastics using scaffolding of skills and concepts. Many of the lessons require distributed practice for students. Although cognitive understanding may come with a single lesson, practice will be necessary to achieve mastery level in performance.

Safety is paramount when students are working in the gymnastics environment. Respect for self and others, proper use of equipment, recognition of the importance of safety, and responsible behavior (Standard 4) are critical to children's safety. Horseplay is not accepted, and crash landings are not permitted.

Traditional, Olympic-style gymnastics requires an abundance of large mats for safe execution of stunts, both on the floor and on equipment. Educational

> ### CRASH LANDINGS
>
> From beginning work in kindergarten through upper-elementary gymnastics, crash landings are not permitted. When children have a crash landing, and they will, they move to the side of the gym, out of the working area, and sit for one minute. By watching the clock on the wall, children know when to reenter the working area for continued gymnastics.
>
> During a gymnastics class when visitors were present, a young child suddenly walked over to the wall and sat down. The adult visitor, thinking the child must be hurt, asked, "Are you OK?" to which the child answered, "Yes, I just had a crash landing!" demonstrating acceptance of responsibility (Standard 4).

gymnastics, however, has areas of focus in balance and weight transfer that can be completed without mats. The first two lessons on balance and the lesson on stretching, curling, and twisting can be taught safely either with or without mats.

The nonlocomotor skills of transferring weight, as well as the actions of stretching, curling, and twisting, are important throughout the development of the foundational skills of elementary physical education. You will find them embedded in the lessons of chapter 8, Manipulative Skills. Balance is critical to all areas of movement, from basic locomotors to advanced gymnastics, dance, games, and sports. Refer to those early lessons for balance as an embedded skill.

CONCEPT OF BALANCE

Bases of Support

Grade K

Standard 1 The physically literate individual demonstrates competency in a variety of motor skills and movement patterns.

Grade-Level Outcome

Maintains momentary stillness on different bases of support (S1.E7.Ka)

Lesson Objectives

The learner will:

- Identify body parts that serve as bases of support
- Maintain balance momentarily on chosen bases of support

Materials and Equipment

- Sufficient space for students to work safely, on floor or mats
- Small individual mats, one per student if available; carpet square for outdoors
- Paper, pencils

(Beginning with the first lesson in gymnastics that uses mats, students are taught safe use, transport, and storage of the mats) (S4.E1, E5, E6.K).

Safety Concern

No disturbing or touching of others as they work is permitted (important safety protocol for gymnastics work at all times). (Standard 4)

Introduction

Today we are going to study balance. What does balance mean? Am I balanced now?

(Stand on one foot and lean forward, waving arms as if about to fall.)

Am I balanced now? (Stand on one foot, extend arms outward from the body, and do not move.) Balance is stillness—no wiggles, no wobbles. Why do I put my arms out? Correct, to help me stand still—to maintain balance.

Briefly introduce balance as one of the major components of gymnastics and an important aspect of game skills, such as kicking, receiving a pass when slightly off balance, and dodging and faking opponents.

BRIGANCE TEST FOR BALANCE

Challenge students to stand on one foot in self-space as you count for three seconds. Extending their arms outward will help them maintain stillness.

This is a task your classroom teacher will probably ask you to do during the school year. Remember the secret of extending the arms for good balance and stillness.

- Balance on the other foot, trying not to wiggle or wobble.

Focus your eyes on a spot on the opposite wall or look at another person; this will help you stay very still.

- Repeat the task with eyes closed—just for fun.
- Repeat the task and choose which foot to serve as the base.
- Balanced on one foot in self-space, use free body parts (arms, one leg) to make the balance different from everyone else—a balance that is uniquely you.

LEARNING EXPERIENCE: BASES OF SUPPORT

Demonstrate the balance of standing on one foot.

When I am balanced on one foot, what body part is touching the mat or floor? Correct—my foot. That is my base of support. When you are seated in self-space, what body part is your base of support? The body parts touching the mat or floor when you balance are called bases of support.

- Have the students demonstrate their favorite balance, as you name the bases of support, emphasizing the various body parts that can serve as bases for gymnastics balances. Then have them balance on a different base or bases of support.
- Have the students create as many safe combinations as they can.

LEARNING EXPERIENCE: BODY IN DIFFERENT POSITIONS

When I observe your balances I notice that some of you created all your balances while standing, others were in a sitting position, and others were lying on the mat or floor. Change your position as you create balances on different bases of support: standing, sitting, lying on the mat.

(If the class has studied levels as a movement concept, refer to the levels of high, middle, and low.)

Assessment

Before we continue our work on balance today, tell your neighbor the criteria for balance. If you heard "holding very, very still," that answer is correct.

LEARNING EXPERIENCE: STILLNESS

Have the students create a balance they think they can hold perfectly still.

Some of you are having difficulty holding your balance; try holding still as if someone is taking a photo of your balance—no wiggles, no wobbles—one thousand one, one thousand two, one thousand three . . . rest.

- Have students repeat the balance with a goal of holding stillness for three seconds. Allow several minutes for students to explore different balances, emphasizing stillness as you provide the three-second count.
- Expand students' balances by selecting various bases of support. (Choose bases of support appropriate to the class and individual skill level, such as feet and hands, two feet, one hand and one foot, two hands, knees and elbows, belly alone, back alone, shoulders and _____, hip and one hand, hip and elbow.)

Gently expand the skill level of children in gymnastics by focusing on the individual and his or her abilities. Use caution in selecting children for demonstrations because others will attempt the balances they see demonstrated, and they may not be ready for that level of difficulty.

LEARNING EXPERIENCE: RECORDING THE FAVORITE

From all the balances attempted today, have the students choose their favorite and repeat the balance, emphasizing stillness and base of support. Provide pencil and paper for each student to illustrate or record that favorite balance. Have the students label the bases of support. (List body parts as bases on the whiteboard to assist with spelling.) Place the students' work in their portfolios.

Assessment

- Observe safety and stillness in balances when students attempt balances.
- Informal assessment is done with pictographs and labeling of bases of support.

Closure

- What was the focus of our lesson today?
- What are the two tests for holding a good balance?
- Tell your neighbor what base of support in gymnastics means.

Reflection

- Can the students balance safely on various bases of support?
- Does the class create a safe environment and respect for others when working in gymnastics?
- Do the students understand stillness when balancing?

CONCEPT OF BALANCE
Shapes, Levels
Grades 1, 2

Standard 1 The physically literate individual demonstrates competency in a variety of motor skills and movement patterns.

Grade-Level Outcomes

- Maintains stillness on different bases of support with different body shapes (S1.E7.1)
- Balances on different bases of support, combining levels and shapes (S1.E7.2a)

Lesson Objectives

The learner will:

- Maintain a balanced position on chosen bases of support for three seconds, demonstrating the four basic shapes (grade 1)
- Maintain a balanced position on chosen bases of support for three seconds, demonstrating different shapes and levels (grade 2)

Safety Concerns

- Disturbing or touching others as they work is not permitted (important safety protocol for gymnastics work at all times). (Standard 4)
- Safe use, transport, and storage of mats (S4.E1, E4, E6.1) (S4.E6.2a.2b)

Materials and Equipment

- Sufficient space for students to work safely, on floor or mats
- Small individual mats (one per student) if available; carpet square for outdoors
- Whiteboard

Introduction

When you first studied balance in kindergarten, we discussed what the word means and established the criteria for balance. Can anyone recall the two criteria? Watch me as I stand on one foot, and tell me whether I am balanced (model by standing in a front scale with arms waving, almost falling over). Was I balanced in that position? No, I was about to fall over. Watch again (model with a firm base of support but arms moving). What about that one? I was not about to fall over, but was I balanced? No. Balance means I can hold the position perfectly still, and I am not about to fall over—not about to lose the balance. The second criterion is being able to hold the position for several seconds; we will say three seconds for our work. Many of you can kick up into a handstand, but only a few of you can hold it for several seconds. You have not mastered a skill unless you can keep it under control and hold perfectly still for several seconds. Tell your neighbor the two criteria for balance in gymnastics.

LEARNING EXPERIENCE: BASES OF SUPPORT

Review bases of support, emphasizing stillness. Have students practice by choosing a variety of bases of support for their balances.

- Select several students with different bases to demonstrate their balances. Have students ask a neighbor to name the body parts used as bases. Write the list on the whiteboard.

Head*	Hands
Knees	Elbows
Belly	Back
Hip	Feet
Shoulders	Base of spine

- Encourage students to try new bases of support as they view the listing on the whiteboard.

When students use the head as a base of support, they must always accompany it with another body part as the base. Students must never attempt to balance on the head alone.

- Have student try these teacher-selected bases of support:

Two hands and two feet	Two hands and one foot
Two feet and one hand	Two elbows and two knees
Two hands, head, and two feet	Two hands, head, and one foot
Shoulders and upper arms	Stomach only
Back only	One foot
Base of spine only	

- Challenge students to use free body parts to create two different balances for each base of support named.

Note: Students who are in competitive gymnastics clubs may need a reminder to save some skills for outside school because other students who are not ready for the skills may attempt them.

LEARNING EXPERIENCE: WIDE TO NARROW

Balances on wide bases of support, such as feet and hands shoulder-width apart, knees and elbows shoulder-width apart

- Balances on narrow bases of support by moving body parts close together
- Discussion with class regarding stability on wide versus narrow base

LEARNING EXPERIENCE: DECREASING THE NUMBER

Balances on wide bases of support, created by the number of body parts serving as bases, such as two feet, two hands

- Balances on narrow bases of support by reducing the number of body parts serving as bases, such as two feet and one hand, one foot and one hand
- Two knees and two elbows decreasing from four to three to two bases of support
- Balances on narrow bases of support with opposition, such as one foot and opposite hand, one knee and opposite elbow

LEARNING EXPERIENCE: MUSCULAR TENSION

What was the difference in your stillness, your balance, when you were on a wide base versus a narrow base? When you were on four body parts as bases versus only two or one body part? Correct. The balance is more difficult. Let's learn a secret for maintaining balance in those difficult situations; it's called muscular tension.

Have students tighten their abdominal muscles while seated in self-space. (Remind them to breathe.) Have them tighten the muscles in their arms and legs yet not change their shape or position on the mat.

- Challenge students to balance on the base of the spine by rocking backward slightly while seated until their feet are not touching the floor. Tightening the abdominal muscles is the key to stillness.
- Have students repeat the wide to narrow balances, emphasizing the tightening of the muscles as the base becomes narrower.

LEARNING EXPERIENCE: BALANCES AND SHAPES

Have students try balances on different bases of support to create wide, narrow, curled, and twisted shapes.

- Teacher-selected shapes with student balance response. Encourage a variety of responses.

- Challenge students to use different bases of support for each of the balances created to demonstrate shapes.
- Students try different bases of support for wide (narrow, curled, twisted) shape. Expand students' skills with balances to demonstrate each of the four shapes.
- Allow several minutes for students to explore balances for each of the shapes and select their best balance for each.
  - Have students demonstrate their best balance for each of the shapes, holding stillness until you give the signal to change to the next balance.
  - Have students repeat the four balances, concentrating on the transition from one balance to the next by performing smooth, purposeful movement in the weight transfer.

LEARNING EXPERIENCE: BALANCES AND LEVELS (GRADE 2)

Review from kindergarten balancing with the body in various positions; review levels from the movement concept lessons.

- Have students create balances at different levels—high, middle, low.
- Direct the students to challenge themselves with balances that require muscular tension to maintain stillness, such as a high-level balance other than standing on one foot, a low-level balance that elevates the body off the mat, and a middle-level balance that is very narrow or on very few bases of support.

LEARNING EXPERIENCE: BALANCES, SHAPES, AND LEVELS (GRADE 2)

Review with the class the many body parts and combinations that can serve as bases of support. Remind them of the many balances to demonstrate shapes that the class created in the previous lesson (or earlier tasks).

- Have students explore body shapes in balances at high, middle, and low levels.
- Challenge students to create a balance using each of the four shapes and at least two levels (high, middle, low).
- Extend the challenge with each of the four shapes and different bases of support at each level, such as wide, narrow, and twisted balances, each with a different base of support at low level, at middle level, and at high level; and curled balances, each with a different base of support at low level and at middle level.

Assessment

Grade 1

Select your four favorite balances to represent the four shapes from all that you tried today. Practice each one again to be sure you can hold it absolutely still for three seconds. When you are confident, ask the person next to you to watch your balances. He or she will watch for the following: stillness, ability to hold position for three seconds, and muscular tension. Your partner will give you a thumbs-up or a thumbs-down, depending on the stability of your balances.

Grade 2

Select your four favorite balances to demonstrate shapes and levels; be sure that each one has a different base of support. Practice each one until you can hold it absolutely still for a three-second count. Get a piece of paper and a pencil from the assignment table. Draw each of your balances and label the base of support and the level. After you complete the drawing, show each balance to the person on the mat nearest you. He or she will give you a $\sqrt{+}$ if the balance meets the two criteria, a $\sqrt{\approx}$ if you still need to practice the balance, and a $\sqrt{-}$ if you cannot hold the balance.

Closure

- What did we add to our study of balance today?
- What are the two criteria for a good gymnastics balance?

Reflection

- Can students hold the gymnastics balances stationary for three seconds with no wiggles, no wobbles, and no loss of balance?
- Can they balance on different bases of support to demonstrate a variety of levels and shapes?
- Do students challenge themselves for a higher skill level, yet being aware of safety?
- What aspects of the lesson do I need to reteach? Which students need individual attention? Which students need challenge at a high level of skill?

Note: All too often, lessons in gymnastics are simply an introduction to the skills for children, an exploration rather than mastery. Many of these lessons require more than one class period for mastery. Do not rush; wait until you observe that the children have mastered the skills before moving on. Gymnastics is no different from games skills in this respect.

INVERTED BALANCES

Grade 2

Standard 1 The physically literate individual demonstrates competency in a variety of motor skills and movement patterns.

Grade-Level Outcomes

- Balances in an inverted position* with stillness and supportive base (S1.E7.2b)
- Combines balances and transfers into a three-part sequence (S1.E11.2)

Lesson Objectives

The learner will:

- Balance in an inverted position on teacher-selected bases of support
- Create and perform inverted balances
- Recognize the concept of alignment in gymnastics balances
- Create and perform a three-part sequence

Safety Concern

*Inverted balances must be presented with differentiated instruction and developmentally appropriate tasks for individual students. Children immediately think of headstands and handstands as the inverted balances; your role is critical in presenting safe, inverted balances for nongymnasts.

Materials and Equipment

Small individual mats, one per student or sufficient large mats for all students to be working simultaneously; carpet square for outdoors

Organization and Management

Established protocol for moving mats, placement on floor, listening position

Introduction

Today, we introduce a new word and a new skill in our work on balance in gymnastics. We are going to explore balancing in inverted positions. Inverted is a big word for "upside down." But when we balance in inverted positions, we do not have to do headstands and handstands. If your head is lower than other parts of the body, you are in an inverted balance for gymnastics.

LEARNING EXPERIENCE: BALANCES AND BASES

Review balances on various bases of support, safety, and criteria for balances. Allow several minutes for students to practice balancing on various bases of support while you review stability and safety protocol.

LEARNING EXPERIENCE: INVERTED BALANCES

As I observed your balances, I noticed that some of them were inverted—your head was lower than other body parts. Show me an inverted, upside-down balance. (Remind students to use a wider base of support for stability.)

- Students balance on shoulders, head, and upper arms with legs extended upward. Introduce the concept of alignment—body parts positioned vertically over the base of support, such as the legs extended upward over the hips.
- Students balance on head, two hands, and one foot, with the other leg extended upward. Introduce the concept of extension—free body parts fully stretched, such as leg extended and toes pointed.

- Students do inverted balances with free body part extensions:
  - Head, one foot, one hand
  - Head and two knees
  - Head, two hands, one knee
- Have students choose their favorite inverted balance. Emphasize that the criteria for a successful balance is stillness for three seconds, not the difficulty of the balance.

Safety Concerns

- When students use the head as a base of support, they must always accompany it with another body part as the base. Students must never attempt to balance on the head alone.
- If children begin to experiment with frog stands, tripods, and headstands as inverted balances, you should teach them the proper mechanics for assuming and maintaining those positions.
- When the head is involved as a base of support, weight must be distributed equally among all the body parts that are bases.

LEARNING EXPERIENCE: ALIGNMENT, EXTENSIONS, AND MUSCULAR TENSION

Earlier in our lesson today, I introduced a new word for our work in balance; the word was *alignment*. Alignment of body parts vertically creates a stable balance.
Have students balance on the shoulders, head, and upper arms and extend the legs upward. (Extending the legs upward over the hips creates alignment and a stable balance.)

Gymnasts have a special trick. When they finish their routines on the mats or on an apparatus, they quickly stand with arms extended upward. We call this the "ta-da" in gymnastics routines, from the cartoon strip Calvin and Hobbs. (Demonstrate as you explain that this position creates proper alignment.) The extended arms are aligned over the shoulders, the shoulders are aligned over the hips, and the hips are aligned over the feet. This alignment creates balance and stability.

- Link alignment to routines with speed, aerials, and rapid exits from pieces of apparatus.
- Link alignment to a perfect score in gymnastics and subtraction from the score for moving the feet. (Demonstrate with a video clip from a gymnastics competition.)
- When students are ready for headstands, alignment will be a major factor in success of the balance.
- Reinforce the concept of extensions in balances:
  - Balance and counterbalance for stability
  - Full extension from trunk through extremities, that is, stretch of leg, pointing of toes, stretch of arm and fingers
- Reinforce the concept of muscular tension:
  - Tightening of the muscles for stillness in balances
  - Tightening of abdominal muscles for stability in inverted balances
  - Tightening of muscles in extended body parts for stillness and form
- Review students' favorite balances on various bases of support, various body shapes, and various levels. Provide cues for alignment, extensions, counterbalance, and muscular tension.
- Students demonstrate three favorite balances, counting aloud the number of seconds they remain still. Offer praise for alignment and extensions.

Note: Muscular tension, alignment of body parts over the base of support, and extensions for counterbalance are critical for the development of good gymnastics balances. They are emerging skills for first and second graders.

LEARNING EXPERIENCE: THREE-PART SEQUENCE

Thus far in our study of balance, you have created balances with various bases of support, balances with shapes, balances at different levels, and some inverted balances. With each of those categories of balances, you chose a favorite. For the culmination of our work today, we will create a gymnastics sequence. A sequence has three parts: a beginning shape, balances or actions in the middle, and an ending shape.

- Beginning shape in standing position
- Balance: student's creative work, choice of balance to demonstrate shape, level, or inversion
- Ending shape: ta-da

Magic Number Three

- Stillness for three seconds
- Three parts in sequence
- Three balances (student's choice of shapes, levels, different bases of support), one of which must be inverted
- Allow several minutes for students to practice balances and choose shapes, levels, or various bases of support for their balances.
  - Class decision on beginning position or shape, review of ending shape, ta-da
  - Individual decision on three balances
- Have the students explore the order of the balances to create smooth transitions between them.
- Allow several minutes for students to practice their sequence from beginning shape to ta-da.
- Group performance with your signal for changing each part of the sequence and each balance.

Assessment

- Informally observe inverted balances.
- Sequences can be recorded on paper or video and assessed informally by a peer. Then you can assess them with established criteria for summative assessment.

Closure

- What was the focus of our lesson today?
- What does the word *inverted* mean?
- If your base of support is narrow and you are having difficulty holding the balance stationary, what can you do to the base to add stability?
- What is alignment in gymnastics? Why is it important?
- Why is extension of free body parts (arms and legs) important?

Reflection

- Can the children balance in an inverted position?
- Are they beginning to balance on narrower bases of support?
- Are they holding the body parts firm with muscles tight?
- Do they have a beginning understanding of extensions and alignment?

CURLING, STRETCHING, AND TWISTING ACTIONS

Shapes

Grades K-2 and Beyond

Standard 1 The physically literate individual demonstrates competency in a variety of motor skills and movement patterns.

Grade-Level Outcomes

- Contrasts the actions of curling and stretching (S1.E10.K)
- Demonstrates twisting, curling, bending, and stretching actions (S1.E10.1)
- Differentiates among twisting, curling, bending, and stretching actions (S1.E10.2)

This lesson is a prerequisite to the outcome for grade 3, Moves into and out of gymnastics balances with curling, twisting and stretching actions (S1.E10.3).

Lesson Objectives

The learner will:

- Identify the actions of stretching, curling, twisting, and bending (grades K, 1)
- Demonstrate the actions of stretching, curling, and twisting (grades K, 1)
- Create balances by stretching, curling, and twisting (grade 2)

Materials and Equipment

Sufficient space for students to work safely, on floor or mats

Safe use, transport, and storage of mats (S4.E1, E4, E6.1) (S4.E6.2a.2b)

Introduction

Earlier in our physical education work, you studied body shapes: wide, narrow, curled, and twisted. Today, we are going to focus on the actions that result in those shapes—the actions of curling, twisting, and stretching.

(Link the actions not only to gymnastics but also to games and dance skills. Link the actions to physical education work in upper-elementary grades and everyday life skills.)

LEARNING EXPERIENCE: STRETCHING, CURLING, AND TWISTING THE TOTAL BODY

With students lying on the floor in self-space, provide the oral signal for an eight-count slow curling, emphasizing total-body involvement and smoothness of the action. Then have students return to starting position.

- Eight count for stretching, then return to starting position
- Eight count for twisting the total body
- Series of three: eight count for curling, eight count for stretching, followed by eight count for twisting of total body

LEARNING EXPERIENCE: STRETCHING, CURLING, AND TWISTING BODY PARTS

Students explore body parts that can curl, bend, stretch, and twist. With guided exploration, lead students to discover and do the following:

- Spine can curl; other body parts can bend.
- Twisting requires rotation of body parts with stationary base.
- Stretching body parts from smallest to largest—fingers and trunk.
- Combinations of actions, such as twist the arms, curl the spine, and stretch the legs.

LEARNING EXPERIENCE: LEVELS, SHAPES, AND ACTIONS (GRADE 2)

Sitting or lying on their mats at low level, students explore stretching to form new balances and new shapes—sometimes changing the base of support, sometimes staying on the original base at low level.

- Students explore curling to form new balances, new shapes at low level.
- They explore twisting to form new balances, new shapes at low level.
- Students repeat the exploration balanced at middle level on their chosen bases of support.
- Standing on one foot, balanced at high level, students explore stretching in different directions, curling the spine forward and to the sides, and twisting free body parts.

LEARNING EXPERIENCE: COMBINING BALANCES AND ACTIONS—A GROUP DANCE (GRADE 2, 3)

In groups of four (S4.E4.1), students create a group statue in which each person in the group balances on his or her favorite bases of support. On a signal (created by you or the group), each person moves to demonstrate stretching, curling, twisting, and bending. On the next signal, they return to original balance as the ending shape.

(This dance can be as complicated or as simple, as long or as short in duration, as you and the class decide. Balances and actions can also be recorded on paper or recorded digitally to be placed in portfolios.)

Variations

- All four students perform the actions of stretching, curling, twisting, and bending at the same time and in the same order.
- Each student selects the action he or she will perform; actions are performed at the same time.
- Each student selects the action he or she will perform. Three students maintain stillness in balances as one student performs. On the signal, the next student performs the action, and so on.

LEARNING EXPERIENCE: COLORS

Name a color, such as red, and ask students to think of the first thing that enters their minds when you say the word.

Shapes

Have students make the shape that best depicts what they thought of when you named the color.

- Younger students usually name an object, such as a playground ball or the gymnasium door.
- Upper-elementary students often name an emotion, such as anger or caring. The shapes they create may not be as definitive as the wide, narrow, curled, and twisted shapes of the younger students.

Actions

- Allow several minutes for the students to explore moving as the object would move.
  - Does it stretch, curl, bend, or twist?
  - Would it roll, bounce, or swing?
  - Would it be heavy or light, fast or slow?

(Red is a playground ball that bounces, a worm that wiggles, paint that splashes. Red is anger that explodes. Its shape is twisted; it darts, pounces, and thrusts into space.)

- Have the students perform the colors dance, beginning with the shape of their representation for red, followed by the movements, and ending by returning to the original shape.
- Challenge students to select a color of their choice. Working alone, with a partner, or in a group, they create a dance of objects or emotions, a story that represents the color.

Object	Shape	Action	Descriptive word
Dragon	Narrow	Crawl	Scales
Bridge	Curved	Swing	Curve
Ice skating	Twisted	Jerky	Crash
Caterpillar	Skinny	Slow	Squirm

Assessment

- Formative: Observe correct action in response to directions and tasks.
- Summative (grade 2): Record group dance for correct stretching, curling, and twisting actions; beginning and ending shapes; and cooperative group work.

Closure

- What was the focus of our lesson today?
- What body part is central in the curling action?
- What happens to create a twisted shape?
- Grades K, 1: Demonstrate each of the actions of stretching, curling, and twisting, as students identify the action.
- Grade 2: In the lesson today, we focused on stretching, curling, and twisting in gymnastics. (Brainstorm situations in sports and dance in which stretching, curling, and twisting are needed: stretching to receive a high pass, twisting to strike a ball with a bat, twisting to keep an opponent away from the ball, curling for protection of a ball just caught, stretching when dancing to leap high in the air using the whole body and extending the arms, curling to roll forward, twisting to avoid being tagged, curling to catch a low ball.) We will review these actions when we are in the midst of lessons in these areas.

Reflection

- Can students correctly perform the actions of stretching, curling, and twisting?
- Can they use the actions to create new balances on selected bases of support?
- Do students work safely at all times in gymnastics? Are there areas where safety needs to be addressed?
- Are individual students attempting unsafe balances?

BALANCE

Muscular Tension, Alignment, Extensions, Stretching, Curling, and Twisting Actions

Grade 3

Standard 1 The physically literate individual demonstrates competency in a variety of motor skills and movement patterns.

Grade-Level Outcomes

- Balances on different bases of support, demonstrating muscular tension and extensions of free body parts (S1.E7.3)
- Employs the concept of alignment in gymnastics and dance (S2.E4.3a)

Lesson Objectives

The learner will:

- Demonstrate muscular tension when balanced on different bases of support
- Extend free body parts for balance and counterbalance
- Align body parts over the base of support for stability
- Transition from balance to balance with purposeful, selected movements

Safety Concerns

- Students must not disturb or touch others as they work. This safety protocol is important for gymnastics work at all times. (Standard 4)
- Safe use, transport, and storage of mats.

Materials and Equipment

Individual mats, one per student, or sufficient large mats for all students to work simultaneously or take turns with one other person (Sequence work can easily facilitate working on and off the mats; the person without a mat can observe for constructive feedback to the person on the mat.)

Introduction

Thus far in our study of balance in gymnastics, you have learned to balance on various bases of support; in wide, narrow, curled, and twisted shapes; and at different levels. We even ventured into inverted balances. As third graders, some of you have been challenging yourself each day with narrower bases of support and inverted balances; others have been practicing balances that you are more comfortable with. Our lesson today is not on creating new balances, but on refining the balances we have, refining them to a "perfect 10" in gymnastics. We will do that by focusing on three concepts you learned as first and second graders: muscular tension, alignment, and extensions.

LEARNING EXPERIENCE: MUSCULAR TENSION

Challenge students to practice the following:

- Narrow bases of support, inverted balances, or previous balances that need a little more practice. Remind them to hold each perfectly still for three seconds.
  - As you walk and observe the students' practice, focus on muscular tension by saying, "I may touch you as I walk past to see whether you have the muscular tension needed for good balance in gymnastics. If the muscular tension is really there, I could lift you or hold you upside down and your gymnastics shape would still be there."

- Demonstrate the best, most difficult balance on bases of support. Remind students that muscular tension will be the key to three seconds of stillness.
  - The best, most difficult balance to illustrate wide, narrow, curled, and twisted shapes. Tightening of the muscles should be visible.
  - The best, most difficult to illustrate low, middle, and high levels. Remind students that a gymnastics balance is a balance that requires muscular tension.
  - The best, most challenging inverted balance for which three-second stillness is possible.

Muscular Tension Sequence

The four balances just completed by students will be a sequence of bases, shapes, levels, and inversion (one balance for each), emphasizing muscular tension and clearly illustrating bases, shapes, levels, and inversion. After several minutes of practice, have the class do a group performance with your signal for changing each balance.

Just for fun, have students add a beginning shape at high level and an ending ta-da.

LEARNING EXPERIENCE: EXTENSIONS

- Challenge students to extend free body parts away from the base of support.
- Balance on base of spine. Legs and arms extended forward in narrow shape, in wide shape, and in combination of narrow and wide.
- Balance on knees and elbows, narrowing base of support to one knee and one elbow (muscular tension). Extension of free leg and arm for counterbalance.

(Counterbalance: Extension beyond the base in one direction requires an extension in the opposite direction.)

- Explore extensions beyond the base in one direction, resulting in a loss of balance.
- Balance on head, two hands, and one foot with free leg extended upward.
- Balance on two hands and one knee with free leg extended upward.
- Balance on one hand and one knee. Explore the extensions needed for counterbalance.
- From all the balances created thus far, have students select their favorite, the one they can hold perfectly still for three seconds. Challenge students to extend free body parts away from the base of support, creating the need for counterbalance extensions.

Extensions Sequence

From all the balances that illustrate extensions, have students select a favorite. Ask them to explore all the possibilities for extensions from that base of support, emphasizing the smoothness of the action as body parts extend from the base and return near the base. The extension actions will create a sequence of movement. Ask these questions:

- How many body parts are free to extend from the base?
- How many different directions? How many levels?

After the extension sequences are complete, have students show the sequence to a partner for suggestions for improvement as well as praise for extensions well done. Working together, partners choose a beginning and ending for the sequence; the sequence begins and returns to that position.

LEARNING EXPERIENCE: ALIGNMENT

Last year we introduced the word ta-da as the ending of gymnastics sequences. Partner A, tell your neighbor what ta-da means in our gymnastics work. Partner B, show your neighbor what ta-da looks like at the end of the gymnastic sequence.

Review with the class: Ta-da is the alignment of body parts over the base of support. Alignment provides stability and stillness in balances. Alignment gives gymnasts a perfect landing in a competitive routine.

- Students balance on shoulders with legs extended upward, with legs bent tucked close to the body, and with legs extended and twisted. Align legs over hips for balance.

The secret to an inverted balance is the alignment of body parts over the base: toes over knees and knees over hips to form a straight line.

- Practice of inverted balances created by the student, emphasizing alignment of body parts and muscular tension for stability
- Balance on head and hands as in a frog stand (knees resting on elbows)
- Tighten abdominal muscles to raise knees and align hips over shoulders

Note: In the early stages of working on inverted balances, teach the skills of returning to the feet or tucking the head and doing a forward or a safety roll out of the balance. Students can use this safety measure any time they lose balance or feel unsafe.

Safety Concern

Differentiated instruction and individual student readiness are critical for inverted balances and all gymnastics work, especially for grade 3 and above.

LEARNING EXPERIENCE: TRANSITIONS

Each student has a large repertoire of balances to illustrate bases of support, body shapes, levels, and inversion. Allow several minutes for students to practice their favorites, using selections from each of the categories.

All the gymnastics work you have done thus far has had me giving the signal to change from one balance to the next. As third graders, you will now do the work on transitions for sequences. You will be in charge of the balances and the transitions between them.

- Have students repeat their favorite balances, being aware of the transitions between the balances as planned, purposeful movement.
- Review stretching, curling, and twisting actions for transition movements.
- Have students experiment with the order of balances to achieve smooth transitions between them.
- Have each student select three favorite balances and place them in the order that allows the smoothest transition from the first to the second to the third.
- Have each student show his or her balances to a partner, emphasizing the switch from the "still photography" of balances to "action recordings" of balances and transitions. The partner observing now provides suggestions for improvement on stillness in balances (muscular tension, alignment, extension) and the smoothness of movements between balances.

Assessment

Informal observation of stillness in balances; muscular tension, alignment, and extensions; smooth transitions

Closure

- Today, we refined balances with muscular tension, alignment, and extensions. Pretend that a new student has arrived in third grade. What would you tell your new classmate about muscular tension in gymnastics? Why is it important?
- Why are extensions important in gymnastics? What is counterbalance?
- How does alignment of body parts help us with inverted balances?

- Think for a moment of your favorite category of balance: shapes, levels, inverted, bases of support. Tell your neighbor why the one you chose is your favorite.
- The new concept today was transitions. What do transitions add to a gymnastics sequence?

Reflection

- Do the students have functional understanding (cognitive and performance) of muscular tension, extensions, and alignment?
- Do they work safely in the gymnastics environment as difficulty is increased and the need for personal responsibility becomes greater?
- Is reteaching needed in some areas? Do some students need individual help to feel secure in gymnastics and to advance?

WEIGHT TRANSFER

Grades K-2

The physically literate individual demonstrates competency in a variety of motor skills and movement patterns.

Many of the skills in gymnastics, such as forward rolls and inverted balances, do not reach maturing stages for students in a single lesson. Distributed practice and reteaching of the skill and critical elements will be needed.

Grade-Level Outcomes

- Rolls sideways in a narrow body shape (S1.E9.K)
- Rolls with either a narrow or curled body shape (S1.E9.1)
- Rolls in different directions with either a narrow or curled body shape (S1.E9.2)
- Transfers weight from feet to different body parts/bases of support for balance and/or travel (S1.E8.2)

Lesson Objectives

The learner will:
- Transfer weight by rolling sideways with a narrow body shape, that is, a log roll
- Transfer weight by rolling sideways with a curled body shape, that is, an egg roll
- Transfer weight by rolling forward with a curled body shape, that is, a forward roll
- Transfer out of balances with a rolling action, that is, a log roll, safety roll, egg roll, or forward roll
- Transfer into balances with a rolling action, that is, a log roll or forward roll

Safety Concern

Rolling skills must be presented with differentiated instruction and developmentally appropriate practice tasks for individual learners. Forward rolls must always be optional for students.

Materials and Equipment

Individual small mats (one per student), or a larger mat shared by students (taking turns for safety)

Introduction

Earlier in our gymnastics study, you practiced balancing on various bases of support, in various shapes, and at various levels. We added the challenge of balancing in an inverted position. Throughout all that work, the emphasis was on body control (tight muscles, alignment) and holding the balance perfectly still for three seconds. That work was fun; the new skills were challenging. But the emphasis was stillness. We talked about the action part of gymnastics; we even worked on smooth transitions between our balances. Today, we will focus on one of the actions of gymnastics—rolling.

LEARNING EXPERIENCE: ROLLING WITH A NARROW BODY SHAPE

With students lying on mats in a narrow body shape, have them roll the length of the small mat, emphasizing the stretched, narrow body shape.

- Roll to the left and roll to the right, traveling the length of the mat.
- Roll slowly with control.
- Roll faster but still maintain control.

Grade 2

- Tight muscles keep the roll straight.
- Hips lead the rolling action.

LEARNING EXPERIENCE: ROLLING WITH A CURLED BODY SHAPE

Position students at the back of their mats, facing you, with the length of their mats in front of them. Standing in a balanced position on two feet, students model the following as you demonstrate:

- Placement of hands on the mat, shoulder-width apart
- Curling of the spine for a rounded shape
- Tucking of the chin into the chest

Return to standing position behind mat; do not complete the roll.

Safety Check: Rolling with a traditional forward roll must always be optional for students. Teacher guidance is needed for individual students: developmental readiness, sufficient arm strength to support body weight momentarily with the hands, and comfort with inverted motion.

- Demonstrate while instructing students:
  - Placement of strong hands on mat
  - Curling of spine
  - Tucking of chin
  - Slight extension of legs to raise bottoms up
  - Head between legs
  - Roll (body in curled position throughout the rolling action)
- Repeat directions and have students perform with you
  1. Hands down
  2. Curling of spine
  3. Tucking of chin (keeping it tucked; head not touching mat)
  4. Bottoms up
  5. Roll

Demonstrate as you talk through steps 1 through 3 with students; observe the class for steps 4 and 5.

Common Errors

- Chin is not tucked or student raises head at last moment, resulting in forward motion—head on mat.
- Student pushes stronger with one hand and one arm collapses, resulting in rolling to one side.
- Student opens from a curled to a straight spine, resulting in a flat back on the mat after the rolling action.

Allow several minutes of practice of forward rolls as students respond to your directions for steps 1 through 5. Walk among the students, looking for commons errors listed earlier; provide individual cues as needed. Refine for quality of movement, emphasizing keeping a round shape throughout roll and no head contact.

LEARNING EXPERIENCE: ROLLING OUT OF BALANCES (GRADE 2)

- Have students balance on knees and elbows as bases of support.
- Students lower the body to the mat and roll sideways with arms and legs tucked close to the body or with a narrow shape.
- Students balance on knees and elbows. They lower one shoulder, tuck arms and legs, and roll out of the balance; that is, they perform a safety roll.
- Students balance on belly as base of support, extending arms and legs in the air. They lower the body to the mat and roll sideways with a narrow shape.

- Students balance on head and hands, frog stand, or balance on head, hands, and one foot. They tuck the head, push with the arms, and roll forward or lower the body to the mat and roll sideways with arms and legs tucked or a narrow body shape.
- Students explore rolling out of other balances and various body shapes.

LEARNING EXPERIENCE: ROLLING INTO BALANCES (GRADE 2)

From standing, squatting, or at low level, students roll into balances on various bases of support, emphasizing the smoothness of the action from the roll into the balance. Explore rolling in different directions and from different positions into balances.

Assessment

- Summative: All students should experience success at a log roll.
- Formative: Record students for whom additional practice will result in successful forward roll; record students for whom a tucked forward roll is not a safe movement.

Closure

- What was the focus of our lesson today?
- Raise your hand if you can successfully roll. That's each and every one of you! You will always have a choice of a narrow or a curled body shape for rolling.
- Why is tucking the chin important for a forward roll?
- Should the head touch the mat when rolling in a curled body shape?
- What role do the hands play in the forward roll?
- Tell your neighbor the five steps in the forward roll.

Reflection

- Are the students aware of the safety factors involved in rolling actions?
- Do they tuck chins and push with the hands when performing the forward roll?
- Can they practice rolling independently, or is your direction still needed through the steps?

WEIGHT TRANSFER

Weight on Hands

Grades 2, 3

This lesson covers an emerging skill for grade 2 and a Grade-Level Outcome for grade 3.

Standard 1 The physically literate individual demonstrates competency in a variety of motor skills and movement patterns.

Grade-Level Outcomes

Transfers weight from feet to hands for momentary weight support (S1.E8.3)

Lesson Objectives

The learner will:

- Transfer weight from feet to hands for momentary balance
- Transfer weight from feet to hands for travel

Materials and Equipment

Enough secure mats for all students to transfer weight from feet to hands

Introduction

Gymnastics centers on two basic skills: balance and transferring weight. Balance provides the stillness; transferring weight provides the actions. The combination of balances and weight transfers creates exciting gymnastics routines on mats and on apparatus. In our last lesson of transferring weight, you practiced traveling across the mat by rolling, transferring weight from feet to rounded back or total body. Today, you will begin learning the skills of transferring weight to hands for travel across the mat. The expert gymnast is highly competent in both of these areas. If only we had the magic formula like Popeye did, you could just eat spinach and have strong arm muscles for taking weight on your hands. It's not that easy, but all your fitness work throughout the year will now pay off in strong arm muscles for taking weight on your hands!

Note: All transfers of weight from feet to hands must be presented with differentiated instruction and developmentally appropriate tasks for individual learners.

LEARNING EXPERIENCE: FEET TO HANDS IN SELF-SPACE

With students standing behind their mats and placing their hands shoulder-width apart on the mat, have them kick up so that their weight is momentarily on hands only. Allow several minutes of practice as students experiment with taking weight on hands. (Being comfortable with this position and being able to return to the floor in a balanced position are critical to further work of weight on hands.)

- In a forward–backward stance with kicking leg extended, students kick one leg upward, keeping the other leg close to the floor.
- Individual goals: count one-alligator, two-alligator, increasing the time for weight on hands. Goal for the day is an increase of one "alligator."
- As students gain confidence in taking weight on hands, challenge them to kick higher.

Safety Concern

If you feel yourself off balance or about to fall over, twist slightly to bring your feet down in a different place. If you kick too far and cannot recover to your feet, tuck and roll.

LEARNING EXPERIENCE: FEET TO A DIFFERENT PLACE

In a forward–backward stance, students transfer weight to hands, twisting the body to bring feet down to a new place.

- Task extension: higher kick, legs together in the air, quarter turn twist of body to bring feet down in a new place
- Variations: quarter turn in each direction, half turn
- Legs extended with a quick snap together and half turn (round-off)

Cue: *Alignment of hips over shoulders for balance.*

LEARNING EXPERIENCE: FEET TO HANDS TO FEET ACROSS THE MAT (GRADE 3)

In a forward–backward stance, students transfer weight from foot to foot, hand to hand, foot to foot for travel across the mat. Allow several minutes of practice as students gain confidence in the transfer from hand to hand; emerging-level cartwheels will appear for some students. (The foot-to-foot landings often begin as two feet landing together rather than one foot landing and then the other; the foot-to-foot landing comes with practice and confidence.)

As you gain confidence in your inverted travel, extend your legs by really stretching them toward the sky. One secret is to reach downward, not outward, for the first hand placement.

Note: This is an emerging skill for third graders and a Grade-Level Outcome for fourth graders. Emphasis for grade 3 is increased time for weight on hands.

Grade 4

Increased time with weight on hands, full extensions of legs: mule kicks, cartwheels, emerging level handstands, focusing on body alignment

Assessment

This lesson is for distributed practice and reteaching with no formal assessment.

Closure

- What new skill did we add today?
- To transfer weight from feet to hands, what body parts require strong muscles?
- What is the most difficult part of taking weight on hands? (List on whiteboard so that students see similar responses and feel at ease because others have difficulty with parts of the skill.)

Reflection

- Can students take weight on hands momentarily?
- Are they accepting responsibility for safety when attempting transfers and inverted skills?
- Are they able to twist slightly to come down safely when off balance?
- Are they beginning to kick legs upward with enough height to have alignment of hips over shoulders?
- Are some students not ready to take weight on hands momentarily? Am I prepared to provide them with developmentally appropriate tasks?

FOCUS▸

Subfocus▸

WEIGHT TRANSFER

Stretching, Curling, and Twisting Actions

Grade 3

Standard 1 The physically literate individual demonstrates competency in a variety of motor skills and movement patterns.

Grade-Level Outcomes

- Moves into and out of gymnastics balances with curling, twisting, and stretching actions (S1.E10.3)
- Employs the concept of alignment in gymnastics and dance (S2.E4.3a)
- Employs the concept of muscular tension with balance in gymnastics and dance (S2.E4.3b)

Lesson Objectives

The learner will:

- Transfer weight into and out of balances by twisting, curling, and stretching
- Create a gymnastics sequence of balances and weight transfers (on mats)

Materials and Equipment

Sufficient mats for all students to work safely

Introduction

Thus far in our gymnastics work, you have balanced with various bases of support, shapes, and levels, and performed balances in inverted positions. Tell your neighbor the two criteria for success in gymnastics balances.

Allow time for peer interaction.

You were introduced to transitions, the movement between balances. Our lesson today focuses on specific types of transitions, moving into and out of balances by stretching, curling, and twisting. To the experienced gymnast, every movement is a planned action, from the beginning shape to the ending ta-da.

LEARNING EXPERIENCE: REVIEW OF STRETCHING, TWISTING, AND CURLING

Standing in self-space, students stretch the arms to reach as far as possible. They stretch the trunk, feeling the tightness of the abdominal and back muscles.

- They curl the spine until the back is round, slowly uncurl, and then curl again.
- They twist the trunk while keeping feet firmly planted in self-space.

LEARNING EXPERIENCE: STRETCHING OUT OF AND INTO BALANCES

Balanced on one foot, with arms extended forward and the free leg backward for counterbalance, students stretch the arms forward until off balance. They "collapse" to the mat into a new balance and new bases of support.

- Allow several minutes for students to explore balancing on various bases of support, stretching in one direction until off balance and transferring weight to a new base of support.

LEARNING EXPERIENCE: TWISTING OUT OF AND INTO BALANCES

- Balanced in a shoulder stand with upper back, head, and arms serving as bases of support, students extend the legs toward the sky. Keeping the legs stretched, they twist the legs and trunk until off balance, resulting in a new balance with different bases of support.

- Balanced on two feet, they twist the trunk in various directions until becoming off balance brings a transfer onto a new base of support.
- Allow several minutes for students to explore balancing on various bases of support, twisting free body parts or the total body, and transferring off balance to a new balance.

LEARNING EXPERIENCE: CURLING OUT OF AND INTO BALANCES

- Balanced on knees and one elbow, students extend the free arm under the body, resulting in being off balance. They tuck body parts close to the body and roll sideways out of the balance.

Variations for Individual Challenges

- Balanced on head and hands (frog stand), students push with the hands, tuck the chin, and roll forward.
- Balanced on hands and one foot, with free leg extended, students tuck the chin, push with the hands, and roll forward.
- Balanced on one foot, students extend the arms forward and the free leg backward for counter-balance, stretching the arms forward until off balance.
  - When "falling" off balance, they lower the body to the mat, stretch into a narrow shape, and roll sideways across the mat.
  - Task extension: When "falling" off balance, they transfer weight to hands, tuck the head, curl the back, and roll across the mat.
- Allow several minutes for students to explore balancing on various bases of support, curling the spine (or tucking arms and legs close to the body), and rolling out of the balance.
- Challenge students to repeat the balances, rolling out of the balance and into a new balance.

LEARNING EXPERIENCE: BALANCES AND ACTIONS

Think of all the many balances you created when we studied bases of support, body shapes, levels, and inversion. Balance in those positions. Use the actions of stretching, curling, and twisting to transfer out of the balances and into new ones.

Allow sufficient time for students to explore and practice transfers out of and into balances as they review bases, shapes, levels, and inversion with transfers.

- Have students select three favorite balances that show transferring weight into and out of the balance by stretching, curling, and twisting. Challenge them within the sequence of three to demonstrate weight transfer by rolling, by stretching, and by twisting.
  - Students then practice for smoothness, best order of balances, and best choices of weight transfers.
  - Peers critique balances for stillness and actions for smoothness.

Assessment

Have students work with partners to prepare a digital recording of the three balances and actions. The focus is on transitions.

Assessment

- Observe throughout for understanding of actions, stillness in balance, and students working to potential.
- Using video presentation outlined earlier, have the class develop criteria for assessment and conduct student self-assessment.

Closure

- What was the focus of our lesson today?
- How was our work on stretching, curling, and twisting today different from when you studied them earlier in gymnastics?
- Tell your neighbor which of the three actions was the most difficult for you. Why? (Ask the class to respond with raised hands to determine the answers for difficulty. Discuss the reasons.)
- Why do we need to transfer weight in gymnastics? Isn't gymnastics all about balances?

Reflection

- Do all students have skills to transfer weight, that is, to make transitions between balances?
- Am I meeting the needs of the highly skilled and the less skilled with tasks presented?
- Is the class working independently and safely as gymnastics work advances?

FOCUS▸ BALANCES AND WEIGHT TRANSFERS: BUILDING A SEQUENCE

Grades 3-5

This lesson is designed to be completed over a series of several classes, not during a single class.

Standard 1 The physically literate individual demonstrates competency in a variety of motor skills and movement patterns.

Grade-Level Outcomes

- Combines balances and transfers into a three-part sequence (i.e., dance, gymnastics) (S1.E11.2)
- Combines traveling with balance and weight transfers to create a gymnastics sequence with and without equipment or apparatus (S1.E12.4)

Lesson Objective

The learner will create and perform a gymnastics sequence of balances and weight transfers on mats (grade 3), optional for grades 4 and 5.

Materials and Equipment

Sufficient mats for all students to work safely

Introduction

Review with the class the work of balance and weight transfer: bases of support, body shapes, levels, inversion, stretching, curling, twisting, muscular tension, alignment, extensions, and transitions.

Relate the gymnastics sequence to sports practice that leads to successful participation in the game as well as to music practice and theatrical rehearsals that lead to the final performance.

Although students have created sequences within class work, the culminating sequence will serve as their summative assessment of the gymnastics work for balance and weight transfer—a creative project that demonstrates skills, cognitive understanding, and the uniqueness of each student.

LEARNING EXPERIENCE: SEQUENCE ON MATS

Students work through the following three parts of the sequence with guided practice of balances and transfers, review of ending shape, and exploration and practice of beginning shape.

- Beginning shape: Students stand at the end (or corner) of the mat. They may select any position they choose with guidance that it should facilitate movement.
- Balances and weight transfers:
  - Grade 3: three balances with different bases of support and weight transfers between balances
  - Grade 4: four balances with different bases of support, each with a different shape—wide, narrow, curled, twisted; and transfers between balances
  - Grade 5: five balances with different bases of support and different shapes, demonstrating the three levels—high, middle, low; at least one inverted balance; and weight transfers of stretching, curling, and twisting
- Ending shape: Ta-da, standing position with arms extended upward, alignment of arms, shoulders, hips, feet

LEARNING EXPERIENCE: STUDENT PROJECT

Following sufficient time for students to explore beginning shape, practice of balances and weight transfers, and review of the ending shape, discuss with the class the final project. Inform students of the components of the project, the criteria for assessment, and the procedures for completion of the assignment.

(Post on the wall charts of the body parts as bases of support, shapes, actions, and levels.)

Discuss with the class the following steps for completion of the gymnastics project:

- Record beginning and ending shape on paper.
- Draw balances on back of paper (stick figures or pictographs) and include transfers.
- Number the balances in order of the sequence.
- Memorize the sequence.
- Have a friend watch a dress rehearsal.
- Come to the teacher for evaluation when ready.

Criteria for Evaluation

- Balances drawn
- Different bases of support for each balance (grade 3)
- Balances and shapes (grade 4)
- Balances, shapes, levels, and inversion (grade 5)
- Balances numbered and performed to match order
- Beginning and ending shapes
- Sequence memorized
- Evidence of concepts of muscular tension, alignment, shapes, levels, and so on as they pertain to gymnastics
- Extra credit: creativity (a touch of me!)

Note: Facilitate final project work by having students prepare an assignment sheet (see sample worksheet). Helpful hints for success: Fold the paper as a three-fold letter, separating parts I, II, and III with the folds. Students focus only on the portion that is assigned for that day, reporting to you for further instructions when they complete that part. Youngsters benefit from actually folding the paper into three sections for concentration on the task.

Begin the sequence work by having students practice balances and weight transfers, record them on the assignment sheet in part II, and put drawings on the back of the assignment sheet. (Observe for students having difficulty understanding directions or working independently; provide individual assistance as needed.)

FINAL GYMNASTICS SEQUENCE FORM

Name: _____ Homeroom: _____

. . . .

Part I: Beginning Shape

. . . .

Part II: Balances and Transfers

Use back of sheet to diagram balances, and label bases of support and transfers.

. . . .

Part III: Ending Shape

From S. Holt/Hale and T. Hall, 2016, *Lesson planning for elementary physical education* (Champaign, IL: Human Kinetics).

Assessment

- Daily assessment of progress on assignment, comments on assignments.
- Summative: The final gymnastics sequence serves as the summative assessment for students' cognitive and performance understanding of balances and weight transfers in gymnastics, as well as the concepts of muscular tension, alignment, shapes, levels, and so on as they pertain to gymnastics.

Note: Complete your assessment of each student's project while students are working on their sequences. Digital recording of sequences is optional for students. Place completed projects in each student's portfolio following your evaluation.

Closure

- Today, we focused on part II of the final gymnastics sequences. Tell your neighbor the requirements for completion of part II.
- Will muscular tension be important when your sequence is being graded? Why?
- Raise your hands if you used extensions in any of your balances. What role do extensions play in maintaining good balance for sequences?
- In our next class we will focus on parts I and III of the sequence—the beginning and the ending.
- In our next class we will focus on practicing or rehearsing the sequences and showing them to a friend before I grade them.
- After I have graded your sequence, you will serve as a coach to help other students with their sequences.

Reflection

- Are students working safely when working independently?
- Do they cognitively understand balances, weight transfers, and the concepts of muscular tension, alignment, and extensions? Can they use them in a sequence?
- Do any students need modifications of the task? Do any students need an extra challenge in their balances and transfers?

FOCUS▶ BALANCES AND WEIGHT TRANSFERS ON LOW EQUIPMENT

Subfocus▶ Partner Relationships

Grades 3-5

Standard 1 The physically literate individual demonstrates competency in a variety of motor skills and movement patterns.

Students are introduced to balances and weight transfers on low equipment only after they display a functional understanding of balances and weight transfers on mats. This lesson, Balances and Weight Transfer on Low Equipment, is designed to be completed over a series of several classes, not during a single class.

Grade-Level Outcomes

- Combines traveling with balance and weight transfers to create a gymnastics sequence with and without equipment or apparatus (S1.E12.4)
- Combines actions, balances and weight transfer to create a gymnastics sequence with a partner on equipment or apparatus (S1.E12.5)

Lesson Objectives

The learner will:

- Combine balances and weight transfers on low equipment
- Combine balances and weight transfers into a sequence on low equipment
- Combine balances and weight transfers into a sequence with a partner on low equipment (grade 5)

Review partner relationships: working in unison or contrast, leading and following, matching side by side, and mirroring by facing each other.

Materials and Equipment

- Variety of low equipment: 12-inch (30 cm) section of vaulting box, low balance beams, benches, low tables, aerobic step boxes
- Sufficient mats to surround equipment for safety

Organization and Management

- Establish protocols for response to signal, listening position, and rotation of stations.
- Set up stations (see examples of low equipment for balances and transfers).

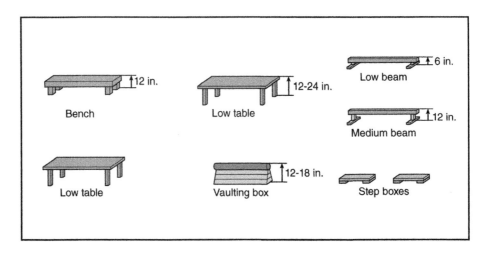

Introduction

During our study of gymnastics, you have balanced on various bases of support and in various shapes and levels; you have transferred weight by stretching, curling, rolling, and twisting; and you have created sequences on mats. Today, we will increase the challenge by applying all those skills to small equipment—tables, benches, beams, and boxes. Safety on the low equipment is our prerequisite to the large gymnastics apparatuses.

Safety Concern

Tell students that they must not disturb or touch others as they work on gymnastics equipment. (Standard 4)

Divide the class into equal groups for stations. Preferably, sufficient equipment should be available so that no more than four or five students are at a station.

- Rotation 1: all students to all stations
- Rotation 2: choice of favorite two stations, no more than five at a station
- Rotation 3: choice of favorite station for sequence work

LEARNING EXPERIENCE: BALANCES ON EQUIPMENT

Review bases of support from lesson on mats and criteria for success.

- Exploration of balances with various bases of support on low equipment. On each rotation to a different station, students begin anew with balances and bases.
- Task extensions: inverted balances on table and vaulting box.

Guided discovery: *Some balances that were easy on the floor are difficult on low equipment, such as one-foot balance, front scale, but some balances are easier on low equipment than on the floor or mat.*

LEARNING EXPERIENCE: WEIGHT TRANSFER ON EQUIPMENT

Review actions of stretching, curling, and twisting; muscular tension; alignment; counterbalance.

- Have students explore weight transfers on equipment.
- Challenge students to transition between balances while remaining on the equipment.

LEARNING EXPERIENCE: MOUNTS AND DISMOUNTS

Have students explore getting onto low equipment.

- Introduce step and spring takeoffs with review of jumping and landing. With a 10- to 15-foot (3 to 5 m) approach to the equipment, students transfer to feet on equipment.
- They transfer to body parts other than feet on equipment, such as knees and hands, upper thighs, stomach.
- Task extension: transfer momentarily to hands only.

Have students explore various ways of getting off low equipment:

- Review of critical elements for safe landings: bending of knees and ankles, and alignment of shoulders, hips, and ankles
- Jumping off with shapes in the air
- Jumping off with quarter and half turns

Task extensions: transfer from feet to hands on equipment for transfer off low equipment; transfer from low-level balance to weight on hands on mat, rolling action for dismount

LEARNING EXPERIENCE: SEQUENCE ON LOW EQUIPMENT

- Approach: Standing approximately 15 feet (5 m) from the bench, low table, or low beam, students may select a locomotor or a weight transfer action to travel from the starting place to the equipment.
- Mount the equipment: Transfer from two feet to two feet, one foot to two feet, one foot to one foot. Task extensions: knee vault, frog stand.
- Balances and weight transfers
  - Grade 3: bases of support
  - Grade 4: bases of support, shapes, levels, weight transfers
  - Grade 5: bases of support, shapes, levels, inversion, weight transfers
- Dismount from low equipment
  - Jumping and landing: two feet to two feet, jump with quarter turn, jump with half turn, jump with shape in the air
  - Task extensions: transfer from feet to hands on equipment for transfer off low equipment; transfer from low-level balance to weight on hands on mat, rolling action for dismount
- Ending shape: ta-da

Following the rotation to all stations, ask students to select their two favorite stations for balances and weight transfers. Allow sufficient time for each student to experiment with balances, weight transfers, and mounts and dismounts at the two stations.

After a discussion of the final project, a sequence on low equipment (the components of the project, the criteria for assessment, and the procedures for completion of the assignment), have each student select his or her best station for the sequence project.

- Review with the class the steps in completing the gymnastics project:
  - Record the approach, mount, dismount, and ending shape on paper.
  - Draw balances and transfers on back of paper (stick figures or pictographs); label bases of support.
  - Number the balances in order of the sequence.
  - Memorize the sequence.
  - Have a friend watch for a dress rehearsal.
  - Come to the teacher for evaluation when ready.

Criteria for Evaluation

- Written work complete
- Sequence memorized and performed as recorded on paper
- Different bases of support for each balance (grade 3)
- Balances and shapes (grade 4)
- Balances, shapes, levels, and inversion (grade 5)
- Sequence matched to skill level of student
- Extra credit: creativity (a touch of me!)

Provide students with the assignment sheet for completing the work on the beam, bench, table, or box they have selected.

GYMNASTICS ASSIGNMENT SHEET FOR LOW EQUIPMENT

Name:_____Homeroom:_____

Low equipment: _____ Partner: _____

Part I

1. Approach to low equipment

2. Mount onto low equipment

Part II

1. Balances: Draw each balance on back of this sheet and label base of support.
2. Weight transfers, transitions, travel

Part III

1. Dismount
2. Ending shape (ta-da)

From S. Holt/Hale and T. Hall, 2016, *Lesson planning for elementary physical education* (Champaign, IL: Human Kinetics).

Assessment

Grade 3

The summative assessment for third graders is the sequence on mats. Sequences on low equipment consist of balances on various bases of support with mounts and dismounts. They can be assessed by a peer or digitally recorded for a self-assessment.

Grade 4

The final gymnastics sequence serves as the summative assessment for students' cognitive and performance understanding of balances and weight transfers in gymnastics, as well as the concepts of muscular tension, alignment, shapes, levels, and so on as they pertain to gymnastics. (Formative assessments have been collected throughout the study.)

Grade 5

The final gymnastics sequence on low equipment is an option for students who prefer the low equipment instead of pieces of apparatus.

Complete your assessment of each student's project by stations while other students continue their work. Digital recording of sequences is optional for students. Place completed projects in each student's portfolio following your evaluation.

Closure

- What was different about our work in gymnastics today? What new challenge was added?
- What is the difference between doing balances on the mats and on the equipment?
- Which pieces of low equipment were best for inverted balances?
- Which shape was easiest? Most difficult?

Grades 4, 5

- Compare your skills of balancing on the mats with balancing on the equipment.
- Compare moving into and out of balances on the mats and on the equipment.

Reflection

- Do students work safely on gymnastics equipment?
- Do they safely come out of balances, both accidental and intentional?
- Are they able to move into and out of balances on the equipment?
- Are they ready with both skills and acceptance of responsibility for the large pieces of gymnastics apparatus?

BALANCES AND WEIGHT TRANSFERS ON APPARATUS

Grades 3-5

Following a successful study of balance on the floor (mats) and balances on low equipment, students are ready for an introduction to balance on large pieces of gymnastics apparatus, which include parallel bars, Olympic balance beams, and vaulting boxes, as well as climbing frames, ladders, inclines, and bridges.

Elementary students are introduced to gymnastics apparatus as each piece becomes developmentally appropriate in size and structure. Early experiences include exploration of the apparatus, safety, body control, and acceptance of responsibility. Young children eagerly await introduction to the "big equipment."

The progression of skills follows closely the progression that occurs on the mats and low apparatus: balances on apparatus, bases of support, transitions between balances, approaches to and mounts onto apparatus, and dismounts from apparatus.

At a more advanced level of skill development, students also study transfers into and out of balances on apparatus, combinations of balances and transfers, as well as transfers onto and off apparatus beyond jumping.

Specific pieces of gymnastics apparatus, such as parallel bars and balance beam, may dictate the types of approaches and dismounts that students can perform safely in elementary physical education. Safety rules pertaining to each piece of apparatus should be posted on the wall near the apparatus. See the following example for the balance beam.

> **Balance Beam Safety Check: Mats in place.**
>
> **Dismounts: All landings on two feet. No crash landings!**

Grade 3

Balances on various bases of support, weight transfer travel on apparatus, approaches with mounts onto apparatus, and dismounts from apparatus (jumping and landing).

Grades 4, 5

Preparation for final gymnastics sequence follows the guidelines established for low equipment: rotation of all students to all stations, choice of two stations, and selection of one station for final project.

- Grade 4: Combining traveling with balance and weight transfers to create a sequence
- Grade 5: Combining actions, balances, and transferring weight to create a sequence alone or with a partner

Final Gymnastics Project on Apparatus

- Approach
- Mount onto apparatus
- Balances, weight transfers, and travel
- Dismount from apparatus
- Ending shape: ta-da

The final project assignment follows the guidelines established for the previous lesson, Balances and Weight Transfers on Low Equipment, for assignment procedures, criteria for sequence evaluation, and sample assignment sheet.

Students will create, record, and perform sequences at their selected piece of apparatus, using skills commensurate with their balance and weight transfer abilities. Differentiated guidelines and developmentally appropriate expectations are critical for students in gymnastics.

CHAPTER 8

Teaching for Competency in Manipulative Skills

This chapter contains a series of lesson plans for each of the manipulative skills found in *National Standards & Grade-Level Outcomes for K-12 Physical Education* (SHAPE America, 2014) for elementary physical education. The lesson plans for each manipulative skill are arranged in a series from simple to complex, moving each learner from the introduction of the skill to mastery of the critical elements (i.e., mature patterns of execution).

Lessons are designed to progress from developing the skill in isolation to using movement concepts and skills in combination, leading to the application of skills in dynamic environments beyond elementary school physical education.

The lesson plans are designed so that students will move through the progression detailed in the Grade-Level Outcomes. The lesson plans are appropriate for the grade levels indicated, based on students' having experienced the earlier lessons in the series. If students have not experienced the earlier lessons in the series, you need to adapt the tasks and redesign the lesson plans for them to master the prerequisite skills and concepts of those particular lessons.

The goal of every task within the lesson plan is student learning, not completion of the written plan within the 30 to 45 minutes of the class. Student learning comes from deliberate, appropriate practice and devoting sufficient time to that practice. Although this process applies to all student learning in physical education, it is true especially for mastering manipulative skills.

Finally, remember that physical education environments vary based on students' previous experiences and the number of days per week allotted to instructional physical education. The manipulative skills included in this text and the depth of the skill development are matched with the National Standards and Grade-Level Outcomes, but the manipulative skills to be taught—as well as depth of skill development for each—will be determined by you as a teacher of elementary physical education. Refer to the sample yearly plan in appendix B for an overview of planning that reflects the breadth and depth of the National Standards.

THROWING UNDERHAND

Pathways

Grades K-2

Standard 1 The physically literate individual demonstrates competency in a variety of motor skills and movement patterns.

Grade-Level Outcomes

- Throws underhand with opposite foot forward (S1.E13.K)
- Throws underhand demonstrating two of the five critical elements of a mature pattern (S1.E13.1)
- Throws underhand using a mature pattern (S1.E13.2)

Critical Elements for Throwing (Underhand Pattern)

- Face target in preparation for throwing action.
- Arm back in preparation for action.
- Step with opposite foot as throwing arm moves forward.
- Release ball between knee and waist level.
- Follow through to target.

Lesson Objectives

The learner will:

- Identify opposite arm and foot (K)
- Throw a hand-size object underhand with opposition most of the time (K)
- Throw a hand-size object underhand demonstrating correct starting position and opposition (grade 1)
- Throw a hand-size object underhand with correct starting position, stepping forward with opposite foot for throwing action (grade 2)
- Throw a ball underhand so that it travels forward toward a target (grades 1, 2)

Safety Concern

Ensure that spacing is adequate for throwing and retrieving.

Materials and Equipment

- Yarn or fleece balls, one per student
- Stickers, one per student
- Station equipment: six hoops, wall tape, geometric shapes, four milk crates or boxes

Introduction

Today, we are going to learn how to be good throwers. What games have throwing in them? (Allow several minutes for student answers.) You will be practicing the underhand throw, sometimes making the ball go in a straight pathway and sometimes in a curvy pathway like a rainbow. We have some targets that will make this practice even more fun.

LEARNING EXPERIENCE: THROWING UNDERHAND—FOCUS ON ARM ACTION

Pretend that you are writing your name on an invisible piece of paper. The hand that you write with will be your throwing hand. Roll your invisible piece of paper into a ball while standing in your self-space.

- Demonstrate an underhand throw with a beanbag or a no-bounce ball, asking students to focus on the swing of your arms as you demonstrate the throw. Repeat the throwing action several times.

Cue: *Tick-tock for arm back and forward.*

- Have students throw the invisible ball to you as they say, "Tick-tock." (Observe for forward and backward action, not sideward across the body.)
- Using a beanbag or a fleece or yarn ball, students practice throwing from behind one boundary line using the tick-tock underhand motion. After each throw, students retrieve and prepare to throw again with the same hand. (Remind students to use their favorite hand each time; some students are still exploring their preferred hand in grades K and 1.)

Safety Check: Remind students to wait for your signal or cue to throw. Younger students have not yet mastered spatial awareness for safety in throwing.

LEARNING EXPERIENCE: THROWING WITH AN ARCH OR CURVED PATHWAY—FOCUS ON RELEASE POINT

Have students repeat the previous task with a focus on the arch or curved pathway (like a rainbow) that the object makes as it travels through the air. After a few minutes of student exploration, discuss point of release and its importance in a curved versus straight aerial pathway. Demonstrate the underhand throw with the point of release for each pathway.

- Allow several minutes for students to practice the release for the curved pathway. Challenge students to throw five times with an arch or curved pathway and five times with a straight pathway, emphasizing the point of release for the type of pathway (grades 1, 2).

LEARNING EXPERIENCE: THROWING UNDERHAND—FOCUS ON OPPOSITE FOOT FORWARD

Have students assume a ready position, with the opposite foot forward (in front of the boundary) before throwing. On your signal, students throw with the underhand throwing action.

Cue: *Opposite foot forward or same foot back. (Some children learn better with this cue.)*

- Students continue practice with self-check of opposite foot forward before each throw. (Stickers on the opposite foot work for children who are struggling.)

LEARNING EXPERIENCE: THROWING FOR DISTANCE

Have students throw the ball, using the underhand throwing action, as far as they can across the work area.

Cue: *Throw really hard.*

  Common error: late release point, resulting in the ball going too high

- Using tape mark or existing lines, create three distance zones approximately 10, 15, and 20 feet (3, 4.5, and 6 m) from starting boundary line.
  - Zone 1 (five tries)
  - Zone 2 (five tries)
  - Zone 3 (five tries)

Have students continue practice of throwing (underhand) for distance; challenge them to throw farther with each attempt.

- Grades 1, 2: Challenge students to tell the person behind them the zone that is their target and then purposely throw so that the ball will land in that zone.
- Grade 2: Discuss with the class the use of the straight pathway versus the curved aerial pathway for distance versus less distance and purposeful landings.

LEARNING EXPERIENCE: THROWING UNDERHAND: FOCUS ON STEPPING FORWARD (GRADES 1, 2)

You are now ready to throw like the big guys, like the pitcher in a softball game. Your starting position will be with feet side by side on the line.

Demonstrate as you verbalize the following: face target with feet side by side, bring throwing arm back, and step opposite as arm comes forward. Repeat the demonstration with spoken description several times. Have the students practice throwing the pretend balls, following your signal for cues and release.

- With your signal, students practice full throwing pattern.
- Add starting position and stepping with the throw. Have students repeat distance zones.

   Note: This lesson plan presents all the critical elements of a mature underhand throwing pattern. Remember that the presentation of all the critical elements is overwhelming for children; present one critical element at a time and follow with practice and success. Move to the next critical element after observing successful execution of the critical element in focus.

LEARNING EXPERIENCE: THROWING TO TARGETS

Students throw underhand to the targets on the wall.

- They use a straight, direct pathway (extending arm toward target).
- They explore increases in distance with focus on accuracy to target. (Remind students that the throw is still underhand.)

LEARNING EXPERIENCE: STATIONS FOR PRACTICE

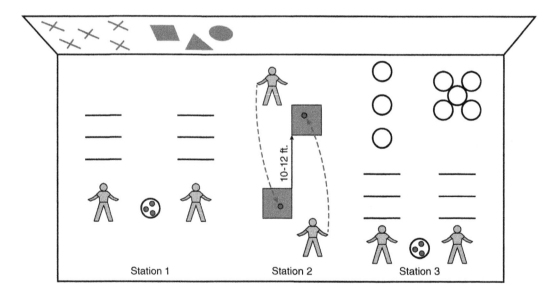

- Station 1: Students throw at the Xs or shapes on the wall; they choose the distance. They continue to practice throwing, alternating turns throwing at the Xs or shapes on the wall.

Grade 2: *The person behind you will observe your throw. He or she will give you 1 point if you throw with the opposite foot forward and an extra point if you hit the target.*

- Station 2: Students throw with a curved pathway so that the ball or beanbag lands in the box or crate; students choose the distance.

- Station 3: Students throw with a curved pathway so that the ball or beanbag lands in a hoop; students choose the distance. They continue to practice throwing, alternating turns, at the different hoop arrangements.

Grade 2: *Tell the person behind you which hoop is your target when throwing for the zone hoops. Give yourself 2 points if the ball or beanbag lands in that hoop.*

Assessment

- Peer assessment: Students give a thumbs-up and award 1 point for stepping with opposite foot.
- Exit slip: Using a drawing of someone holding a ball with feet side by side, have students place an X on the foot that should step (K and 1).

Closure

- What was the focus of our lesson today?
- What is important to remember about our feet on the underhand throw?
- If the ball is in my right hand, which foot is my opposite (grades K and 1)?
- What determines whether you should use a straight or a curved aerial pathway for the underhand throw (grade 2)?

Reflection

- Are students using arm and foot opposition most of the time?
- Are students (grades 1 and 2) stepping as the arm comes forward?

THROWING UNDERHAND

Movement Concepts, Partner Relationships

Grades 3-5

Standard 1 The physically literate individual demonstrates competency in a variety of motor skills and movement patterns.

Grade-Level Outcomes

- Throws underhand to a partner or target with reasonable accuracy (S1.E13.3)
- Applies skill (S1.E13.4)
- Throws underhand using a mature pattern in nondynamic environments (closed skills) with different sizes and types of objects (S1.E13.5a)
- Throws underhand to a large target with accuracy (S1.E13.5b)

At the end of grade 2, students should be able to demonstrate the critical elements of the underhand throwing pattern. According to the scope and sequence suggested in *National Standards & Grade Level Outcomes for K-12 Physical Education* (SHAPE America, 2014), students in grade 3 have left the emerging stage and entered the maturing stage for the underhand throw. In grades 3 through 5, students should continue to be engaged in practice experiences in which they can refine the underhand throw. These practice experiences are usually embedded in other lessons.

The following are sample underhand throwing experiences appropriate for students in grades 3 through 5:

- Into targets (hoops, crates, boxes)
- To partners
- At wall targets
- At a wall with force (as if pitching a softball)
- To a batter
- To a partner who is striking with a paddle or small tennis racquet
- Rolling to hit objects such as in bowling, bocce, or other target games
- Specific skills such as "pitch out" in a keep-away game (using different sizes and types of balls)

CATCHING

Throwing Underhand

Grades K-2

Standard 1 The physically literate individual demonstrates competency in a variety of motor skills and movement patterns.

Grade-Level Outcomes

- Drops a ball and catches it before it bounces twice (S1.E16.Ka)
- Catches a large ball tossed by a skilled thrower (S1.E16.Kb)
- Catches a soft object from a self-toss before it bounces (S1.E16.1a)
- Catches different sizes of balls self-tossed or tossed by a skilled thrower (S1.E16.1b)
- Catches a self-tossed or well-thrown large ball with hands, not trapping or cradling against the body (S1.E16.2)

Critical Elements for Catching

- Extend arms outward to reach for ball.
  - Thumbs in for catch above the waist.
  - Thumbs out for catch at or below the waist.
- Watch the ball all the way into the hands.
- Catch with hands only; no cradling against the body.
- Pull the ball into the body as the catch is made.
- Curl the body slightly around the ball.

Lesson Objectives

The learner will:

- Move arms outward and position hands ready to catch a ball tossed by a skilled thrower (grades K, 1)
- Catch with hands only (grades 1, 2)

Safety Concern

Ensure that spacing is adequate for students to toss and catch to themselves.

Materials and Equipment

- Different types of large (7- to 8.5-inch [18 to 22 cm]) lightweight balls that will bounce (plastic, rubber, foam), different hand-size balls, beanbags
- Station equipment: net (6 by 8 feet [180 to 240 cm]), two inclines made of cardboard or plastic

Introduction

The skill we are working on today is catching. The focus is catching with your hands only. You will have many different kinds of balls to catch. Watch as I toss to myself and catch. I toss it just slightly above my head, let it bounce once, and then catch it. Watch again. What do I do with my arms and hands? (Allow time for responses from students and introduce "ready hands and arms" and catching with hands only.)

LEARNING EXPERIENCE: TOSSING AND CATCHING A LARGE BALL AFTER A BOUNCE

Focus on an easy toss. Standing in self-space, students toss balls gently upward (using two hands, lifting arms, and releasing just before the ball is at eye level), let the ball bounce one time, and then catch it.

Cues: *Toss, bounce, catch.*

Allow several toss and catches for students to perform the gentle toss to self correctly.

- Have students continue the same task by focusing on catching with hands only. (Demonstrate an incorrect cradle catch.) Remind students to bend their elbows slightly and not have stiff arms.

Cue: *Hands only.*

- Continue with emphasis on watching ball to hands.

Cue: *Watch the ball. (Remind students that "Watch the ball" is a cue that even college athletes in basketball, football, soccer, and baseball hear the coach say every day.)*

- Challenge students to see how many consecutive catches they can make with the sequence: toss, bounce, catch.

LEARNING EXPERIENCE: TOSSING AND CATCHING A LARGE BALL WITHOUT THE BOUNCE

Focus on using hands only. Allow several minutes for students to continue the same task of tossing and catching, but without the ball bouncing. As you observe students catching without the bounce, you will notice catching above the head at high level and in front of the body at middle level. When you observe catching at different levels, introduce catching with thumbs in and thumbs out.

Cues: *Thumbs in. (for catching above the waist), thumbs out (for catching at or below the waist)*

- Allow several minutes for students to practice tossing and catching at different places in relation to the body to explore thumbs in and thumbs out.

LEARNING EXPERIENCE: TOSSING TO THE WALL AND CATCHING (GRADE 2)

The focus here is on ready hands and quick feet. Have students toss the ball to the wall and catch it after it bounces one time. Allow several minutes of practice for control of force on the wall toss.

Cue: *Ready hands.*

- Students continue practice of toss, bounce, and catch against the wall. Remind them of the critical elements introduced and practiced thus far: watching the ball and catching with hands only. When you observe students reaching consistently for the ball, they are ready for the next critical element: pulling the ball in toward the body.

Cue: *Reach and pull.*

- Task extension: Students catch the ball before it bounces, moving purposely to be always in position for the catch.

Cue: *Quick feet.*

LEARNING EXPERIENCE: TOSSING AND CATCHING A SMALL BALL

Focus is on hands being closer together and fingers closing around the ball. In self-space, students toss a small ball upward above the head and catch it before it touches the floor.

Cues: *Venus flytrap. Catcher's mitt. Baseball glove.*

- Demonstrate catching a small ball with the heels of hands close together and fingers closing around the ball after contact. Demonstrate an example of the ball bouncing out of the hands after the catch because of failing to close the fingers.
- Students continue practice with emphasis on the two-hand catch, not catching with one hand. Emphasize reaching for the ball, not waiting for the ball to come into the body.

Grades 1, 2

Challenge students to make 5, 10, or 15 consecutive catches. Students might need a reminder about thumbs in and thumbs out for a toss above the head when keeping score.

LEARNING EXPERIENCE: STATIONS FOR PRACTICE (AND TEACHER ASSESSMENT)

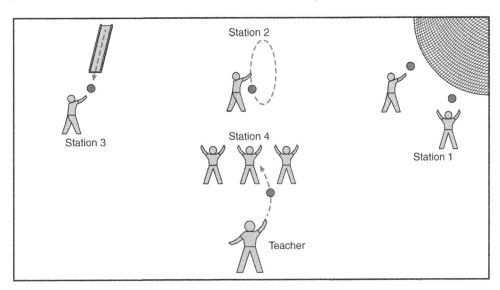

Station 1

Students toss and catch a large ball (7 to 8.5 inches [18 to 22 cm]) into a net suspended approximately 6 feet (180 cm) off the floor, with the back corner higher than the front edge so that the ball rolls off.

- K: after one bounce.
- Grade 1: with or without a bounce
- Grade 2: before the ball bounces

Station 2

Students practice catching a variety of balls. They make five catches and then change to a different ball.

- K, grade 1: with or without a bounce
- Grade 2: without a bounce

Station 3

Use a slide with raised edges or a long box with ends removed and back against a wall to create a slight incline. Students toss the ball to the slide and catch it as it rolls down.

- K: after one bounce.
- Grade 1: with or without a bounce
- Grade 2: before it bounces

Station 4

Assessment station. Use a large ball for K and both large and small balls for grades 1 and 2. You toss the ball underhand. Students catch after a bounce the first turn and then in the air on the second turn. Observe and assess the following:

- K: arms extended, ready for catch, and visual tracking of ball
- Grade 1: catching with hands only
- Grade 2: reaching for the ball, thumbs in or thumbs out for correct catch, beginning to reach and pull the ball into the body

Assessment

Teacher checklist of preceding criteria for assessment.

Closure

- What skill did we focus on today?
- Do we catch with hands only or with arms and hands?
- Show me the correct position for arms. Remember: bent slightly, not stiff.
- Why do we close fingers around a small ball after the catch?

Reflection

- Do the children place their arms and hands in ready position for catching?
- Do they extend the arms to catch with hands only, or do some still cradle the ball?

FOCUS▸

CATCHING

Subfocus▸ Underhand Throwing, Partner Relationships, Levels

Grades 2, 3

Standard 1 The physically literate individual demonstrates competency in a variety of motor skills and movement patterns.

Grade-Level Outcomes

- Catches a self-tossed or well-thrown large ball with hands, not trapping or cradling against the body (S1.E16.2)
- Catches a gently tossed hand-size ball from a partner, demonstrating four of the five critical elements of a mature pattern (S1.E16.3)

Critical Elements for Catching

- Extend arms outward to reach for ball.
  - Thumbs in for catch above the waist.
  - Thumbs out for catch at or below the waist.
- Watch the ball all the way into the hands.
- Catch with hands only; no cradling against the body.
- Pull the ball into the body as the catch is made.
- Curl the body slightly around the ball. (Specific only to certain catches.)

Lesson Objectives

The learner will:

- Catch a self-tossed ball at different levels with proper hand position, using reach and pull
- Catch large balls, self-tossed and from partner, with hands only, using reach and pull (grade 2)
- Catch a well-tossed ball from a partner, with ready hands and with hands only, using proper hand position, and reach and pull (grade 3)

Safety Concern

Ensure that spacing is adequate for tossing and catching.

Materials and Equipment

Different types of large (7- to 8.5-inch [18 to 22 cm]) lightweight balls (plastic, rubber, foam), different hand-size balls

Introduction

In our last lesson, you practiced catching with your hands only. Most of the catches were at a middle level. But when we play in games and sports, the ball doesn't always come exactly where we want it to: right to us. To be successful in sports and playing games, we must be able to catch in different positions and at different levels. Today, you will begin catching balls that don't come to your "sweet spot" for catching. You also will throw and catch with a partner, which always makes practice more fun.

LEARNING EXPERIENCE: REVIEW PRACTICE OF CATCHING

Students toss and catch to self. Observe for critical elements: catching with hands only, watching the ball into the hands, correct position of hands with thumbs in or thumbs out, and reach and pull. Review and reteach as necessary.

- Discuss with the class the importance of reaching for the ball (e.g., extending one's reach by even 1 inch (2.5 cm) makes a difference in getting the rebound in basketball and making the catch in many games). Have students practice reaching for and pulling the ball into the body as they continue their tossing and catching in self-space.
- Challenge students to toss the ball high and wide so that they must extend their arms for the catch—in front, to the right, to the left—while keeping one foot in self-space.

Cue: *Reach for the ball.*

- After several minutes of practice, add pulling the ball in.

Cue: *Reach and pull.*

LEARNING EXPERIENCE: REVIEW CATCHING OFF THE WALL

From a distance of 10 to 12 (3 to 3.5 m) feet from the wall, students throw the ball and catch the rebound. Allow several minutes of practice for students to control the force of the throw for the distance from the wall.

Cue: *Reach and pull.*

- Have students explore throwing and catching at different angles and at different heights.

Cues: *Reach and pull. Use quick feet.*

- Challenge students to vary the force of the throw, creating catches at middle and low height, and near and far from the wall.

LEARNING EXPERIENCE: CATCHING AT DIFFERENT LEVELS

Students focus on correct hand position and hands-only catches by tossing and catching to self.

- Students toss the ball above the head so that the catch is at a high level, above the head.
- They toss the ball at middle level, to practice "sweet spot" catches.
- They catch at a low level (below the knees), just before the ball hits the ground.

Remind students to toss the ball above their heads but to wait until it reaches a low level before catching it.

(Option: Students who are struggling with the timing of the low-level catch can let the ball bounce first.)

Self-Assessment

Have students take a 30-second test at their favorite level. The goal is two or fewer misses. Students challenge themselves to repeat the assessment at another level.

LEARNING EXPERIENCE: PARTNER GENTLE TOSS AND CATCH WITH LARGE PLAYGROUND-TYPE BALL

Position students in two lines facing partners, approximately 8 to 10 feet (2.4 to 3 m) apart. Allow several minutes for students to practice tossing the ball to their partners at chest height, using a gentle toss, with emphasis on catching.

Cues: *Ready hands. Thumbs in. Hands-only catches.*

- After 10 catches, partner B takes two steps backward and practice continues. (Remind the class that the emphasis is on catching: They should use gentle throws and no further increase in distance.)
- After two minutes of practice with partners, have all students in line A remain stationary, while students in line B rotate one position to the right, resulting in new partners (see diagram). Begin practice again with new partners and at the original starting line. Continue this rotation every two minutes for several rotations of partners.

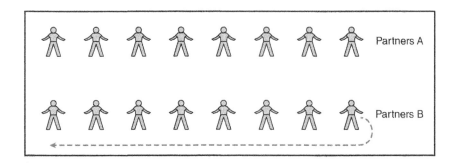

Grade 3

Students toss the ball to partner's right so that he or she must stretch to catch it. They repeat the toss to the partner's left.

Safety Check: More space between groups of students may be needed.

Students toss the ball above the partner's head so that the catch is at high level, above the head.

- Students toss higher so that the partner has to stretch arms upward for the catch.
- Students can challenge the partner by not announcing where the toss will go: high level, middle level, to the right, to the left. The catcher must react quickly to make the catch.

Assessment

- Self-assessment: 10 catches or 30-second test
- Match picture with level of catch: thumbs in or out
- Written test on cues

Closure

- What was the focus of our catching today?
- Show me the hand position for high-level catches, for low-level catches.
- Why should you always pull the ball in to complete a catch?
- Why is catching at different levels important?

Reflection

- Do students stretch for high-level catches?
- Are hands in proper positions?
- Do they reach for the ball rather than wait for it to come to them?
- Do they pull the ball in?

FOCUS▸

CATCHING

Throwing Overhand, Stretching and Twisting Actions, Spatial Awareness

Grades 4, 5

Standard 3 The physical literate individual demonstrates competency in a variety of motor skills and movement patterns.

Grade-Level Outcome

Catches a thrown ball above the head, at chest or waist level and below the waist using a mature pattern in nondynamic environments (S1.E16.4)

Critical Elements for Catching

- Extend arms outward to reach for ball.
  - Thumbs in for catch above the waist.
  - Thumbs out for catch at or below the waist.
- Watch the ball all the way into the hands.
- Catch with hands only; no cradling against the body.
- Pull the ball into the body as the catch is made.
- Curl the body slightly around the ball. (Specific only to certain catches.)

Lesson Objectives

The learner will:

- Toss and catch to self while demonstrating stretching and twisting actions
- Catch a well-thrown ball from a partner, demonstrating stretching and twisting actions
- Catch a ball at different levels with all the critical elements of a mature pattern
- Catch a self-tossed ball while walking or jogging in general space

Safety Concern

Ensure that spacing is adequate for tossing and catching.

Materials and Equipment

A variety of kinds and sizes of balls, beanbags

Introduction

Our lesson today focuses on catching in different places around the body and at different levels. In games and sports, the ball does not always come directly to us; sometimes, we have to stretch or even twist to make a catch. Today, you will practice with different balls, different levels and positions, and with different partners.

LEARNING EXPERIENCE: CATCHING AT DIFFERENT LEVELS

The focus is on all critical elements of a mature catch. Allow sufficient time for practice of skill and observation of critical elements.

- Students practice catching at middle level while staying in self-space:
  - Catching for 30 seconds with no mistakes
  - Using different types of balls

- Have students practice high-level catches, stretching arms upward and pulling the ball in. (Emphasize stretching into a narrow shape.)
- Challenge students to try jumping to reach even higher. Discuss a rebound in basketball, a football player's jumping catch, and a soccer goalkeeper's pulling in the ball after the catch.
- Have them use different types of balls.

Self-Assessment

- How many catches can student make out of 10 attempts without the jump?
- How many out of 5 can they make with the jump?

Peer Assessment

Peers watch for stretch and pulling the ball in.

- Students practice low-level catches, at the last second before the ball hits the floor or ground.
- Have them use different types of balls.

LEARNING EXPERIENCE: CATCHING IN DIFFERENT PLACES AROUND BODY (FRONT, BOTH SIDES, BEHIND)

- Allow several minutes for students to explore twisting and stretching to make catches, reminding them to pull the ball in after each catch.
- Have students:
  - Keep one foot planted as if glued to the ground and stretch to the point of being off balance to make catch in front
  - Toss and stretch to the side, one hand only (right and left)
  - Stretch high to catch and stretch low to catch
  - Toss the ball to the side and slightly behind the body and then twist to make the catch

LEARNING EXPERIENCE: TRAVEL, TOSS, STRETCH, AND CATCH

Students walk in general space, looking for open space. They toss the ball forward, stretch, catch, and pull it in:

- At different levels
- Jumping to catch at high level: stretch, reach, and pull

Safety Concerns

Ensure that students are aware of others in general space.

- Students toss the ball to the right, take a slide step, stretch, and catch. They repeat to the left.
- When you observe students tossing and catching successfully while walking, add the skill of jogging in general space to the toss and catching at different levels.
- Spatial awareness is critical with the combination of jogging, tossing, and catching at different levels.

LEARNING EXPERIENCE: PARTNER TOSS AND CATCH

Working in pairs, have students throw and catch while pretending to play first base in baseball or softball, tossing the ball so that the partner must stretch forward to make the catch:

- To the right
- To the left

Backward game: Partner A turns his or her back, twists, and looks over the right shoulder, offering a two-hand target. Partner B tosses the ball for the Partner A to catch. They reverse roles.

- They repeat to the left.
- Ultimate challenge: When you see students being successful at standing to catch, add the skill of walking or jogging away from the partner for the over-the-shoulder catch.

Safety Check: Everyone jogs and passes in the same direction.

These tasks serve as a prerequisite to the throwing and catching lessons that follow for small-sided practice environments and with both partners moving. (Outcome S1.E16.5b)

Assessment

Observe students' execution of critical elements.

Closure

- What was our new catching skill today?
- Why is it important to catch the ball in different places around the body?
- When might you need to catch with one hand?

Reflection

- Do the children stretch and pull the ball in?
- Are they able to toss the ball to self or partner to elicit the stretch?

THROWING OVERHAND

Force

Grades 2-4

andard 1 The physically literate individual demonstrates competency in a variety of motor skills and movement patterns.

Grade-Level Outcomes

- Throws overhand demonstrating two of the five critical elements of a mature pattern (S1.E14.2)
- Throws overhand demonstrating three of the five critical elements of a mature pattern in nondynamic environments (closed skills) for distance and/or force (S1.E14.3)
- Throws overhand using a mature pattern in nondynamic environments (closed skills) (S1.E14.4a)

Critical Elements for Throwing (Overhand Pattern)

- Hip and spine rotate side to target in preparation for throwing action.
- Arm back and extended, and elbow at shoulder height or slightly above in preparation for action; elbow leads.
- Step with opposite foot as throwing arm moves forward.
- Hip and spine rotate as throwing action is executed.
- Follow through toward target and across body.

Lesson Objectives

The learner will:

- Throw a ball with an overhand throwing action
- Throw an object for distance or force with an overhand throwing action starting side to target, stepping with opposition (grade 2)
- Throw an object for distance or force with an overhand throwing action starting side to target, stepping with opposition, attempting to use proper arm action (grade 3)
- Throw an object for distance or force with an overhand throwing action using hip and spine rotation, arm back in preparation, stepping with opposition, rotating hip and spine as throw is executed (grade 4)

Safety Concern

Ensure that spacing is adequate for throwing and retrieving equipment.

Materials and Equipment

- Small-size limited-bounce balls (indoor softballs, Wiffle balls, or similar), one per student
- Fleece or no-bounce balls, one per student
- Large wall targets (paper is best to add the "pop" sound)
- For outdoor tasks, one bucket or crate of 8 to 10 old tennis balls, three beanbags or three marker cones for each group

Introduction

Previously, you learned to throw underhand. Today, you will practice using an overhand pattern. The skill is used in many games and sports for distance, force, and accuracy. Some games use throwing to people, and other games require throwing at goals or targets. Today, you will practice throwing with force—learning how arms, legs, and trunk work together to create a really good throw.

LEARNING EXPERIENCE: THROWING OVERHAND FOR DISTANCE

The focus is on starting side to target and stepping with opposition. Using a fleece ball or no-bounce ball, students throw overhand from behind one boundary line, stepping with the opposite foot. (Remind students to retrieve and wait for the next signal to throw.)

- Students continue practice with focus on starting side to target, placing feet shoulder-width apart, and then stepping with opposition.
- Grade 4: Students start by facing the target and then rotate hip and spine into side-to-target position.
- Have students increase distance of the throw, focusing on having the arm way back in preparation.
- Grade 4: Students focus on combining the twist with having the arm back.

LEARNING EXPERIENCE: THROWING OVERHAND FOR FORCE

The focus is on stepping with opposition, with the arm way back. Using a limited-bounce ball (indoor softballs, Wiffle balls, or similar), students throw hard against the wall from a distance of approximately 15 feet (4.5 m). (Use tape or spots on floor for starting lines).

Space limitations may require this to be done with partners or groups of three.

- Students repeat tasks, throwing at large paper targets, focusing on force.

Peer Assessment

Evaluating partner stands beside thrower for good observation.

- Grades 2, 3: Give 1 point for arm way back and 1 point for hitting the target.
- Grade 4: Give 1 point for hip and spine rotation and 1 point for hitting the target.

  Note: Present the next critical element only after you observe success at the critical element that has been the focus of the students' practice. This lesson has presented all the critical elements leading to a mature pattern for the overhand throw. Students will not master overhand throwing in a single lesson. A series of lessons and distributed practice throughout the year are necessary for student success.

LEARNING EXPERIENCE: DISTANCE THROW (OUTDOORS, GRADES 3 AND 4)

The focus is on the rotation of hip and spine for preparation and execution, and arm back and extended. Divide the class into groups of three. Each group needs a bucket or crate of 8 to 10 tennis balls, three beanbags, or three small marking cones (see diagram). One student is the thrower (with the bucket or crate of balls); the other two are positioned "in the field." Fielder 1 collects the balls and places them in another container or location; fielder 2 uses beanbags or marking cones to mark the farthest throw.

- Students throw the balls for distance, increasing the distance with each throw and trying to set a personal best.

Cues: *Face the field. Twist into side to target. Take arm way back. Step or "crow hop" before throwing.*

If space allows, students can work independently in their groups and rotate roles after all balls have been thrown. If space is a concern, students throw on your signal.

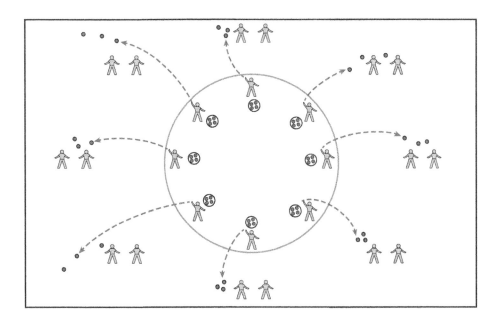

Assessment

- Peers evaluate the critical element that is the focus of the task.
- Exit slip (grades 3, 4): What is the purpose of the hip and spine rotation in the overhand throwing pattern for force or distance?

Closure

- What skill did we focus on today?
- How is it similar to the underhand pattern?
- Watch me throw and see whether you can tell me what I need to keep practicing. (Vary the critical element observation for grades 2, 3, and 4 based on Grade-Level Outcomes.)
- Throwing for distance and force takes lots of practice. Find a ball and a place at home or at recess to practice.

Reflection

- Are students demonstrating opposition when they throw overhand? Are they stepping with opposition at they throw (grades 3, 4)?
- Grade 2: Do they stand side to target in preparation for throwing?
- Grade 3: Are some students beginning to use the rotation of the hips and spine into the side-to-target preparation position and again in executing the throw?
- Grade 4: Are most students using the rotation of the hips and spine into the side-to-target preparation position and again in executing the throw?
- Is the arm going back with the elbow at shoulder height or slightly above in preparation for throw action, and is the elbow leading the execution of the throw?

FOCUS▸

Subfocus▸

THROWING OVERHAND

Accuracy, Force

Grades 4, 5

| **Standard 1** | The physically literate individual demonstrates competency in a variety of motor skills and movement patterns. |

Grade-Level Outcomes

- Throws overhand using a mature pattern in nondynamic environments (closed skills) (S1.E14.4a)
- Throws overhand using a mature pattern in nondynamic environments (closed skills), with different sizes and types of balls (S1.E14.5a)
- Throws overhand to a partner or at a target with accuracy at a reasonable distance (S1.E14.4b)
- Throws overhand to a large target with accuracy (S1.E14.5b)

Critical Elements for Throwing (Overhand Pattern)

- Side to target in preparation for throwing action.
- Arm back and extended, and elbow at shoulder height or slightly above in preparation for action; elbow leads.
- Step with opposite foot as throwing arm moves forward.
- Hip and spine rotate as throwing action is executed.
- Follow through toward target and across body.

Lesson Objectives

The learner will:

- Throw an object for force with an overhand throwing action using hip and spine rotation, placing arm back in preparation, stepping with opposition, rotating hip and spine while executing the throw, and following through to target (grade 4)
- Throw with varying degrees of force to match distance from target
- Explain the concept of adjusting force for accuracy and distance
- Throw with accuracy to targets and partners
- Throw with accuracy and proper force, demonstrating a mature pattern of execution to targets and partners (grade 5)
- Throw balls of different sizes and types with the critical elements of a mature pattern (grade 5)

Safety Concern

Ensure that spacing is adequate for throwing and retrieving equipment.

Materials and Equipment

- Hand-size, limited-bounce balls (e.g., indoor softballs, Wiffle balls), one per student
- 5- to 7-inch (13 to 18 cm) high-density foam balls, one for each set of partners
- Balls of different sizes and types
- Paper wall targets

Equipment for Stations

- Four sticky hand paddles with felt tennis balls
- Four hoops and hoop stands

- Paper wall targets, each target with three different colors—large, 4 feet by 4 feet (120 cm by 120 cm); medium, 2 feet by 2 feet (60 cm by 60 cm); small, 1 foot by 1 foot (30 cm by 30 cm)
- 12 bowling pins
- Two benches

Introduction

In the previous throwing lesson, you worked on throwing overhand with force and distance. Who can share the critical elements that we learned? Today, we will continue to practice force, but now we will combine force and accuracy.

Sometimes, you might need to alter your throwing form to be accurate. Watch as I demonstrate throwing to someone close compared with throwing to someone far away. (Have students focus on your arm position for a throw to someone close, when you take your arm just beyond your head, compared with your arm position way back when throwing far.) Was my throwing form and arm position the same for each throw? Why not?

Altering the form to meet the task goal: After students have the mature pattern of a manipulative skill, they are ready for tasks that might require altering the form of the skill. The goal of the task (e.g., accuracy to ensure that a partner can receive an object) might require a reduction of force, which alters the form of the skill. These alterations are often necessary when students perform skills in dynamic environments.

LEARNING EXPERIENCE: THROWING FOR FORCE

- Focus on preparation and execution. Using a limited-bounce ball, students throw hard against the wall at the large targets (lines or spots on the floor for distance of approximately 15 feet [4.5 m]).
- Allow several minutes of practice to review critical elements: rotating side to target as arm goes back, uncoiling, and stepping with opposite foot.

Cue: *Overexaggerate the coiling motion.*

(Observe and offer individual assistance as needed.)

LEARNING EXPERIENCE: THROWING FOR ACCURACY AND FORCE

Focus on follow-through. Students throw from the 15-foot (4.5 m) line at the medium targets with force, emphasizing following through across the body.

- Self-challenge and assessment: If successful on three or more of five throws, students continue throwing from this distance. If not, they move closer and reduce force to find distance for accuracy. Students take a step back when successful. Have students continue to explore distance needed for both force and accuracy with the medium target.
- Students repeat the previous task with the small target.
- Grade 5: Students try the two previous learning experiences with different types and sizes of balls for throwing.

LEARNING EXPERIENCE: VARYING FORCE TO MATCH DISTANCE

Students, in pairs, stand approximately 4 feet (120 cm) across from each other in the middle of the gym or work area. Using a 5- to 7-inch (13 to 18 cm) high-density foam ball, they throw overhand to partner, who attempts to catch it. After each person throws, both partners take a step back. They continue throwing and stepping backward to the distance of the gym or work area; they reverse direction and move forward while continuing throwing until back in starting space. If a catch is missed, practice continues from that distance point. The emphasis is matching force to distance. (If the teaching space does not allow space for the entire class, have half the students observe for critical elements and then change roles.)

- Discuss with students how the distance changed the amount of force used and the need for the mature pattern of an overhand throw. (If space dictates dividing the class into groups, this question is excellent for observers.)

LEARNING EXPERIENCE: STATIONS FOR PRACTICE

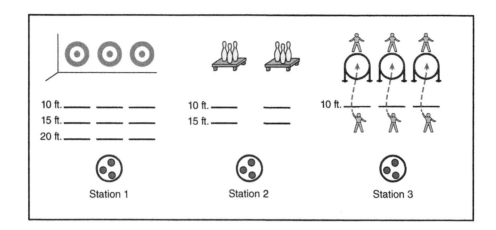

- Station 1: Students make five throws from each starting distance to wall targets. They have their choice of size of target (large, medium, small) or distance (grade 4). They use the designated target size and five throws from each distance to compare accuracy (grade 5).
- Station 2: Students throw with force to knock down the bowling pins.
- Station 3: Pitching station. From a distance of 10 to 12 feet (3 to 3.5 m), students throw so that the catcher can be successful—pitcher to catcher. Place a hoop standing upright in a hoop stand. One partner is the catcher and squats behind the hoop with the sticky paddle. The other partner is the pitcher and throws overhand until the batter strikes out (in the hoop three times) or walks (outside the hoop four times). Hitting the hoop is a foul ball.

If sticky paddles and hoop stands are not available, use a ball that the catcher will be able to catch safely with partners in position as pitchers and catchers. The catcher places hand where the throw is to come for accuracy. If the catcher successfully catches the ball without moving the hand, the pitch is a strike. If the catcher moves the hand to catch the ball, the pitch is a ball.

Assessment
- Peers assess critical elements. (Focus on single element for assessment.)
- Use a checklist to identify what critical elements are evident consistently.

Closure
- What skill did we focus on today?
- What changed about your throw when you were close to your partner or the target? Why?
- Name a sport in which throwing hard or far is important. Be specific about why throwing for distance is important in this sport.
- When is it more important to be accurate? When are both equally important?
- Becoming a good thrower takes lots of practice. Practice at home and at recess.

Reflection
- What critical elements are consistently evident?
- Do students demonstrate functional understanding of adjusting force for accuracy?

PASSING AND CATCHING

Force, Levels

Grades 4, 5

Standard 1 The physically literate individual demonstrates competency in a variety of motor skills and movement patterns.

Grade-Level Outcomes

- Catches a thrown ball above the head, at chest or waist level, and below the waist using a mature pattern in nondynamic environments (closed skills) (S1.E16.4)
- Catches with accuracy, both partners moving (S1.E16.5b)
- Throws to a moving partner with reasonable accuracy in nondynamic environments (closed skills) (S1.E15.4)
- Throws with accuracy, both partners moving (S1.E15.5a)

Critical Elements for Catching

- Extend arms outward to reach for ball.
    - Thumbs in for catch above the waist.
    - Thumbs out for catch at or below the waist.
- Watch the ball all the way into the hands.
- Catch with hands only; no cradling against the body.
- Pull the ball into the body as the catch is made.
- Curl the body slightly around the ball. (Specific only to certain catches.)

Critical Elements for Throwing (Overhand Pattern)

- Side to target in preparation for throwing action.
- Arm back and extended, and elbow at shoulder height or slightly above in preparation for action; elbow leads.
- Step with opposite foot as throwing arm moves forward.
- Hip and spine rotate as throwing action is executed.
- Follow through toward target and across body.

Lesson Objectives

- Catch a ball thrown by a partner
- Extend to catch and curl to protect a caught ball
- Pass a ball with reasonable accuracy to a partner

Safety Concern

Ensure that spacing is adequate for throwing and catching.

Materials and Equipment

- Playground or youth-size basketballs, one per student
- Variety of balls and objects for throwing, such as youth-size footballs, flying discs, hand-sized balls, 6- to 7-inch (15 to 18 cm) foam balls

Introduction

You have practiced throwing and catching earlier in the year and in previous grades. Let's review the critical elements of catching and the overhand throw. (Allow several minutes for student recall and review.) Today, we are going to make the catching more challenging, much like in a game. We will use the term passing for our throwing. For passing, some of the critical elements are the same as for throwing overhand and some are similar to throwing underhand. When passing the ball in a game, you want to make sure that your teammate can catch it.

LEARNING EXPERIENCE: REVIEW OF CATCHING A LARGE BALL AT DIFFERENT LEVELS

Use playground balls or youth-size basketballs. Students are scattered in self-space, tossing the ball and jumping to catch it.

- Students stretch to catch at a higher level.

Pretend that the ball is a rebound in basketball (emphasis on extension and timing the jump).

- They continue practice of catching at high level, emphasizing pulling the ball in and curling body to protect the ball.

   Students travel in general space, toss high, extend, catch, and pull it in.

Cue: *Curl and protect.*

LEARNING EXPERIENCE: WALL PASS

Students push the ball with two hands from the chest, step forward, and catch the rebound off the wall after one bounce. (Demonstrate the chest pass, using a pushing action with fingers spread on the outside of the ball and thumbs in.)

- Have students explore the force needed to make the ball bounce once and come back to them.
- Students continue practicing the chest pass, extending arms to make the catch, pulling the ball into the body, and curling around it, as if to keep an opponent from taking the ball from them.

LEARNING EXPERIENCE: PARTNER PASS

Partners face each other, approximately 10 feet (3 m) apart. They pass to each other, aiming for the chest area, using the chest pass they just practiced. Allow several minutes for exploration of the force needed for the ball to travel to the partner while allowing the partner to catch.

Cue: *Accuracy is important. Aim for chest.*

   Note: Remind students of the two-hand push from the chest to the partner's chest with the simultaneous step action. Receivers may need a reminder of ready hands—fingers spread, thumbs in, at chest level.

- After 10 combined catches, both partners take a step back and then continue to pass and catch.
- They continue increasing distance to determine maximum distance for accuracy.

Self-Assessment

When both partners can pass accurately and catch 8 out of 10 chest passes, they have reached maximum distance.

- Select a different object (football, flying disc, or other type of ball). Students repeat the passing and receiving challenge, beginning at the original starting point and extending the distance as before.
- Discuss with students the match between type and size of ball and type of throw: chest pass, overhand throw, and underhand throw. (A few minutes of instruction and practice on throwing a football or flying disc will be necessary here.)

Cue for receivers: *Position hands as target.*

Cue for throwers: *Pass to target.*

- Each time partners discover maximum distance, they switch to a different object for throwing and catching.
- Students change partners to discover force and distance for each new partner (Standard 4).

Discuss games play and importance of throwing passes so that receivers can catch them.

LEARNING EXPERIENCE: PARTNER PASS AND CATCH IN DIFFERENT LOCATIONS AROUND BODY

With object of partners' choice, receiver positions hands as target above the head. Thrower tosses the ball in a curvy, rainbow pathway so that receiver can reach to catch.

- Receiver catches at high level, pulls the ball into the body, and curls to protect it.
- Receiver catches at low level with thumbs turned out, pulls it in, and curls to protect the ball.
- Challenge partners to target throws to the left or to the right and to high or low levels.
- Challenge them further to strive for personal best in distance, accuracy, or level.

Assessment

Students make journal entry with description of reason for success—accuracy and force.

LEARNING EXPERIENCE: PASSING AND RECEIVING WITH RECEIVER ON THE MOVE (GRADE 5)

Safety Check: Spatial awareness is critical with partners moving; outdoor open field is best.

Receiver points in the direction of travel and takes two or three steps to the right; the pass is made in front of receiver.

- Review of leading the receiver as practiced in previous lessons. The target is now the space in front of the receiver. Allow several minutes of practice because timing when to release the throw is difficult.
- Receiver reaches, pulls it in, and then prepares to become the thrower. (It is best to use a "break" signal to help with timing of when to move.) Remind students that only the receiver is moving; the passer is stationary.
- Receiver repeats to the left, traveling two to three steps.
- Receiver increases speed of going both right and left, each time providing a target.
- Students explore different types of balls and a flying disc.

(Receiver is traveling only two or three steps. Emphasis is on throwing a lead pass and being accurate for ease of catching.)

LEARNING EXPERIENCE: CATCHING AND TRAVELING

Partners stand side by side facing the same direction. Partner A is the first passer, and partner B is the first receiver. The receiver combines a pathway design (combination of straight, curved, or zigzag movements) moving away from the thrower and providing a target for the thrower. The thrower leads the receiver when the target is signaled.

Safety Check: All students move in the same direction across the gymnasium or field.

- After the reception, the receiver jogs back to the thrower and they change roles.

Catching over the shoulder with a twisted body shape. Repeat the preceding except this time the receiver jogs slowly away from the passer traveling in a straight pathway. When ready, the receiver twists the body and provides a two-hand target over one shoulder. The passer attempts to pass to the receiver's target hands.

Cue for passer: *A lead pass will allow the receiver to continue jogging.*

Cue for receiver: *Twist only the upper trunk so that the feet can continue jogging forward.*

- Students practice at a short distance and increase distance only with success. (Remind students that accuracy, not distance, is the key to success.)

Assessment

Journal entry: Why do you need to alter the force based on distance? Why might you alter the force with some partners or teammates?

Closure

- Why is it important in some situations to curl around the ball after pulling it in?
- What did you do differently in your throw when you were close to someone compared with when you increased the distance?
- What situation or object required you to face your partner when you were throwing? What situation or object required side to target?

Reflection

- Are the students extending to make catches?
- Do they pull it in and curl around it?
- Are the students throwing with at least 80 percent accuracy?
- Do they appear to have a functional understanding of how much force is needed in varying situations?
- Are fifth-grade students leading the receiver and timing their throws?

FOCUS▶ PASSING AND CATCHING IN DYNAMIC ENVIRONMENTS

Subfocus▶   Spatial Awareness, Partner Relationships

Grade 5

Standard 1 The physically literate individual demonstrates competency in a variety of motor skills and movement patterns.

Grade-Level Outcomes

- Catches with accuracy, both partners moving (S1.E16.5b)
- Throws with accuracy, both partners moving (S1.E15.5a)
- Throws with reasonable accuracy in dynamic, small-sided practice tasks (S1.E15.5b)

Critical Elements for Catching

- Extend arms outward to reach for ball.
  - Thumbs in for catch above the waist.
  - Thumbs out for catch at or below the waist.
- Watch the ball all the way into the hands.
- Catch with hands only; no cradling against the body.
- Pull the ball into the body as the catch is made.
- Curl the body slightly around the ball. (Specific only to certain catches.)

Critical Elements for Throwing (Overhand Pattern)

- Side to target in preparation for throwing action.
- Arm back and extended, and elbow at shoulder height or slightly above in preparation for action; elbow leads.
- Step with opposite foot as throwing arm moves forward.
- Hip and spine rotate as throwing action is executed.
- Follow through toward target and across body.

Lesson Objectives

The learner will:

- Catch a ball thrown by a partner with both partners moving
- Pass a ball with reasonable accuracy to a moving partner
- Throw a ball with reasonable accuracy against a passive defensive player
- Catch a ball against a passive defensive player
- Throw and catch with reasonable accuracy while others are trying to defend and intercept

Safety Concern

Ensure that spacing is adequate for throwing and catching on the move.

Materials and Equipment

- Playground or youth-size basketballs, one per student
- Variety of balls and objects for throwing, such as youth-size footballs, flying discs, hand-sized balls
- 6- to 7-inch (18 to 22 cm) foam balls

- Marker cones
- Five hoops

Introduction

You have practiced throwing and catching to yourself, and passing and catching with stationary partners and with the receiver moving a few steps. Today, we are going to make our passing and catching more as they happen in a game. We will increase travel, distance, and speed, and add defensive players.

LEARNING EXPERIENCE: REVIEW PASSING AND CATCHING WITH A PARTNER

Students attempt to perform 10 successful passes to and from a partner at a distance of 10 to 15 feet (3 to 4.5 m).

- They increase the distance and complete 10 more passes.
- They repeat tasks with different ball or object.

Cue for receiver: *Give a target, reach, and pull.*

Cue for passer: *Look for the target.*

- Students pass and catch at high and low levels, to the right, and to the left.

LEARNING EXPERIENCE: REVIEW PASSING AND CATCHING ON THE MOVE

Partners stand side by side facing the same direction. Partner A is the first passer, and partner B is the first receiver. The receiver creates a pathway design moving away from thrower, while providing a target for the thrower. The thrower leads the receiver when the target is signaled. After the throw and catch are completed, the receiver returns to the starting position and roles are switched.

Safety Check: All students move in the same direction across the gymnasium or field.

- Catching over the shoulder with a twisted body shape. Receiver jogs slowly away from the passer traveling in a straight pathway. When ready, the receiver twists the body and provides a two-hand target over one shoulder. The passer attempts to pass to the receiver's target hands. Students increase distance only with success.

Cue for passer: *A lead pass will allow the receiver to continue jogging.*

Cue for receiver: *Twist only the upper trunk so that the feet can continue jogging forward.*

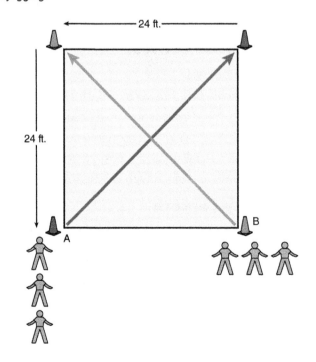

LEARNING EXPERIENCE: PARTNERS GIVE-AND-GO

With spray paint on field or tape on floor, create squares approximately 24 feet by 24 feet (7 m by 7 m). Use four cones (two of one color and two of a different color) to mark the square (see diagram).

Divide the class into groups with partners, based on the number of squares created. Two partners practice the give-and-go; students waiting observe for target hands and leading the receiver.

Partner A, the passer, positioned in one corner of the square, slaps the ball and gives the spoken signal for travel. Partner B, positioned at a cone of the different color, begins travel to the matching-color cone across the square. Partner B provides the hand position target; partner A leads the receiver with a pass. After partner B gains possession of the ball, partner A waits for the signal and begins travel to the opposite diagonal corner. Partner B throws the leading pass. After each set of two passes, new partners begin their practice.

- Students have their choice of using aerial or bounce pass.
- Students have their choice of type of ball or disc to use.
- Challenge students with the addition of a passive defense. When the pass is made, the defensive player travels to a position between passer and receiver.
  - Defender uses body position only and cannot use arms or hands to intercept the pass.
  - Defender positions body in pathway, not close to passer.

LEARNING EXPERIENCE: PASSING AND CATCHING ON THE MOVE

On one end of the gymnasium or field, position partners about 12 feet (3.5 m) apart. The partners travel down the field passing and receiving the ball. When partners complete the pass and receive series, they wait until the remaining students in the group have arrived before returning. Each set of partners begins travel after the partners directly in front have made two passes.

- Emphasize leading the receiver, gaining control, and returning the pass.
- Students have their choice of ball or disc.
- Add the option of combining the skill of dribbling with a playground ball or basketball.

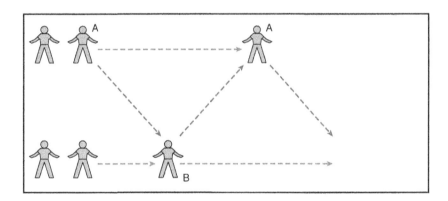

LEARNING EXPERIENCE: CATCHING AGAINST A MOVING DEFENDER

Students repeat the previous task with a third student playing the role of a defender attempting to intercept the ball.

- Receiver uses changes in pathways and speed to create open space.
- Thrower times throw to match receiver being open.
- Defender is positioned in space between thrower and receiver.

LEARNING EXPERIENCE: PASSING, CATCHING—INTERCEPTING

Divide the practice floor or field into four quadrants. Scatter five hoops in each quadrant. Divide the class into groups of five or six students who have similar throwing and catching skills. For each quadrant, three students stand in hoops and two hoops are empty. Two students are scattered in open space within the quadrant (see diagram).

Offense (students in hoops) begins throwing and catching the ball. Thrower must be in a hoop to pass; receivers can extend one step outside the hoop to catch. Receivers are free to travel between hoops but must have at least one foot in the hoop when making the catch.

Defense can move anywhere in the area but may not make contact with a person or with the ball in a person's hand.

- After 45 to 60 seconds of practice, switch offense and defense. Provide several minutes of practice for skills and strategy of open spaces.
- Offense scores 1 point for every complete pass; defense scores 1 point for every interception or incomplete pass. After one team has 7 points, switch offense and defense.

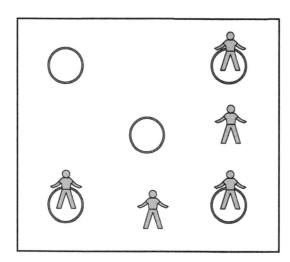

Assessment

Passing and Catching on the Move and Passing, Catching—Intercepting provide excellent environments for authentic assessment that focuses on critical elements, not scoring. Tell students in advance the focus of the observation or assessment. Compare the authentic assessment with earlier formative assessments of critical elements in nondynamic environments.

Closure

- What happened to the skills today when we added more game-like situations?
- Why do the skills decrease in game-like situations?
- Why do we say throwing and catching are two sides of the same coin?
- Name the games or sports in which throwing and catching are important skills.

Reflection

- Do students have a comfortable skill level of throwing and catching? Are they competent and confident in their skills?
- Do I need to revisit passing and catching without defenders?

KICKING ALONG THE GROUND

Distance or Force

Grades K-2

andard 1 The physically literate individual demonstrates competency in a variety of motor skills and movement patterns.

Grade-Level Outcomes

- Kicks a stationary ball from a stationary position, demonstrating two of the five elements of a mature kicking pattern (S1.E21.K)
- Approaches a stationary ball and kicks it forward, demonstrating two of the five critical elements of a mature pattern (S1.E21.1)

Critical Elements for Kicking for Distance or Force

- Arms extend forward in preparation for kicking action.
- Contact with ball is made directly below center of ball (travel in the air); contact with ball is made directly behind center of ball (travel on the ground).
- Contact the ball with shoelaces or top of foot for kicking action.
- Trunk leans back slightly in preparation for kicking action.
- Follow through with kicking leg extending forward and upward toward target.

Lesson Objectives

The learner will:

- Kick a stationary ball from a stationary position so that it travels along the ground (K)
- Approach a stationary ball and kick it along the ground (grade 1)
- Extend arms in preparation and contact the ball directly behind center for the kicking action (K, grade 1)
- Extend arms in preparation and contact the ball directly behind center with the shoelaces for the kicking action (grade 2)
- Adjust the force of the kicking action to match the distance from the target or partner (grade 2)

Safety Concern

Ensure that spacing and awareness of others is adequate for kicking and retrieving balls.

Materials and Equipment

- Kicking balls*, one per student
- Plastic tape
- Hoops, five or six
- Empty plastic bottles, liter size
- Large, colorful target
- Rope suspended 3 to 4 feet (90 to 120 cm) above floor

*After a year or two of use, inexpensive plastic balls become partially deflated and cannot be reflated, but they are excellent for kicking. Mark each with a large "K" so that the children know that these balls are for kicking practice.

Organization and Management

See diagram for stations.

Introduction

Today, we are going to do a special lesson on kicking. You will learn to kick balls along the ground; later in the year, you will be able to kick balls along the ground and in the air. Can you think of a game or sport that has kicking as one of the skills? Soccer players kick the ball along the ground and in the air. Football players learn to punt and to place kick. Kicking is an important part of a playground game of kickball. Everyone, both boys and girls, needs this skill.

Kicking, like all motor skills for children, cannot be mastered in a single lesson. Revisiting the skill throughout the year is the key. Introduce new components of the skill as you observe mastery of critical elements.

LEARNING EXPERIENCE: WALL KICK

Focus on contact with top of foot. Place a ball, one per student, on a tape mark approximately 10 feet (3 m) from the wall. Standing beside the ball, on your signal, students kick the balls to the wall and then retrieve them, placing the ball back in position for the next kick. For safety, have all students kick when you give the signal. Remind them to be aware of others when retrieving balls.

Practice of kicking outdoors can be done against a backboard or fence. Kicking along the ground or grassy area fosters correct execution of critical elements because force is needed for travel.

- Allow several practice kicks as you observe for contact point on the foot.
- Have students repeat the task with focus on contact with the shoelaces, or top, of foot; allow several minutes of practice.

Cue: *Shoelaces.*

- Have students practice kicking with the other foot and then alternating kicks with right and left foot to determine dominant foot for kicking.
- Continue practice with focus on starting position of nonkicking foot beside the ball. (The position of the nonkicking foot beside the ball will aid the student in using the top of the foot.)

Cues: *Shoelaces. Kicking foot behind; nonkicking foot beside.*

- Place tape marks on the wall approximately 3 feet (90 cm) from the floor. Have students practice kicking the ball to the wall for contact below the tape line.

Cue: *Watch the ball (for contact behind center).*

- Allow several minutes of practice, observing for critical elements and giving individual assistance as needed.

Assessment

Students have a friend observe kicking for the following:

- K: Are you watching the ball? Did you contact the ball with shoelaces?
- Grades 1, 2: Are you contacting with shoelaces behind the ball so that it travels along the ground? Is the nonkicking foot directly beside the ball?

If your friend can say yes to both of these questions, take two giant steps backward and kick again. You are now kicking from a distance of approximately 15 feet (4.5 m) from the wall! (Tape marks on the floor at distance of 15 feet.)

Cue: *Arms out for good balance (as the kick increases in force).*

- Challenge students to kick the ball hard enough for it to travel to the wall and return to them. (Students may need a reminder that this is still a kick of a stationary ball from a stationary position—no running approach.)

- Allow several minutes of practice with choice of distance. The goal is to produce straight pathways, have the ball travel along the ground, and use sufficient force for the ball to return.

LEARNING EXPERIENCE: APPROACH AND KICK (GRADES 1, 2)

Place the kicking balls on the tape line 10 feet (3 m) from the wall as before. Have students take one regular step back from the ball. From this starting position, they take a step-hop on to the nonkicking foot to land beside the ball on the nonkicking foot and kick the ball with the other foot. On your signal, they kick and retrieve.

Cues: *Hop beside. Arms out for good balance.*

Allow a few minutes of practice, observing for critical elements and giving individual assistance as needed.

Grade 2

Continue using the setup of the previous task. Have students take three giant steps back from the ball. From this starting position, they approach the ball and kick to the wall. On your signal, they kick and retrieve.

Cues: *Watch the ball (until it contacts your shoelaces). Hop beside, kick behind.*

A demonstration is helpful here to illustrate the crash that will occur if contact is made on the top of the ball from a running approach or if the nonkicking foot does not step-hop into position beside the ball.

- A common error in this kick is running to the ball, stopping, and then kicking.
- The kick should be a continuation of the approach right into the step-hop, without stopping. Continue practice, emphasizing the running approach and the step-hop action.

Cue: *Run, run, run, kick.*

- Challenge students to kick to the wall with the running approach, straight pathway, and sufficient force for the ball to return. After performing three successful kicks, students take three giant steps backward and continue.

LEARNING EXPERIENCE: STATIONS FOR PRACTICE

The stations are designed to practice kicking a stationary ball along the ground. At each station, students have a choice of distance. For all stations, for grade K, ball and kicker are stationary; for grade 1, students have a choice of being stationary or using a running approach; for grade 2, they use a running approach.

At each station, students quickly retrieve the ball after their kick, being aware of others, and return to the starting line for another kick.

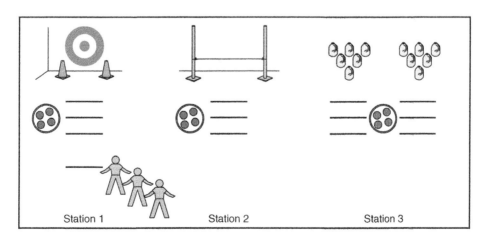

- Station 1: Soccer target. Students place the ball on the line from which they wish to kick. They approach the ball with three or four running steps and kick the ball toward the wall so that it hits the wall between the marker cones.
- Station 2: Under the clothesline. Students kick the ball so that it travels along the ground and contacts the wall under the suspended rope.
- Station 3: Kick bowling. Students stand behind the kicking ball at the tape line. They kick the ball along the ground so that it travels to the jugs, and they see how many jugs they can knock over.

Assessment

Conduct formative teacher and peer assessment to guide individual assistance as well as plan for the next lesson on kicking.

Closure

- What was the focus of our lesson today?
- What two types of kicking did you practice?
- Place your hand on the part of your foot that should contact the ball for the kick.
- Where on the ball do you contact for a kick along the ground?
- Grades 1, 2: Where should your nonkicking foot land?
- Grade 2: Why is the step-hop on the nonkicking foot important?

Reflection

- Can the children kick a stationary ball from a stationary position and send it along the ground?
- Do they contact the ball with the top of the foot, with the shoelaces?
- Does the nonkicking foot consistently land beside the ball?
- Can they approach a stationary ball and kick it along the ground?

KICKING ALONG THE GROUND AND IN THE AIR
Partner Relationships, Force
Grades 2-4

This lesson has two parts.

The physically literate individual demonstrates competency in a variety of motor skills and movement patterns.

Grade-Level Outcomes

- Uses a continuous running approach and kicks a moving ball, demonstrating three of the five critical elements of a mature pattern (S1.E21.2)
- Uses a continuous running approach and intentionally performs a kick along the ground and kick in the air, demonstrating four of the five critical elements of a mature pattern for each (S1.E21.3a)
- Uses a continuous running approach and kicks a stationary ball for accuracy (S1.E21.3b)
- Kicks along the ground and in the air using mature patterns (S1.E21.4)

Critical Elements for Kicking for Distance or Force

- Arms extend forward in preparation for kicking action.
- Contact with the ball is made directly below center of ball (to travel in the air); contact with ball directly behind center of ball (travel on the ground).
- Contact the ball with shoelaces, or top of foot, for kicking action.
- Trunk leans back slightly in preparation for kicking action.
- Follow through with kicking leg extending forward and upward toward target.

Lesson Objectives

The learner will:

- Extend arms in preparation and contact the ball directly behind center with the shoelaces to kick the ball along the ground
- Extend arms in preparation and contact the ball slightly below center with the shoelaces to kick the ball in the air
- Kick with accuracy at varying distances to large targets or partners
- Use a running approach to kick a moving ball
- Use a running approach to kick a stationary ball, demonstrating a step-hop
- Action and follow-through (grades 3, 4)

Safety Concern

Ensure that spacing and awareness of others is sufficient when kicking and retrieving balls.

Materials and Equipment

Kicking balls, one per student

Introduction

Earlier in the year, we worked on kicking balls along the ground. Who can tell me the keys to a successful kick—arms, contact on ball? (Younger students benefit from your demonstrating each of the previously learned critical elements.) *Today, we will add kicking through the air and kicking to partners. Do we ever need those two skills in games or sports?* (Take examples from students.)

PART I—INDOORS, ALONG THE GROUND

LEARNING EXPERIENCE: REVIEW OF KICKING

Have students practice kicking to the wall (on your signal)—stationary ball and stationary kicker. After a couple of minutes of kicking on signal, they progress to independent kicking. Students retrieve, check for space awareness, and continue practice without waiting for your signal.

Assessment

Practice early in the lesson provides an excellent time for you to observe critical elements and offer individual or class feedback as needed. This formative assessment early in the lesson directs the teaching to either progression or reteaching for remediation.

- Students continue practice of kicking with choice of distance, 10 feet (3 m) or 15 feet (4.5 m) from the wall (tape marks on the floor for starting position).
- Have students practice kicking to the wall with the running approach. Again, they kick on signal and progress to independent practice based on your observation of safety and accuracy of kicks.

(Observe students kicking a stationary ball with a running approach. Is the class ready for progression to a moving ball and a moving kicker?)

- Students choose kicking practice—stationary ball and stationary kicker, stationary ball and running approach, distance from wall.
- Challenge students to produce straight pathway to wall and sufficient force for ball to travel back to kicker at starting position.

LEARNING EXPERIENCE: PARTNER KICKS FOR ACCURACY—RUNNING APPROACH, STATIONARY BALL

Students select a partner with whom they want to practice kicking. They position themselves approximately 15 to 20 feet (4.5 to 6 m) apart. Partner A places the ball 3 to 4 feet (90 to 120 cm) in front of his or her standing position. Partner A approaches the ball and kicks it along the ground, sending it to partner B. Partner B then places the ball on the ground, approaches it from 3 to 4 feet, and kicks it back to partner A.

Remember, use a running approach and kick directly behind the ball.

Safety Concern

Position students so that all kicking is done in the same directions across the gymnasium or work area.

Task Extensions

- Kicking the ball from a stationary position or with a running approach
- Being far from the partner or closer
- Challenge students to kick the ball 10 times to their partner so that it travels along the ground and the partner does not need to move more than one or two steps to collect the ball. For added challenge, after five successful kicks, receiver takes a giant step backward.

Ultimate Accuracy

Partner A kicks the ball with the choices listed earlier; partner B stands with feet shoulder-width apart. The kicker attempts to send the ball along the ground in a straight pathway so that it travels between the receiver's legs. Partner B collects the ball and becomes the kicker; partner A is then the receiver. Allow several minutes of practice. (If indoor work area does not have a wall area behind kickers, organize task with three per group: kicker, receiver (target), and fielder positioned behind receiver to collect the ball as needed. Rotate positions after five kicks.)

LEARNING EXPERIENCE: RUNNING APPROACH, MOVING BALL

With partners facing each other, approximately 15 feet (4.5 m) apart, partner B gently rolls the ball toward partner A, who uses a running approach to kick the ball back to partner B. After five practice kicks, receiver and kicker switch positions.

Cues: *Watch the ball. Run, run, run, kick. Contact the ball directly behind center for travel along the ground.*

Safety Concern

For this first attempt at kicking with the running approach and moving ball, emphasize accuracy, not force.

Note: The distance between the partner rolling the ball and the kicker is determined by skill of the partner executing the underhand roll as well as space and safety concerns. Distance will vary for grades 2, 3, and 4.

- As students become comfortable with the running approach and moving ball, the distance between partners can be increased to provide challenge.
- Challenge students to kick with sufficient force and accuracy for the receiver to collect the ball with only one or two steps from self-space (grade 2) or without moving from self-space (grades 3, 4). Remind students that all kicks are along the ground.

Assessment

- Summative assessment of critical elements relative to kicking a stationary ball from a stationary position and kicking a stationary ball with a running approach
- Formative assessment of critical elements relative to kicking a moving ball with a running approach and accuracy to target or partner
  - Grade 2: three of five critical elements
  - Grade 3: four of five critical elements
  - Grade 4: mature pattern

Closure

- What was the focus of our lesson today?
- What new skill did we add to kicking?
- Tell your neighbor the most difficult type of kick for you: stationary ball and stationary kicker, stationary ball and moving kicker, or moving ball and moving kicker. Why is that one the most difficult for you?

Reflection

- Are students able to keep the ball on the ground for all three types of kicks?
- Do students have control of their bodies during and after the kicking action; that is, are they in balance?
- Are they ready for kicking through the air?
- Are they ready for the punt to be introduced (grade 3)?

PART II—KICKING OUTDOORS, ALONG THE GROUND AND IN THE AIR

The practice of kicking outside creates opportunities for kicking with increased force, for height, for refinement of critical elements, and for practice in an authentic environment.

Materials and Equipment

Partially deflated balls, one per student

Safety Concern

Ensure that students have spatial awareness for kicking and retrieving balls. (See the Inside-out Circle diagram for organization and management.)

LEARNING EXPERIENCE: REVIEW OF KICKING ALONG THE GROUND

- Have students practice kicking a stationary ball as stationary kicker, using maximum force for distance. Allow several minutes for students to establish maximum distance with a straight pathway to partner.

  Have student practice kicking a stationary ball using a running approach, focusing on critical elements:
- Kicking really hard for maximum distance
- Kicking for accuracy in straight pathway to partner

Cues: *Extend arms (for balance). Make contact directly behind ball.*

LEARNING EXPERIENCE: KICKING THROUGH THE AIR

All of your work thus far has been on kicking the ball along the ground. You are now ready for kicking the ball for travel through the air. Watch as I demonstrate the kicking action. (Demonstrate several kicks for travel of the ball through the air.) What is different about this kick? What is the same for kicking along the ground and through the air?

After several minutes of class discussion, introduce the new critical element: contact slightly below center of the ball.

Students practice kicking to their partners so that the ball travels through the air. Allow several minutes for exploration of the aerial kick.

Cues: *Contact the ball below center. Run, run, run, kick. Watch the ball.*

The combination of kicking with force and the running approach will lead to the introduction of the step-hop as contact is made for the kick, and the resulting follow-through. Demonstrate several times.

- Allow several minutes of practice as students focus on the step-hop action and high follow-through of the kick. The follow-through should be demonstrated because the height of the leg action is critical for an aerial kick.
- Observe new critical elements and provide individual assistance as needed.

Aerial Kick for Accuracy

Have students practice kicking through the air to determine range of kick. After several kicks with partners, challenge students to kick so that the partner can catch the ball. Remind each set of partners that they can determine the distance for the kick and the catch.

Aerial Kick for Distance (Grades 3, 4)

Use outdoor spray paint to create three distance zones. Partners A stand behind the kicking line with several balls each; partners B are the retrievers positioned in the zones.

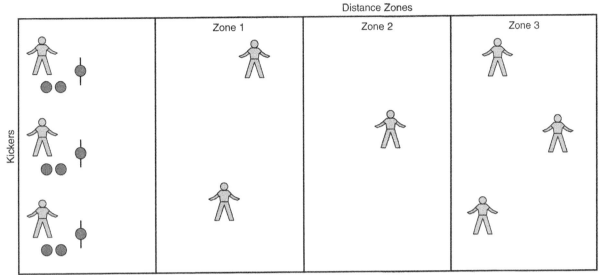

Kicker stands approximately five or six steps behind the ball. With a running approach, he or she kicks the ball through the air for maximum distance. (Each kicker has three balls.) Retriever collects the balls after all three have been kicked. Partners switch positions as kicker and retriever.

Aerial Kick for Distance and Accuracy (Grade 4)

Have each student determine his or her best distance for accuracy and attempt to kick all three balls to that distance zone. Challenge students to tell their partners the distance zone that will be the target and then attempt to kick all three balls to that zone.

Assessment

The Grade-Level Outcomes for kicking (SHAPE America, 2014) are a reminder that distributed and deliberate practice is needed for mastery of skills:

- Grade 3, kicking through the air, four of five critical elements
- Grade 4, kicking through the air, mature pattern

Kicking to distance zones can easily become the assessment. Focus on the critical elements, not the distance of the kick.

Closure

- What was the focus of our lesson today?
- Tell your neighbor the key to kicking the ball in the air versus kicking the ball along the ground.
- What does the step-hop add to the kicking?
- What is the difference in the follow-through for kicking along the ground and through the air?

Reflection

- How well did students develop the skill of kicking along the ground outdoors as compared with kicking indoors?
- Was the introduction of kicking through the air appropriate for this class?
- Do the students understand the role and importance of each of the critical elements?
- Can the students (grade 4) adjust force to achieve the desired distance for the kick?

FOCUS▸

Subfocus▸

PUNTING

Force, Aerial Pathways

Grades 3-5

Standard 1 The physically literate individual demonstrates competency in a variety of motor skills and movement patterns.

Grade-Level Outcomes

- Kicks along the ground and in the air, and punts using a mature pattern (S1.E21.4)
- Demonstrates mature patterns in kicking and punting in small-sided practice task environments (S1.E21.5)

Critical Elements for Punting

- Use a step-hop approach, becoming momentarily airborne.
- Arms extend forward and drop the ball as kicking leg moves forward.
- Extend kicking leg and foot; contact the ball with shoelaces, or top of foot, for punting action.
- Trunk leans backward in preparation for punting action.
- Follow through with kicking leg extending forward and upward just beyond waist level.

Lesson Objectives

The learner will:

- Drop a ball and make contact for the punting action (grade 3)
- Punt a ball successfully with a forward flight (grade 4)
- Punt a ball, demonstrating all the critical elements of a mature pattern (grades 4, 5)
- Punt a ball with purposeful direction and force to achieve target (grade 5)

Safety Concern

Ensure that outdoor space is sufficient for punting and retrieving balls.

Materials and Equipment

- Partially deflated balls, one per student
- Domes to designate personal space for each kicker

Introduction

Today, we begin the kicking that most of you have been waiting for—the spectacular kick that you see in sports—the punt. Punting is very much like the other forms of kicking: running approach, contact with shoelaces, follow-through. Oh, yes, and what is probably most important: Watch the ball! What is different for the punt? The ball does not touch the ground before the kick. Watch as I demonstrate the punting action.

Demonstrate several times, asking students to focus on a single critical element as you kick—shoelaces, follow-through, and the drop of the ball.

LEARNING EXPERIENCE: RELEASE AND CONTACT

Students are scattered in general space with a kicking ball on the ground beside each one. Have students extend their arms as if holding the ball for kicking and extend the kicking foot to create a flat surface with the shoelaces. On your signal, students open their arms to drop the pretend ball and kick it through the air. They repeat several times, emphasizing the drop action.

- With students holding the kicking balls in readiness for kicking, on your signal:
  - Ready: They extend the arms, holding the playground ball between the hands.
  - Drop: They drop the ball (they do not toss it) onto the extended foot. (The ball should land on the foot and fall to the floor.)
- Demonstrate the drop. Emphasize the dropping action and the extended kicking foot with verbal cues. On your signal, students practice several times.
- Have students bend the kicking leg behind them and practice the timing of the drop and contact point. Retrieve and repeat.

Cues: *Drop. Touch. No kick.*

Tap Punt

Have students practice the release and contact skill by performing a slight tap punt into open space. (Remind students that the ball should not go above the head.) On your signal, students practice several times with observation of drop release.

Cues: *Drop. Shoelaces.*

LEARNING EXPERIENCE: STEP-HOP, EXTEND

Arrange the class with partners facing each other at a distance of approximately 30 feet (10 m). Place the balls beside the kickers. Kickers are all on one side, and retrievers are on the opposite side, facing their partners.

Earlier in the year, you learned the step-hop action for skilled kicking. The step-hop is especially important for a good punt. We will practice with our pretend balls to review the step-hop action.

- Have the students extend their arms as if holding the ball for kicking. On your signal, they take one step forward, release the pretend ball, and kick it with the other foot. They repeat several times, emphasizing step right and kick left or step left and kick right.
- Have students kick harder, emphasizing the lift of the body from the floor and the extension of the kicking leg.

Cues: *Step-hop. Extend.*

Observe for successful step-hop action and extension of kicking leg. Reteach and provide individual assistance as needed.

- When students are ready, have them begin punting deflated balls. On your signal, kickers punt the ball to partners; retrievers collect balls and wait for the signal to punt back to partners.

Cues: *Drop or release. Contact with shoelaces. Watch the ball.*

For students struggling with the timing, suggest that they let the ball bounce first. It becomes a drop, bounce, punt action. With success, encourage the punt without the bounce.

Safety Concern

Ensure that students have spatial awareness of others when punting and retrieving balls.

- Have students continue practice of punting on signal, emphasizing a single critical element, such as watch the ball, extend foot for contact with shoelaces, drop or release the ball—no upward toss. Observe for common errors.

Note: When younger students are introduced to the skill of punting, they may miss the ball completely, punt the ball backward over their heads, and occasionally fall to the ground. Enjoy the experience with them and assure them that with practice comes skill.

Three-Step Approach

Students punt the ball with a three-step approach by beginning on the nondominant foot, taking three steps, and punting: left, right, left, punt; or right, left, right, punt.

Cue: *Step-hop.*

LEARNING EXPERIENCE: PUNTING FOR ACCURACY (GRADES 4, 5)

Have students punt with sufficient force and accuracy so that the receiver can collect the ball by taking only one or two steps from self-space.

- Students punt so that the receiver can catch the ball by taking only one or two steps from self-space.
- Challenge students to punt so the receiver can catch the ball without moving from self-space.

LEARNING EXPERIENCE: PUNTING FOR DISTANCE

Use outdoor spray paint to create three distance zones. Partners A stand behind the kicking line with several balls each; partners B are the retrievers positioned in the zones.

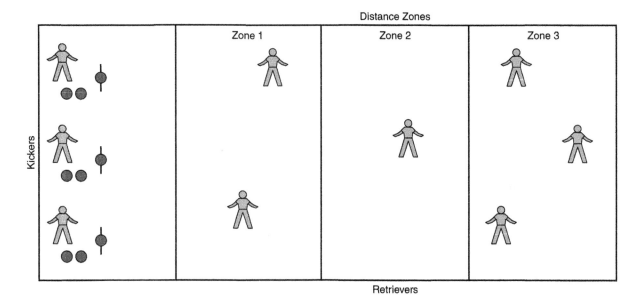

Punter stands approximately three to four steps behind the starting boundary and uses a three-step approach to punt the ball for maximum distance. (Each punter has three balls.) Retriever collects the balls after all three have been kicked. Partners then switch positions as punter and retriever.

Punting for Distance and Accuracy

Have each student determine his or her best distance for accuracy and attempt to punt all three balls to that distance zone.

- Challenge students to tell their partner the distance zone that will be the target and then attempt to kick all three balls to that zone.

Purposeful Punting: Direction, Force, Accuracy (Grade 5)

Challenge students to punt for placement to the right, to the left, and with designated distance. Punter stands approximately three to four steps behind the starting boundary; partner is positioned in the zone that is the target for the punt. With a three-step approach, the punter attempts to kick the ball to the receiver. (Each punter has three balls.) Retriever collects the balls after all three have been kicked. Partners switch positions as punter and receiver.

	Zone 1 – Left	Zone 2 – Left	Zone 3 – Left
Kickers	Zone 1 – Right	Zone 2 – Right	Zone 3 – Right

Receivers

Assessment

- Formative assessment of punting throughout the year
- Summative assessment of critical elements of punting (grade 4)

Closure

- What was the focus of our lesson today?
- You have now learned four types of kicking. Working with your neighbor, name all four types. Hint: You learned a couple of them before this year.
- Listed on the whiteboard are the four types of kicks. Listed on the left are different sports and games that use kicking. Working together, let's see whether you can match the sport or game skill with the type of kick needed (grade 5). This task can easily become a cognitive assessment of kicking.

Reflection

- Are students able to make contact with the ball before it touches the ground (grade 3)?
- Do some critical elements need reteaching?
- Grade 4: Is the class approaching mature patterns of punting in nondynamic environments?
- Can students adjust force for distance and accuracy?
- Grade 5: Can students vary force and direction for placement of the punt?
- Can students match the sport or game skill with the type of kick needed?

Classroom Integration

Discuss the angle of the trajectory of the ball on the punt for zones 1, 2, and 3, that is, the graphing of angles and pathways.

FOCUS> DRIBBLING WITH FEET

Subfocus> Space Awareness, Force, Time, or Speed
Grades K-2

Standard 1 The physically literate individual demonstrates competency in a variety of motor skills and movement patterns.

Grade-Level Outcomes

- Taps a ball using the inside of the foot sending it forward (S1.E18.K)
- Taps or dribbles a ball using the inside of the foot while walking in general space (S1.E18.1)
- Dribbles with the feet in general space with control of ball and body (S1.E18.2)

Lesson Objectives

The learner will:

- Tap or dribble a ball with the inside of the foot sending it forward (K)
- Tap or dribble a ball with the inside of the foot while walking in general space (grade 1)
- Dribble (with feet) with increases in force and distance (grade 2)
- Tap or dribble a ball with alternating feet, inside of the foot, while moving in general space (grades 1, 2)
- Dribble (with feet) a ball in general space with control of ball and body (grade 2)

Safety Concern

Ensure that students have spatial awareness of others when traveling in general space with the tap or dribble of balls.

Materials and Equipment

Slightly deflated playground balls, soccer balls, and plastic balls (one per student)

Introduction

Today, we begin the study of a very different kick—the gentle kick often called a tap or dribble of a ball along the ground as in soccer. Throughout the year, you will learn the correct technique of a soccer dribble, the skill of trapping or slowing the momentum of the ball, and kicking to score a goal. Today, we will focus on the tap or dribble for control of the ball.

LEARNING EXPERIENCE: TAP OR DRIBBLE

Standing in self-space, students gently tap the ball with the inside of the foot—left, right, left, right—so that it travels from side to side between the feet.

We will call this a tap or dribble to distinguish it from a kick with the top of the foot.

- Students tap or dribble the ball with the inside of the foot so that the ball travels forward.

Cue: *Gentle taps.*

- Students tap or dribble the ball so that it moves forward yet stays within 2 to 3 feet (60 to 90 cm) of the body at all times
- They alternate feet while tapping or dribbling and moving forward.

Cue: *Gentle taps.*

LEARNING EXPERIENCE: CONTROL OF BALL AND BODY

- Students tap or dribble in general space, keeping the ball within 2 to 3 feet (60 to 90 cm) at all times.

Cue: *Watch the ball.*

- Have students move at slow speed, changing pathways to avoid others.

If you were soccer players, you would be taught the skill of trapping, or gaining control of the ball, while tapping or dribbling and traveling. Today, we will stop the ball by placing one foot on top of the ball.

- Have students continue tapping or dribbling the ball, moving slowly in general space. On your signal, have students stop the ball by placing one foot on top of the ball.
- Challenge students to stop the ball within three seconds of the signal. Give a one thousand one, one thousand two, one thousand three count.

Grades 1, 2

Students independently practice the tap or dribble combined with stopping the ball and then continue the tap or dribble while walking in general space. Challenge students to practice the task with a slow jog (grade 2).

LEARNING EXPERIENCE: GAINING CONTROL OF THE BALL WITHOUT COMING TO A COMPLETE STOP (GRADE 2)

Dribbling with the feet in general space, students "check" the travel any time they approach another person or change directions.

- Dribbling in general space, students maintain the ball within 2 to 3 feet (60 to 90 cm) while traveling. On your signal, students "check" the forward momentum of the ball, pause briefly, and then continue to tap or dribble and travel. Discuss with the class the importance of keeping the ball within 2 to 3 feet (60 to 90 cm) for stopping, changing direction, and so on.
- Challenge students to dribble and travel in general space for 30 seconds without losing control of ball or bumping another person.
- Increase the challenge with irregular interval signals to "check" the momentum of the ball.
- Allow 60 to 90 seconds for the travel segment.

  Divide the class into two groups, each student with a partner. One partner stands with legs apart to create a wide tunnel; the other partner is the dribbler. The dribbler tries to tap the ball through the partner's tunnel and then proceed through other tunnels.

Cues: *Inside of foot. Gentle taps.*

  Observe for gentle taps, not kicks, and gaining control of the ball before continuing to dribble.

- After 60 to 90 seconds, have partners exchange places.
- Students enjoy counting the number of tunnels they successfully pass through. For loss of ball or collision, subtract 2 points.

LEARNING EXPERIENCE: INTRODUCTION TO KICKING ACTION (INSIDE OF FOOT)

With students positioned approximately 5 feet (150 cm) from the wall or fence, have them gently kick the ball, using the tap action of the dribble.

Cues: *Inside of foot. Kick.*

  Note: This kicking action is an extension of the tap or dribble, with increased force. It is in preparation for passing to a partner, grade 3.

Assessment

Observe for formative assessment of progress toward outcomes appropriate for grade level.

Closure

- What skill was the focus of our lesson today?
- Why do we call this skill a tap or dribble instead of kicking?
- What does "checking" the momentum mean?
- Why is it an important skill?
- Tell your neighbor which is more difficult: the tap or dribble or "checking" the momentum. Why?

Reflection

- Do students understand the concept of using gentle taps for the dribble?
- Can they keep the ball within 2 to 3 feet (60 to 90 cm) of the body when tapping or dribbling?
- Do they have control of the ball and their body when moving with the tap or dribble?

DRIBBLING WITH FEET

Time, Pathways, Directions, Space Awareness

Grades 2-4

Standard 1 The physically literate individual demonstrates competency in a variety of motor skills and movement patterns.

Grade-Level Outcomes

- Dribbles with the feet in general space with control of ball and body (S1.E18.2)
- Dribbles with the feet in general space at slow to moderate jogging speed with control of ball and body (S1.E18.3)
- Passes and receives ball with the insides of the feet to a stationary partner, "giving" on reception before returning the pass (S1.E19.3)
- Dribbles with the feet in general space with control of ball and body while increasing and decreasing speed (S1.E18.4)
- Receives and passes ball with the insides of the feet to a moving partner in a nondynamic environment (closed skills) (S1.E19.4a)
- Receives and passes a ball with the outsides and insides of the feet to a stationary partner, "giving" on reception before returning the pass (S1.E19.4b)
- Dribbles in combination with other skills (e.g., passing, receiving, shooting) (S1.E20.4)

The lengthy listing of Grade-Level Outcomes is a reminder that students do not master skills in a single lesson. Distributed and deliberate practice, not game play, is essential for students to reach the maturing level of skills.

Lesson Objectives

The learner will:

- Dribble the ball in general space with control of ball and body
- Dribble the ball with control progressing from slow to moderate speed of travel
- Increase and decrease speed of travel while dribbling (grade 4)
- Pass and receive passes with inside of feet in nondynamic environments
- Combine dribbling and traveling with shooting for a goal (grade 4)

Safety Concern

Ensure that students have spatial awareness of others and are in control of ball and body.

Materials and Equipment

- Slightly deflated playground balls, one per student
- Soccer balls, optional
- Plastic balls (grade 2)
- Marker cones

Introduction

Earlier in our work on the dribble, you practiced the skill with a focus on control of ball and body, a skill that becomes increasingly difficult as the speed of your travel increases and others are moving in general space at the same time. Today, we will focus on purposely changing speed, direction, and pathways as you dribble. We will practice passing and receiving with a partner as an added challenge.

LEARNING EXPERIENCE: REVIEW OF DRIBBLE IN GENERAL SPACE

Emphasis is on control of ball and body (ball within reach, no collisions).

- Students dribble in general space for several minutes. (Observe class and provide individual remediation as needed.)

Cue: *Control of speed.*

- Increase the difficulty of the task by placing marker cones throughout general space; the more cones that are used, the greater the challenge is. Have students dribble in general space, keeping control of ball and body as they avoid other students and cones.

Cues: *Ball within reach. "Check" speed.*

- Have students "check" the forward movement of the ball each time they come within 3 feet (90 cm) of another person or a marker cone.

   (Remind students that "checking" the speed does not mean coming to a complete stop; rather, it is a momentary pause before continuing travel.)

Assessment

The following provides a self-assessment of dribbling and control skills. The purpose of the activity is to dribble the ball in general space with no collisions or loss of the ball. The activity is called Keeping It Perfect: Zero, Zero. Everyone begins with a perfect score of zero. A negative point is earned if the dribbler

- bumps into another person or the ball that the person is dribbling,
- bumps into a marker cone, or
- loses control of the ball he or she is dribbling.

   Allow approximately 30 seconds of dribbling and then pause for students to calculate their individual scores mentally. Repeat for the same or an increased amount of time. (Time segment depends on age and skill of students; the aim is challenge, not frustration.)

How did you do? Remember your score. We will try to improve it another day.

LEARNING EXPERIENCE: INCREASING AND DECREASING SPEED (GRADES 3, 4)

Remove the marker cones from general space. Have students dribble in general space and explore increasing and decreasing speed. Remind them to control ball and body.

Cues: *Ball within reach. Awareness of others.*

- Have students begin with a slow to moderate speed of dribbling in general space. On your signal, students increase speed, emphasizing control. Then, on your signal, students decrease speed, returning to slow to moderate speed while continuing to dribble throughout general space.

Cue: *Control.*

- On your signal, students begin dribbling in general space with their personal selection of speed. At 30-second intervals, provide the signal for an increase or decrease in speed. (Students will be traveling at different speeds, as some increase and others decrease with each signal.)

Cues: *Increase or decrease. Maximum speed with control.*

LEARNING EXPERIENCE: CHANGES IN DIRECTIONS, PATHWAYS, SPEED

Dribbling in general space, students change speed each time they come within 3 feet (90 cm) of another person.

Cue: *Check and continue travel.*

- Students change direction each time another person is within 3 feet (90 cm)—to the left, to the right, backward, and then forward again.

Did you know that you can gently tap the ball with your heel, sending it backward to change directions?

Demonstrate as students continue practicing dribbling and changing directions and pathways.

- Students change pathways (straight, curved, zigzag) while in open spaces. Have them mentally create a pathway map while standing in self-space—a combination of straight, curved, and zigzag pathways. On your signal, students begin to dribble and travel the pathway maps they designed. Have the students "follow the leader" using a partner's pathway map.

If another dribbler enters your pathway space, pause briefly and then continue; don't change your map.

LEARNING EXPERIENCE: PASSING AND RECEIVING

Passing

The kicking action for today is passing to a partner; accuracy and correct force will be important. The kick is an extension of the dribble with the inside of the foot—a dribble with more force so that the ball travels to your partner.

Partners are scattered in general space. With students positioned approximately 10 feet (3 m) from partners, have them kick the ball so that the partner receives within personal space.

Cues: *Watch the ball. Use inside of foot for the kick. Contact directly behind the ball for travel along the ground.*

Allow several minutes of practice as students explore force needed. Observe for individual or class remediation.

Receiving

Pinpoint the importance of receiving by demonstrating or describing common errors, such as balls that rebound off the receiver's foot, kicks that are missed completely, and kicks that do not travel toward partners. Demonstrate as you explain the concept of "giving" to absorb the force of the kick, control of the ball, and readiness to kick. Continue practice of passing and receiving with partners, emphasizing "giving" when receiving the pass: give, tap dribble for quick control, and return the pass.

Cues: *Watch the ball. Give, tap, and pass.*

Receiving Partner on the Move

Partner A is the passer, positioned in self-space. Partner B, positioned beside the kicker, begins traveling slowly forward. Partner A kicks the ball to partner B, who is traveling forward. The receiver gains control and dribbles back to the stationary partner. Passer and receiver change roles. They continue practice, alternating kicker and receiver.

Common Errors

- Receiver stops to receive the pass.
- Kicker sends the pass to the receiver as if he or she were stationary.

Safety Concern

Ensure that students have spatial awareness as they are passing and receiving while traveling.

- After several minutes of exploration, discuss the concept of passing ahead of the receiver—leading with the pass.

Cues: *Pass to partner. Not a distance kick. Lead the receiver 4 to 5 feet (120 to 150 cm).*

Note: Leading the receiver is a challenge to all learners because the speed of travel dictates the force of the kick as well as the pathway of the receiver. Beginners and advanced soccer players benefit from and enjoy the practice.

LEARNING EXPERIENCE: DRIBBLING AND KICKING TO THE WALL, TO A PARTNER (GRADES 3, 4)

Students dribble in a defined personal space, approximately 8 feet (2.5 m) from the wall or fence. On your signal, they send the ball to the wall, using the inside of the foot for the kicking action.

- They alternate feet for the kick to the wall with each signal. Allow several minutes for practice of combined skills.
- They dribble and kick to the wall with shoelaces (top of the foot). Discuss force and angles (grade 4).

Grade 4

- Students dribble in "limited" general space (partner approximately 5 to 6 feet [150 to 180 cm] to the side, also traveling). On your signal, they increase the force of the tap to send the ball to the partner with the inside of the foot.
- They independently practice dribbling and passing to partner.

Cues: *Space awareness. Control of ball and body.*

Assessment

In an elementary physical education class, many children have been in soccer leagues since preschool; other children have never experienced a tap or dribble. Formative assessment will be important throughout the lessons to provide assistance and challenge for student growth.

Closure

- What was the focus of our lesson today?
- What new skills did we add to the tap or dribble and gentle kicks?
- Why is it important to pass to the open space ahead of the receivers when they are moving?
- Is the pass a distance kick? Is the pass the same as kicking for a goal? Tell your neighbor what the difference is and why each is important.

Reflection

- Have students reached a maturing pattern of tapping or dribbling?
- Can they pass and receive with correct form for each?
- Do some students need individual attention to continue practice? Do some students need challenge to continue engagement in the class practice?
- Are they ready for dynamic practice situations?

KICKING

Grade 5

Standard 1 The physically literate individual demonstrates competency in a variety of motor skills and movement patterns.

Standard 2 The physically literate individual applies knowledge of concepts, principles, strategies and tactics related to movement and performance

Grade-Level Outcomes

- Demonstrates mature patterns in kicking and punting in small-sided practice task environments (S1.E21.5)
- Passes with the foot, using a mature pattern, as both partners travel (S1.E19.5a)
- Receives a pass with the foot using a mature pattern as both partners travel (S1.E19.5b)

Kicking, like many skills, requires revisiting and practice as the learner progresses through the emerging stage (grades K-2). In grades 3 and 4, students must experience deliberate practice opportunities to reach the mature kicking pattern. Kicking with intent (high or low), kicking with accuracy, and punting are a part of these experiences. Additional related skills taught in grades 3 and 4 include passing and receiving with the inside of the foot.

In grade 5, students should continue to be engaged in practice experiences where they can apply kicking, punting, and passing and receiving skills. Application of the skills requires cognitive engagement and decision making. Standard 2 speaks to the need for students in grade 5 to apply knowledge of concepts, principles, strategies, and tactics to their movement performance.

Examples include the following:

- Combines spatial concepts with locomotor and nonlocomotor movements for small groups in gymnastics, dance, and game environments (S2.E1.5)
- Combines movement concepts with skills in small-sided practice tasks in game environments, gymnastics, and dance with self-direction (S2.E2.5)
- Applies movement concepts to strategy in game situations (S2.E3.5a)
- Analyzes movement situations and applies movement concepts (e.g., force, direction, speed, pathways, extensions) in small-sided practice tasks in game environments, gymnastics, and dance (S2.E3.5c)
- Applies basic offensive and defensive strategies and tactics in small-sided practice tasks (S2.E5.5a)

Situational kicking experiences in small-sided invasion game play provide opportunities for analysis of situations and decision making relative to

- where to kick the ball,
- how much force to place behind the kick,
- what type of kick to use (inside of foot for pass or instep for force or distance),
- whether to use an aerial or ground kick,
- how to use space for travel within the game, and
- what basic offense or defense strategies and tactics to use.

Student learning in grade 5 will best occur with deliberate practice orchestrated by the teacher rather than game play that has no purposeful intent or that benefits only the highly skilled. Deliberate practice suggestions for kicking include the following:

- Target practice from different angles, heights, and distances and varying the complexity (e.g., stationary ball, rolled ball, dribble and kick, dribble and pass, punting)
- Target practice (as preceding) with moving targets or people
- Punt Over (game designed to punt into the opponent's end zone)
- Cone Soccer (objective to knock over the opponent's cone and protect own cone)
- 2v1 keep-away (offensive advantage)
- 3v2 keep-away (with or without scoring goals)
- 3v2 keep-away (add scoring goals and a goalkeeper)
- Student-created games that involve kicking and decision making

DRIBBLING WITH HANDS

Space Awareness, Force

Grades K-2

The physically literate individual demonstrates competency in a variety of motor skills and movement patterns.

Grade-Level Outcomes

- Dribbles a ball with one hand, attempting the second contact (S1.E17.K)
- Dribbles continuously in self-space using the preferred hand (S1.E17.1)
- Dribbles in self-space with preferred hand demonstrating a mature pattern (S1.E17.2a)
- Dribbles using the preferred hand while walking in general space (S1.E17.2b)

Critical Elements for Dribbling With Hands

- Knees slightly bent.
- Opposite foot forward when dribbling in self-space.
- Contact ball with finger pads.
- Firm contact with top of ball.
  - Contact slightly behind ball for travel.
  - Ball to side and in front of body for travel.
- Eyes looking "over," not down at, ball.

Lesson Objectives

- Dribble a ball in self-space with multiple contacts (K)
- Dribble a ball with preferred hand in self-space with opposite foot forward and contact with finger pads (grade 1)
- Dribble a ball with preferred hand in self-space with opposite foot forward, contact with finger pads, and ball at waist height (grade 1)
- Dribble a ball with preferred hand in self-space with opposition, finger pads, waist height, and eyes looking over, not at, the ball (grade 2)
- Dribble a ball with control of ball and body, while walking in general space (grade 2)

Materials and Equipment

Playground balls, one per student

Introduction

Today, we will begin work on the skill of dribbling. There are three types of dribbling: dribbling with the hands like a basketball player, dribbling with the feet like a soccer player, and dribbling as you tap a puck with a hockey stick. The focus of the lesson today will be dribbling with the hands. What sport uses that skill?

Grades 1, 2: Review dribbling work from previous years.

LEARNING EXPERIENCE: BOUNCE, CATCH (KINDERGARTEN)

Students are scattered throughout general space, each with a playground ball. Demonstrate as you have the students bounce the ball in front of their bodies with both hands, catching the ball after each bounce. They repeat several times using both hands.

Common errors are bouncing on the toes and bouncing too hard or too soft.

- Students continue practice of bouncing and catching, spreading feet apart to avoid bouncing on the toes.
- They bounce and catch, emphasizing pushing with the hands as compared with slapping the ball. Demonstrate for the class and verbalize the push as practice continues.
- Students continue bouncing and catching, emphasizing pushing the ball with the force needed for the bounce to return to waist height—not over the head, not below the ankles.

Cue: *As Goldilocks says, "Just right."*

- Challenge students to bounce and catch five times without moving from self-space: bounce, catch, one; bounce, catch, two; and so on.
- They bounce the ball two times before the catch: bounce, bounce, catch.
- They bounce the ball in front of the body without catching it after each bounce (model).

Cues: *Feet apart, waist high. Push (don't slap) the ball.*

LEARNING EXPERIENCE: DRIBBLING WITH ONE HAND

Students dribble the ball in self-space with one hand, focusing on staying in self-space. Provide several minutes of practice as students explore position of feet, height of ball, and preferred hand.

- Feet are shoulder-width apart, and opposite foot is forward.

Cue: *Same foot back, opposite foot forward.*

- Students dribble with right hand for 30 seconds and with left hand for 30 seconds. (Young children often have difficulty establishing dominant, or preferred, hand.) Allow several minutes of practice to establish preferred hand for dribbling.

Cue: *The hand that holds crayon or scissors.*

- Students dribble with preferred hand, emphasizing push of the ball. Demonstrate the pads of the hands versus the fingertips (place fingers together, palms not touching—finger pads).

Cue: *Pads, pads, push, push.*

- Students perform 5, 10, or 15 consecutive dribbles with preferred hand. (Observe for opposite foot forward, push of the ball.)
- Review force needed for ball to return to waist height for continuous dribbles.
- Students dribble the alphabet (with you leading orally).
- They dribble students' names; students dribble as you spell the student's name—one bounce per letter (every student, every name).

LEARNING EXPERIENCE: DRIBBLING CHOICES

Have students do 90 seconds of individual choice: bounce, catch in self-space, dribbling with two hands in self-space, dribbling with preferred or nonpreferred hand in self-space, dribbling and walking in general space.

Assessment

Observe for progress on critical elements.

Closure

- What was the focus of our lesson today?
- Why is it important to keep your feet apart when dribbling?

- Why do we want the dribble to be at waist height? What happens if it goes too high? Too low?
- Raise high in the air the hand that is your preferred hand for dribbling.

Reflection

- Are students able to dribble in self-space with one hand with consecutive dribbles?
- Do students push the ball rather than slap it for the dribble?
- Are they able to keep the ball within their self-space when dribbling with the preferred hand?

LEARNING EXPERIENCE: REVIEW OF DRIBBLING IN SELF-SPACE (GRADES 1, 2)

Students scattered throughout general space dribble in self-space with preferred hand.

Cues: *Opposite foot forward. Pads, pads, push, push.*

Observe for feet position and pushing action of hand. Provide class or individual assistance as needed.

- Students continue dribbling in self-space, emphasizing height of ball between knees and waist. Discuss what happens when ball is too high, above shoulders, and using low-level dribble for tricks.

LEARNING EXPERIENCE: DRIBBLING WITH HEAD UP (GRADES 1, 2)

Students continue dribbling in self-space, looking over the ball, not down at the ball.

Cue: *Head up, eyes forward.*

- Standing in self-space, students focus on a spot on the wall—a line, a block, a picture. They continue dribbling, keeping eyes on that spot, for 30 seconds without losing the ball or moving from self-space.

Cue: *Head up, eyes forward.*

Without moving from your self-space, look directly at a person close to you—eyeball to eyeball. Begin dribbling in your self-space, keeping your eyes focused on that new partner. If you see your partner look down at the ball, say his or her name aloud; if you look down at the ball, you will hear your name.

LEARNING EXPERIENCE: DRIBBLING AND TRAVELING (GRADES 1, 2)

Students in self-space dribble with opposite foot forward, pushing the ball and keeping eyes focused forward. Introduce the critical element of keeping knees bent in readiness to travel. Demonstrate the dribble action with straight legs and knees locked and with bent knees; discuss readiness to run really fast and readiness to move. Allow several minutes of dribbling with preferred hand. Observe critical elements (grade 2, mature pattern).

- Students dribble and walk in general space. Position large cones throughout general space; more cones means greater challenge.

Cue: *Head up, eyes forward.*

- They continue dribbling and walking, avoiding contact with another person or a cone.
- They need to dribble with control of ball and body—no loss of ball, no contact with another person or cone.
- Challenge class with Magic 10. Students dribble and walk in general space for 30 seconds. Each student has 10 points; a point is subtracted if the student loses the ball or bumps into another dribbler or a cone. Goal is to complete the 30 seconds with 8 or more points. Increase to 60 seconds, reminding students that the travel is walking.
- For ultimate challenge, students have choice of walking or jogging slowly (grade 2).

Assessment

Observe critical elements when students are dribbling in self-space; observe critical elements when they are traveling (grade 2).

Closure

- What was the focus of our lesson today?
- What new components did we add to dribbling compared with last year (grades 1, 2)?
- Why is bending the knees important when you dribble in self-space?
- Why is keeping your head up and looking forward important when you dribble and travel?

Reflection

- Do the students have a mature pattern of dribbling in self-space (grade 2)?
- Which critical elements need attention (grade 1)?

DRIBBLING WITH HANDS

Grades 3, 4

andard 1 The physically literate individual demonstrates competency in a variety of motor skills and movement patterns.

Grade-Level Outcomes

- Dribbles and travels in general space at slow to moderate jogging speed with control of ball and body (S1.E17.3)
- Dribbles in self-space with both the preferred and the nonpreferred hand using a mature pattern (S1.E17.4a)
- Dribbles in general space with control of ball and body while increasing and decreasing speed (S1.E17.4b)

Critical Elements for Dribbling With Hands

- Knees slightly bent.
- Opposite foot forward when dribbling in self-space.
- Contact ball with finger pads.
- Firm contact with top of ball.
  - Contact slightly behind ball for travel.
  - Ball to side and in front of body for travel.
- Eyes looking "over," not down at, ball.

Lesson Objectives

The learner will:

- Dribble in self-space with the preferred and the nonpreferred hand with control of the ball (grade 3)
- Dribble in self-space with the preferred and the nonpreferred hands with all the critical elements of a mature pattern (grade 4)
- Dribble and travel in general space to open spaces with control of ball and body
- Dribble in general space with the preferred hand increasing and decreasing the speed of the travel
- Dribble in different places around the body
- Dribble with the body in different positions

Materials and Equipment

Playground balls, one per student

Introduction

In our previous lessons on dribbling, you demonstrated excellent dribbling skills in self-space with your preferred hand. You traveled in general space without losing the ball or bumping into others who are also dribbling. Today, we will add to the complexity of the skill by changing pathways and directions, and increasing and decreasing the speed of your travel. You will also work on dribbling with both the preferred and the nonpreferred hand. To be really good at dribbling, you need to be skilled with both hands.

LEARNING EXPERIENCE: REVIEW OF DRIBBLING IN SELF-SPACE

- Students are scattered in general space dribbling with the preferred hand. Observe critical elements from previous lessons.
- Positioned in general space with view of wall clock, students dribble with preferred hand, watching the clock and timing for one minute.

Cue: *Heads up, eyes forward.*

- Students, positioned where they can see you, dribble in self-space with preferred hand and maintain visual contact with you as you move about the perimeter of the room. (Students may turn in self-space to maintain visual contact but may not travel from self-space.)

LEARNING EXPERIENCE: DRIBBLING WITH NONPREFERRED HAND (SELF-SPACE)

Students are scattered in general space in position to dribble with preferred hand.

Cue: *Opposite foot forward, same foot back.*

Have students hold the ball in the hand they are going to use for dribbling; you observe for correct foot position. Discuss with students the "pocket" created with the ball slightly to the side, as if protected. This placement of dribbling will be important when a defense is added.

- Have students, in self-space, switch the ball to the nonpreferred hand for dribbling. Problem solving: Ask students what happens to their foot position when they switch hands for dribbling in self-space. Provide several minutes of practice dribbling with the nonpreferred hand. Remind students that critical elements and cues are the same for preferred and nonpreferred hand. (Observe as students are practicing; allow a switch to preferred hand if they display frustration.)
- Students dribble for 30 seconds with preferred hand and 30 seconds with nonpreferred hand. They continue switching hands on 30-second intervals or as multiple mistakes and frustration appear.

Cue: *Switch hands, switch feet.*

(This is an excellent time to teach the pivot for the feet for students in grade 4.)

- Students perform independent practice with preferred and nonpreferred hand, emphasizing correct position for feet, push of the ball, and eyes forward. (Students often want to switch hands after only 2 or 3 dribbles; set a minimum limit of 8 to 10 dribbles before the switch.)

Dribbling Challenges

Each dribbling lesson begins with a review and practice of dribbling in self-space to broaden the students' dribbling skill base. Throughout the year, tasks may be selected from the following during the warm-up and review portion of the lesson. The tasks provide additional practice for the students with enough challenge to prevent their becoming bored with "just dribbling."

- They dribble the playground ball with the body in different positions.
- They dribble the ball in different places in relation to the body—front, sides, back, between legs, around the body, and so on.

Grades 4, 5

- Students dribble between the legs, making a figure-eight pathway with the ball.
- They dribble around the body, making a circular pathway with the ball.
- They hold the ball at low level between the legs, one hand in front and one hand in back; they switch the hands from front to back without dropping the ball.
- Keeping the ball at low level between the feet, they dribble two times with the hands in front and then two times with the hands behind. The dribble is front—left, right; back—left, right.
- They dribble two playground balls at the same time and switch hands without losing control of either dribble.

LEARNING EXPERIENCE: BALL AND BODY: PLACES AND POSITIONS

Students are scattered in general space with sufficient personal space to dribble standing, kneeling, or lying on the floor. Provide several minutes for exploration as students dribble with the body in different positions, at different levels.

- Dribbling with right hand, dribbling with left hand
- Dribbling in different places around the body—in front, on the sides, behind, and around the body
- Combinations of places and positions
- Challenge students to create a sequence of three or four dribbling tricks that they can perform in self-space. They record drawings of dribbling tricks and place in their portfolios for later use.

LEARNING EXPERIENCE: DRIBBLING AND TRAVELING

Have students dribble and travel in general space with control of ball and body—no collisions, no loss of ball. Provide one to two minutes for dribbling and traveling; observe critical elements.

Cues: *Control speed. Head up, eyes forward.*

Dribbling with emphasis on ball position—slightly to side and in front of the body

Cue: *Front, side "pocket."*

Starting and Stopping

Students dribble in general space, starting and stopping travel on your signal, while continuing the dribble.

On my signal, begin dribbling and traveling with control of ball and body. When you hear the signal, stop your travel but continue to dribble in self-space. When you hear the next signal, begin traveling and dribbling again. The task is to maintain the dribble while starting and stopping. The combination of starting and stopping while dribbling is one way to fake the opponent in a game.

Cues: *Bent knees. Ready to travel.*

Discuss with students the difference on the angle of the push when stationary (directly above the ball) and when traveling (slightly behind the ball).

Open Spaces

When dribbling in general space, students should always be looking for open spaces. Allow several minutes of dribbling and traveling as students look for open spaces, dribble to those spaces, pause to look for another open space, and continue to travel.

Cue: *Head up, eyes forward.*

When you see an open space, dribble quickly to that space, stop and dribble five times in that self-space as you visually find a new open space, then travel quickly to that open space. The sequence is travel and dribble to open space, stationary dribble 1-2-3-4-5, travel and dribble to open space, stationary dribble.

- Remind students they may travel and dribble as fast or as slowly as they choose. Control is the name of the game.

Note: As discussed previously, students do not master critical elements in a single lesson, nor do they progress as fast as we expect them to; they need more practice. When attempting a large leap, such as moving from dribbling in self-space to dribbling in general space, the loss of control is evident. Children may need additional experiences or extended practice with the new component. Simply note in your lesson plan book how far the class progressed and begin the next lesson with a review and practice for mastery before moving to any new material. This lesson contains several suggested tasks for each new component of the skill progression, thus giving you options for continued practice of the skill.

LEARNING EXPERIENCE: INCREASING AND DECREASING SPEED

Students dribble and travel in general space, increasing and decreasing the speed of their travel.

When traveling and dribbling, and especially when increasing speed, the dribbling hand needs to be slightly behind, not on top of, the ball.

- Students dribble and travel at the speed they choose. On your signal, they increase or decrease speed. Each drumbeat will call for a switch in speed, either an increase or a decrease.
- Combining changes in speed, directions, and pathways, students dribble in general space and avoid collisions.

LEARNING EXPERIENCE: CONTROL OF BALL AND BODY

- Travel and dribble at the maximum speed that still shows control with no collisions and no loss of the ball.
- Travel and dribble at the best speed for maintaining control of the ball (personal choice).
- Circle Switch: Dribble while traveling from circle to circle, avoiding collisions and loss of the ball.

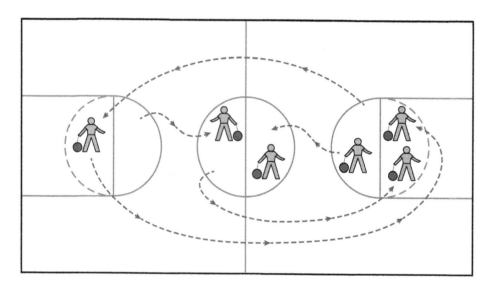

Students dribble in self-space in a chosen circle. On your signal, they travel and dribble to another circle with control of ball and body, stop in that circle, and dribble in self-space. On your signal, they travel and dribble again. Grade 4: Switch the dribbling hand with each travel signal.

The previous task can easily be adapted to indoor or outdoor space with no circles. Corner Switch provides the same challenge for students. They use the four corners of the work space, emphasizing speed of travel and changes in pathways to avoid other dribblers.

LEARNING EXPERIENCE: BALL GYMNASTICS

For a nontraditional application of dribbling skills, students perform a ball gymnastics routine that is designed by you (grade 3) or by a small group of students (grade 4).

- Grade 3: You create a group routine for students (see sample routine at end of this lesson).
- Grade 4: Students in groups of three or four use dribbling tricks that each student placed in his or her portfolio and combine them for individual and group performance.

Assessment

- Observe critical elements—stationary and traveling.
- Checksheet of Dribbling Challenges easily becomes an assessment. Include a space for students to add date of mastery and initials of person who observed the skill; add space at bottom of check sheet for students to create and record new tricks.
- Evaluation of dribbling skills, integration and evaluation of Standard 4 in routines (grade 4).

Closure

- What new skills did we add to our study of dribbling today?
- Why is being able to change speed important when you travel and dribble?
- Why is it important to keep the ball to the side rather than in front of you when you dribble in relation to others?
- Pretend that a new student who has just entered our school today knows nothing about dribbling. What would you tell the student for him or her to be successful at dribbling?

Reflection

- Do students travel and dribble with control of ball and body?
- Can they identify the factors contributing to their loss of control when traveling?
- Has the class mastered looking over, not down, at the ball when dribbling?
- Are fourth graders maturing in their dribbles with the nonpreferred hand as well as the preferred hand in self-space?

LEARNING EXPERIENCE: SAMPLE ROUTINE—BALL GYMNASTICS (GRADE 3)

Group dribbling routine (4/4 time): Children are scattered in self-space with sufficient space to stretch and dribble without bumping others.

Dribble right hand 4 counts; dribble left hand 4 counts.
Dribble right hand 2 counts; dribble left hand 2 counts.
Dribble right hand 1 count, left hand 1 count, right hand 1 count, left hand 1 count.

In a lunge position to the left, dribble with the right hand 4 times.
Pivot into a lunge position to the right, dribble with the left hand 4 times.
Repeat.
Slide to the left, 4 slide steps, dribbling with the right hand.
Slide to the right, 4 slide steps, dribbling with the left hand.
Repeat.

Extend the arms to the side (shoulder height), ball resting in the right hand. Lift the ball above the head. The left hand comes above the head. Gently toss to the left hand. Bring the ball down to shoulder height with the ball resting in the left hand.

Repeat with the left arm.
Repeat.
Dribble with the right hand 3 times and then bounce under the right leg.
Dribble with the left hand 3 times and then bounce under the left leg.
Repeat.
Dribble 3 times in front of the body, clap 1 time, and catch.
Repeat 3 times.
Dribble right hand 4 counts; dribble left hand 4 counts.
Dribble right hand 2 counts; dribble left hand 2 counts.
Dribble right hand 1 count, left hand 1 count, right hand 1 count, left hand 1 count.

FOCUS▸

Subfocus▸

DRIBBLING WITH HANDS

Partner Relationships, Combination Skills

Grade 5

Standard 1: The physically literate individual demonstrates competency in a variety of motor skills and movement patterns.

Grade-Level Outcomes

- Combines hand dribbling with other skills during 1v1 practice tasks (S1.E17.5)
- Dribbles with hands or feet with mature patterns in a variety of small-sided game forms (S1.E20.5)

Critical Elements for Dribbling With Hands

- Knees slightly bent.
- Opposite foot forward when dribbling in self-space.
- Contact ball with finger pads.
- Firm contact with top of ball.
  - Contact slightly behind ball for travel.
  - Ball to side and in front of body for travel.
- Eyes looking "over," not down at, ball.

Lesson Objectives

The learner will:

- Dribble in self-space and general space, demonstrating the critical elements of a mature pattern with both the preferred and the nonpreferred hands
- Combine dribbling with other skills in a routine of dribbling skills
- Dribble while keeping the body between the ball and obstacles or opponent
- Combine dribbling with other skills in one-on-one practice tasks of the games environment

Materials and Equipment

- Playground balls, one per student
- Youth basketballs, optional
- Hoops, one per set of partners

PART I—BALL HANDLING WITH RHYTHM

Introduction

In our previous lessons on dribbling, you demonstrated excellent dribbling skills in self-space with both the preferred and nonpreferred hand. You practiced tricks of dribbling with the ball and body in different positions and places. Today, you will combine those skills into a dribbling and ball handling routine with music. Raise your hand if you have ever seen the Globetrotters in a live performance, online, or on television. You will be the "(Name of school) Globetrotters" with your dribbling routines.

LEARNING EXPERIENCE: REVIEW OF DRIBBLING SKILLS

Play the song "Sweet Georgia Brown" (Globetrotters theme) while students find personal space for dribbling. Provide several minutes of practice as students review dribbling with the body in different positions, at different levels, and in different places around the body.

- Dribbling in self-space to the beat of the music (4/4 time)
- Dribbling to places and in positions to the beat of the music

Review tricks used previously (e.g., figure eight, hand switch between legs, front to back hand dribbles, between the legs). Previous dribbling tricks were stored in students' portfolios; retrieve those for review.

LEARNING EXPERIENCE: BALL HANDLING ROUTINE (HARLEM GLOBETROTTERS)

With a partner, in a small group, or working alone, students create a routine that uses different dribbling skills. Dribbling may be combined with throwing and catching, as well as traveling.

Student decisions include floor patterns, skills or tricks to be performed, directions of travel, and partner and group relationships (e.g., side by side, mirroring, together versus follow the leader).

Provide sufficient time for students to create routines, practice with and without music, and record for assessment. (Routines can be drawn on paper or digitally recorded and placed in students' portfolios as dribbling artifacts.)

Students need time to develop creative work in games, gymnastics, or dance. Plan an extended period of design, practice, and recording of routines before demonstration of the final product and assessment—self, peer, or teacher.

PART II—DRIBBLING AGAINST A DEFENSE

Introduction

In our previous lessons on dribbling, you demonstrated excellent dribbling skills in self-space with both the preferred and nonpreferred hands. You practiced dribbling while changing speed, pathways, and directions. Your practice today will focus on using those skills while dribbling against a defense—an opponent who is attempting to gain possession of the ball.

LEARNING EXPERIENCE: REVIEW OF DRIBBLING SKILLS

- Dribbling in self-space with preferred and nonpreferred hands, looking at clock, partner, teacher
- Dribbling in general space with personal changes in speed, directions, and pathways

LEARNING EXPERIENCE: PROTECTING THE BALL

Today, we add a new challenge to the dribbling skill—protecting the ball from the opponent. When an opponent is trying to get the ball from you, where should the ball be in relation to the opponent to prevent him or her from taking it? (Student responses: as far away as possible, on the opposite side.) You want to keep your body between your opponent and the ball.

With cones scattered throughout general space, students dribble through the space, purposely approaching cones with ball on outside of body in relation to cone.

Cue: *Body between.*

- Students approach cones to the right and to the left, switching hands to position body between ball and cone.
- They use different pathways and switch hands in preparation for approaching the cones.
- Introduce the "shield," the raising of the nondribbling arm to provide even more protection of the ball. Basketball players do this when they dribble near opponents.

Cue: *Body between, shield up.*

LEARNING EXPERIENCE: AGAINST A DEFENSE

Windmills

Divide the class in half. Group A, the defenders, are in stationary positions scattered throughout general space. Demonstrate defensive position with knees bent and arms extended with one arm up and one arm down (windmills). Group B, the dribblers, dribble throughout general space, passing the "windmills" only on the arm-up sides. Defenders (windmills) position arms before the dribblers begin their turn.

Cues for dribblers: *Body between. Shield up when dribbling past defenders.*

- Dribblers and windmills change roles after 30 seconds.
- Challenge the defense to move arms up and down; challenge the dribblers now to decide the better pathway for traveling past the defense.
- Defense cannot move feet, only arms.
- Offense maintains possession of the dribbling for 30 seconds; on your signal, they switch positions.

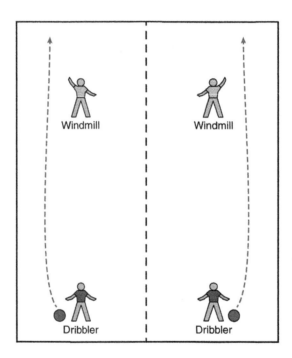

Defense in the Hoops

Group A stands inside hoops scattered throughout general space; group B dribbles. Defensive players can attempt to deflect the ball from the dribblers as they pass, but one foot must remain in the hoop at all times. Offensive players must make good decisions for travel (speed, pathways) and protect the ball (body between and shielding).

- Defensive players must always have one foot inside the hoop.
- Offensive players must maintain possession of the dribbling for 60 to 90 seconds; on your signal, they switch positions.

LEARNING EXPERIENCE: ONE-ON-ONE DRIBBLING (OFFENSE, DEFENSE)

Partners stand approximately 3 feet (90 cm) from each other, each with a ball for dribbling. On your signal, both start dribbling. Each dribbler is both offense and defense. As an offensive player, student protects the ball and maintains the dribble. As a defensive player, student tries to gain possession of the ball that the partner is dribbling.

Cues for offense: *Shield and protect. Low dribble.*

Cue for defense: *Quick hands.*

Offense and defense: The only contact allowed is with the ball. If students wish to keep score, each partner begins with 5 points. One point is subtracted each time loss of control occurs (ball goes astray, dribble stopped, partner deflects ball). Two points are subtracted if opponent gains possession of the ball and continues dribbling with a ball in each hand! If body contact occurs, play begins anew.

LEARNING EXPERIENCE: DRIBBLE TAG

Two or three students are selected as taggers. Everyone, including the taggers, is dribbling. On your signal, students beginning dribbling in general space (five seconds early start for dribblers), avoiding the taggers. Taggers may deflect the ball or tag the opponents. If a player is tagged, loses control of the ball, double dribbles, or stands in self-space for more than three dribbles, he or she freezes and holds the ball above the head. Other students look for frozen players to "defrost."

Maintain the dribble at all times.

Select new taggers every one to two minutes. Increase the challenge by increasing the number of taggers.

Alternate defrost: If tagged, dribblers move outside the dribbling area, dribble 20 times with preferred hand and 20 times with nonpreferred hand and then return to the game.

Assessment

- Peer or teacher observation and portfolio submission of the ballhandling (Globetrotter) routine
- Observe how well students protect and control the ball and body against single and multiple defense

Closure

- What critical component did we add to dribbling skill today that you will need in a game situation?
- Why is body protection and shielding important?

Reflection

- Do students control the ball in the more dynamic environment?
- Do students protect the ball most of the time?
- Do they appear to anticipate the need to protect in the dynamic game-like environment?
- Are they ready to begin combining dribbling and passing?

VOLLEYING UNDERHAND

Space Awareness, Force

Grades K-2

This is an introductory lesson for kindergarten and a review lesson for grades 1 and 2.

Standard 1 The physically literate individual demonstrates competency in a variety of motor skills and movement patterns.

Grade-Level Outcomes

- Volleys a lightweight object (balloon), sending it upward (S1.E22.K)
- Volleys an object with an open palm, sending it upward (S1.E22.1)
- Volleys an object upward with consecutive hits (S1.E22.2)

Critical Elements for Volleying (Underhand)

- Face the target in preparation for the volley.
- Opposite foot forward.
- Flat surface of hand for contact with the ball or object.
- Contact with ball or other object made between knee and waist level.
- Follow through upward and to the target.

Lesson Objectives

The learner will:

- Volley a balloon with an open, flat palm
- Volley a balloon, sending it upward
- Volley a balloon with different body parts
- Volley a balloon upward with consecutive contacts (grade 2)

Safety Concern

Ensure that students have spatial awareness as they are visually tracking vertical flight of balloon or object.

Materials and Equipment

- Lightweight round balloons, one per student for K and grade 1
- Heavy, round balloons, one per student for grade 1
- Heavy balloons or small beach balls, one per student for grade 2

Introduction

Kindergarten: *Today, we introduce a new skill, a new word for many of you—the volley. Any idea what that word means? To volley is to send an object upward or forward through the air by hitting it with a chosen body part. Today, we will volley with one hand.*

Grades 1, 2: *Last year you were introduced to a new skill, a new word in physical education—the volley. Who can tell the class what the word volley means? When I say the word volley, most of you immediately think of the sport of volleyball. The skill of volleying is also used as an underhand striking pattern for handball; with feet, head, and thighs in soccer; and in hacky sack. You will learn each of the different types of volley. Today, we will concentrate on the underhand striking pattern of a volley.*

LEARNING EXPERIENCE: VOLLEYING UPWARD

Students are scattered in general space, each with an inflated balloon. Have students volley, or strike, the balloon with the preferred hand so that it travels upward. They catch it after each volley.

Cue: *Watch the balloon.*

- Demonstrate for the class the flat surface of the open hand and the upward motion of the arm for striking, emphasizing the flat surface and low to high action of the arm. Have students continue the single volley action, attempting to stay in self-space as they volley the balloon.

Cues: *Flat surface. Low to high (arm action).*

Grades 1, 2

- Volleying with the nonpreferred hand
- Volleying to a height above the head

LEARNING EXPERIENCE: CONSECUTIVE HITS

Students volley the balloon upward in self-space, keeping the volley pattern going (not catching the balloon).

Cues: *Low to high. Above the head. Contact directly underneath. Control the force (grades 1, 2).*

- Students try to volley five consecutive hits.
- Challenge students to count their consecutive hits for a personal best.

Remember that if the balloon touches the floor, the count begins anew.

LEARNING EXPERIENCE: DIFFERENT BODY PARTS

- Volleying the balloon with body part designated by you, catching after each volley (head, elbow, thigh, inside of foot, shoulder, nose)
- Volleying with a combination of designated body part and hand, such as, hand, head, hand, head; hand, elbow, hand, elbow

In the early stages of body part volleys, students can use the hand as the intermittent volley surface. Children enjoy head, nose, thigh, foot inside, foot outside, shoulder, and, just for fun, bottom!

Cue: *Self-space. Flat surface. Upward.*

Grade 2

Have students create a volley sequence with the skills they wish to highlight of their personal volleys. (Record on paper or digitally; place in portfolio.)

Cues for advanced volleys: Foot to foot. Knee to foot.

Assessment

- Observe critical elements.
- Place volley sequence in portfolio (grade 2).

Closure

- What was the focus of our lesson today?
- What part of the hand should contact the ball? Show me the correct hand position (open palm, flat surface).
- Show me the correct swing of the arms for the volley you did today.

Reflection

- Do the students contact the ball with open, flat palms?
- Do they track the balloon visually until they make contact?

Revisitation and review lesson on volleying: age-appropriate striking of a variety of lightweight balls such as beach, foam, and plastic balls as well as volleybirds and hacky sacks

VOLLEYING UNDERHAND, WITH A BOUNCE

Partner Relationships, Force, Space Awareness

Grades 3, 4; Grade 5 Application

Standard 1 The physically literate individual demonstrates competency in a variety of motor skills and movement patterns.

Grade-Level Outcomes

- Volleys an object with an underhand or sidearm striking pattern, sending it forward over a net, to the wall, or over a line to a partner, while demonstrating four of the five critical elements of a mature pattern (S1.E22.3)
- Volleys underhand, using a mature pattern in a dynamic environment (e.g., two square, four square, handball) (S1.E22.4)

Critical Elements for Volleying (Underhand)

- Face the target in preparation for the volley.
- Opposite foot forward.
- Flat surface of hand contacts the ball or object.
- Contact with ball or object between knee and waist level.
- Follow through upward and to the target.

Lesson Objectives

The learner will:

- Volley a ball with an underhand striking pattern, sending it forward to a wall
- Volley a ball with an underhand striking pattern, sending it forward over a line to a partner
- Volley a ball with an underhand striking pattern, sending it forward over a net to a partner
- Volley a ball with changes in force to create offensive strategies (grade 4)

Materials and Equipment

- Lightweight plastic balls, 8.5 inches (22 cm), one per student
- Wall space for volleying
- Tape lines on wall approximately 3 to 4 feet (90 to 120 cm) above floor
- Tape line on floor
- Low nets, optional

Introduction

The last time you worked on the skill of volleying, you practiced the volley in self-space, keeping balloons, lightweight balls, and even hacky sacks and volleybirds in the air by always hitting them with a flat surface and always sending them upward. Today, we will introduce another type of volley: the volley of sending the ball forward and allowing one bounce between hits. This is the skill you use in four square at recess, the skill of handball games.

LEARNING EXPERIENCE: DROP, BOUNCE, VOLLEY

With students standing in a circle, demonstrate as you review the correct position of the hand (open palm, flat surface) and introduce the forward and backward swing of the arms. Have students model the skill as you demonstrate and observe for correct arm action and hand position.

Cues: *Flat surface. Forward–backward stance.*

- Position students around the perimeter, facing the wall approximately 6 to 8 feet (2 to 2.5 m) from the wall, each with a ball for volleying. Have students perform single-hit volleys, sending the ball to the wall and catching it after each volley pattern. Demonstrate with this pattern: drop, bounce, hit, bounce, catch.

Cues: *Flat surface. Forward–backward stance.*

- Students continue single-hit volleys. Observe to learn whether you need to provide class or individual assistance. Have students target the wall area just above the tape line as they continue the single-hit volleys.

Where on the ball do you need to make contact for it to travel forward and upward to the wall? (Discuss with the class the difference in contact for upward flight and contact for forward flight.)

Cues: *Forward and backward arm swing. Follow through to target.*

- Challenge students to perform five single hits without making a mistake—ball travels to wall slightly above tape line and returns to sender with one bounce. Allow several minutes for students to explore amount of force needed for travel to the wall, bounce, and catch.

Cue: *Amount of force (as Goldilocks says, just right).*

Assessment

Observe critical elements and provide individual assistance or reteaching as needed.

LEARNING EXPERIENCE: CONSECUTIVE VOLLEYS

When students feel confident about single hits (target to wall, stance, flat surface), they begin consecutive hits. Remind class that not everyone has to be doing consecutive hits; single hits are acceptable until student is ready for practice of consecutive hits.

- Two consecutive hits: drop, bounce, volley, bounce, volley, bounce, catch.
- Challenge students to increase the number of consecutive hits by one after previous challenge is easy to perform, that is, three volleys, four volleys, and so on.

Does the ball always come directly back to you? (Sometimes to the left, to the right, shorter distance in front.) Move your feet to be always in position behind the ball for the volley.

Cue: *Quick feet.*

- Consecutive hits, alternating right and left hand (grade 4).

Personal Best

Have students perform consecutive volleys to set a personal best—the highest number of volleys they can perform without making a mistake.

- Match or increase personal best
- Challenge for next day of practice: better than personal best

LEARNING EXPERIENCE: WITH A PARTNER (COOPERATIVE)

Have students select a partner with whom they choose to work or with whom they have never worked (Standard 4). Students now perform consecutive volleys to the wall, alternating hits with partner.

Cue: *Space awareness (I hit, you hit).*

- Students try to perform five consecutive partner hits.
- They practice for highest cooperative score. Challenge students to achieve higher score of volleys with partner than volleys alone.

- Introduce sidearm striking pattern as students begin moving into different positions to volley the ball after the partner has hit. They do consecutive partner volleys with underhand or sidearm striking pattern depending on position of ball and body.

LEARNING EXPERIENCE: AGAINST A PARTNER (COMPETITIVE, GRADE 4)

Now the partner with whom you cooperated will be your competitive partner. You will still be doing consecutive, alternating hits, but you are now trying to volley the ball so that your partner has difficulty completing the volley.

Allow time for several practice volleys, emphasizing accuracy for the each partner.

Students can use several offensive strategies:

- Changing the force of the volley—sometimes short, sometimes deep within the designated space
- Changing the height of the volley—sometimes high, sometimes just above the tape line
- Creating an angle with the volley—not hitting with a direct rebound pathway to the partner

Partner Choice: Cooperative or Competitive

Allow three minutes for partners to play either a cooperative game for a high score or a competitive game (with or without a score).

- Partner decisions: boundaries, side, back, and on the wall; what determines a point (whether score is kept).
- Teacher decisions: Game must center on the underhand volley with a bounce; partners must alternate hits—no doubles.

Students switch partners or game choice at end of three minutes of playing time.

Handball Challenge (Grade 5)

Older students may enjoy the challenge of playing different partners in the competitive game. Pair students for the first game. At the conclusion of each game, match the winners and the nonwinners for the next round of games. Writing partners' names on the whiteboard (flipchart) is helpful. Students then circle the winner (no score) and continue to find new partners (winners versus winners; nonwinners versus nonwinners).

Students enjoy a challenge day when they can replay partners or test the best, including you. Again, the competition is by choice. This competitive class challenge works equally well for over-the-line as well as against-the-wall volleying.

LEARNING EXPERIENCE: OVER A LINE, OVER A NET (GRADES 3-5)

Students can practice all of the partner tasks over a line on the floor (two square, four square) or over a low net. The skill is the same—underhand volley with a bounce. Both net and line games provide excellent dynamic environments for practice of the underhand volley pattern (grades 3, 4) as well as the strategies of force and angles (grades 4, 5). Younger students enjoy creating new games with the underhand volley. Give all students the option of cooperative or competitive practice or play.

Assessment

- Observe critical elements in isolation for formative assessment.
- Assess design of original games using the skill of the underhand volley (grade 3).
- Use authentic assessment in cooperative (grades 3, 4) and competitive (grades 4, 5) environments.

Closure

- What was the focus of the lesson today?
- How was this volley different from the one you studied earlier?

- Model each of the critical elements, asking students to describe the correct performance of each, such as contact hand, arm swing, follow-through, and so on.
- Tell your neighbor your choice for the underhand volley—cooperative or competitive. Why?

Challenge your friends to a game of two square or four square at recess to practice your underhand volley skills.

Reflection

- Are third graders approaching mature patterns of execution with the underhand volley with a bounce?
- Do fourth and fifth graders demonstrate mature patterns in the dynamic environments of game-like situations with partner?

Note: The lesson plan for the underhand volley, as with many of the skills lessons, presents more tasks and learning experiences than can be completed in a single lesson. Do not rush through the lesson to complete the lesson plan; you want to avoid being like the classroom teacher who is intent on completing the textbook with or without student learning. Student learning is the basis for advancing to the next level of complexity.

VOLLEYING OVERHEAD

Body Awareness, Relationship of Body Parts

Grades 4, 5

Standard 1 The physically literate individual demonstrates competency in a variety of motor skills and movement patterns.

Grade-Level Outcomes

- Volleys a ball with a two-hand overhead pattern, sending it upward, demonstrating four of the five critical elements of a mature pattern (S1.E23.4)
- Volleys a ball using a two-hand pattern, sending it upward to a target (S1.E23.5)

Critical Elements for Volleying (Overhead)

- Body aligned and positioned under the ball.
- Knees, arms, and ankles bent in preparation for the volley.
- Hands rounded; thumbs and first fingers make triangle (without touching) in preparation.
- Ball contacts only the finger pads; wrists stay firm.
- Arms extended upward on contact; follow through slightly toward target.

Lesson Objectives

The learner will:

- Volley a ball upward to the wall with an overhead volley pattern
- Volley a ball upward over a net with an overhead volley pattern
- Volley a ball upward and forward to a partner with an overhead volley pattern

Materials and Equipment

- Lightweight balls, one per student (plastic or beach balls)
- Volley trainers, optional
- Tape line on wall at height between 6 feet and 7 feet (180 and 210 cm)
- Nets or suspended stretch ropes at heights between 6 feet and 7 feet (180 and 210 cm)

Introduction

When we first introduced the skill of volleying (kindergarten and first grade), you immediately thought we were going to play volleyball. You volleyed balloons with different body parts while in self-space. The focus was always contacting with a flat surface. In third grade, we introduced the underhand volley with a bounce as in four square and handball; you volleyed against a wall, over a line, and over a low net. Today, we will introduce still another type of volley—the overhead volley—a skill you will use in middle school physical education and perhaps in a recreational sport. Can you guess the name of the sport that uses the overhead volley? Volleyball.

LEARNING EXPERIENCE: READINESS TO VOLLEY

Toss, Catch

Students are scattered in general space, each with a plastic or beach ball (grade 5: plastic balls, beach balls, and volley trainers).

The ready positions of the body and of the hands are important for the overhead volley.

Demonstrate while explaining to students the body position (slight front–back stance with knees, ankles, and arms bent) and the position of the hands (hands rounded, thumbs and first fingers making a triangle but not touching).

Model as students demonstrate readiness with body and hands positions.

- Students assume ready position, toss the ball upward gently, and catch with finger pads in triangle, or volley, position.
- They continue toss and catch, catching directly over the nose with the triangle.

Cues: *Ready position. Triangle. Finger pads.*

Volley, Catch

With ready position of body and hands, students toss the ball, extend arms to volley upward, and then catch the ball. The pattern is toss, volley, catch. Provide several minutes of practice as students attempt the gentle toss and volley with finger pads to produce upward flight of ball in self-space.

Cues: *Triangle. Extension of arms on contact. Volley above the head. Catch above the nose.*

Volley, Catch to the Wall

Standing 3 to 4 feet (90 to 120 cm) from a wall, students repeat the toss and volley catch pattern, emphasizing readiness of body and hands. (The extension of the arms is now slightly forward and up.) Allow several minutes of volleying with single hits to the wall; remind students of cues.

Cues: *Finger pads. No palms, no slap, no sound. Extend to target. Forward and up.*

The Power of the Legs

Demonstrate the overhead volley with legs straight in contrast to the volley with knees and ankles bent. Extreme example: arms and legs extend with no bending. Contrast the power of the volley with arms, knees, and ankles bent in preparation and extension on contact. Have students continue the single-hit volleys. Observe for readiness of legs, arms, and hands.

Cue: *Ready legs, ready hands.*

- Challenge students to volley the ball above the upper tape mark (7 feet [210 cm]) as they practice readiness and extension of arms and legs.

LEARNING EXPERIENCE: CONSECUTIVE VOLLEYS

Students volley the ball to the wall for two hits: toss, volley, volley, catch. Students practice the overhead volley for two consecutive hits. Observe triangle of hands and finger pad contact and bending of knees and arms in preparation.

Do you remember when you practiced the underhand volley to the wall and we focused on the importance of quick feet? Just as the ball did not always come directly back to you then, neither does it always come directly back to you in the overhead volley. Move your feet to be always in position for the volley.

Cue: *Body behind and under the ball.*

- Students continue the overhead volley above the tape mark.

Cue: *Upward extension of arms.*

Assessment

Observe for critical elements. Don't rush students into a higher number of consecutive volleys or more advanced skills until they master the basics of the overhead volley.

- Challenge students to perform three volleys, four volleys, five volleys, and so on.
- Grade 5: Challenge them to seek their personal best for consecutive volleys.

In a game-like situation, only one volley is needed. Focus on making it your best each time.

LEARNING EXPERIENCE: VOLLEY TO A TARGET (GRADE 5)

Partners are positioned in general space, facing each other approximately 4 to 5 feet (120 to 150 cm) apart; close proximity is important for emphasis on vertical flight of the ball. Partner A tosses the ball upward and volleys to partner B, who catches the ball. Partner B then self-tosses and volleys. Common errors are using one-hand hits, slapping the ball, and using incorrect force for distance.

Although these tasks appears to be an easy transition for students, skills often regress significantly; be prepared for reteaching and remediation.

- Challenge students to volley so that partner can catch the ball without moving from self-space.

LEARNING EXPERIENCE: OVER A NET

The learning experience is appropriate only if students have a high success rate on single volleys to a partner in general space. Nets or stretch ropes are suspended 6 to 7 feet (180 to 210 cm) above floor or ground. Partners face each other 3 to 4 feet (90 to 120 cm) from net on either side. They continue single overhead volleys from self-toss to a partner over the net, emphasizing hands, arms, and legs in preparation and extension of arms and legs for volley.

- Students volley so that partner can catch without moving from self-space.
- Accuracy challenge: Volley 10 singles to partner.
- Receiving partner chooses position, such as aligned with partner, to the right, to the left, near, far; volley must now travel to partner with accuracy.

Assessment

- Observe critical elements.
- Grade 5: Students decide whether to volley to wall target or volley to partner for accuracy.

Closure

- What was the focus of our lesson today? What did we add to the skill of volleying?
- I have just arrived as a new student in our school today. As I model, tell me what I need to know to be successful at the overhead volley.
- You now have three types of volley skills: body parts to body parts in self-space, underhand volley with a bounce, and overhead volley. Tell your neighbor which was easiest, which was most difficult, and why.

Reflection

- Have fourth graders mastered four of the five critical elements of the overhead volley in a non-dynamic situation?
- Can fifth graders perform the overhead volley from a self-toss with accuracy to a target or partner? Are fifth graders ready to advance to overhead volleys in dynamic situations?
- Are the students achieving height on the volley?

VOLLEYING OVERHEAD

Partner Relationships

Grade 5

Standard 1	The physically literate individual demonstrates competency in a variety of motor skills and movement patterns.

Grade-Level Outcome

Volleys a ball using a two-hand overhead pattern, sending it upward to a target (S1.E23.5)

Critical Elements for Volleying (Overhead)

- Body aligned and positioned under the ball.
- Knees, arms, and ankles bent in preparation for the volley.
- Hands rounded; thumbs and first fingers make triangle (without touching) in preparation.
- Ball contacts only the finger pads; wrists stay firm.
- Arms extend upward on contact; follow through slightly toward target.

Lesson Objectives

The learner will:

- Volley a lightweight ball consecutively with a partner over a net
- Volley a lightweight ball consecutively upward and forward to partners or targets in a small group

Materials and Equipment

- Plastic balls, one per student
- Volley trainers, one per two students, if available
- Tape line on wall at height of 6 to 7 feet (180 to 210 cm)
- Net or suspended stretch rope at height of 6 to 7 feet

Introduction

In previous lessons, you practiced the overhead volley from a self-toss and with a partner tossing. Today, you will practice the overhead volley in game-like situations. The overhead volley is one of the skills of volleyball—a game for middle school, recreational activities, and high school sports. Let's begin with a review of the critical components of the overhead volley. Tell a partner two of the critical elements you remember about the overhead volley. Let's share and see whether we remembered all of them.

LEARNING EXPERIENCE: REVIEW OF THE WALL VOLLEY

Demonstrate the wall volley and review the critical elements:

- Body is aligned under the ball.
- Knees, ankles, and arms are bent in preparation and extends on contact.
- Hands are rounded, and only finger pads are used to push the ball upward and to the wall.

Partners are positioned around the perimeter, facing the wall. Each set of partners has a plastic ball or volley trainer. As one partner volleys to the wall above the tape line, the other partner observes for the selected critical element (selected and called out by you).

Allow three turns of consecutive volleys before having partners change roles. Observe and provide feedback. Tell students that you are listening to the volleys and do not want to hear slaps or similar sounds.

LEARNING EXPERIENCE: PARTNER TOSS AND VOLLEY

Partners are positioned in general space. Partner A tosses the ball high to partner B, who volleys back to partner A, focusing on aligning the body under and behind the ball. After five tosses, partners change roles. (Remind students of the importance of a high toss; a toss that is not high enough will not result in an overhead volley.) The pattern is toss, volley, catch.

Cues: *Under the ball. Finger pads, no palms. No slap or sound.*

- Moving into position: Partner A now tosses the ball to the right, left, or a few steps in front of partner B so that the partner must move, align the body under the ball, and volley back to the partner.

Cue: *Under the ball.*

- Consecutive volleys to a partner: If your observation indicates that students are successfully volleying with body and hands in proper position and extension on contact, introduce consecutive partner volleys with a goal of three consecutive volleys with partner. The pattern is self-toss, volley, volley, volley, catch.

Cues: *Good height to partner. Good volley in return.*

LEARNING EXPERIENCE: PARTNERS OVER A NET

Partners face each other on opposite side of a net, approximately 4 to 5 feet (120 to 150 cm) from the net. Have students repeat the previous task with single volleys to a partner over a net, emphasizing using the legs for more power by bending and extending on contact. The pattern is toss, volley, catch.

Cues: *Under the ball. Bend and extend legs.*

- Introduce stepping forward and shifting weight as the volley is made to create the forward–backward stance. Students continue single volleys to partner over the net.

Cues: *Toes to target. Behind the ball and square to target.*

Consecutive Volleys With a Partner

Partner A tosses to self and then volleys to partner B, who volleys over the net with a goal of three consecutive volleys. The pattern is self-toss, volley, volley, volley, catch. Partner B then begins the series with the self-toss. Students continue series of three for several minutes as you observe for critical elements.

Cues: *Quick feet. Under the ball. Forward and backward. Toes to target.*

- Students continue series of three with emphasis on high volleys.

Cue: *Bend and extend. Arms and legs.*

Note: Introduce the following tasks only if you observe mastery of critical elements for consecutive volleys with a partner.

LEARNING EXPERIENCE: CONSECUTIVE VOLLEYS: TRIANGLES AND SQUARES

In groups of three (triangles) and four (squares), students volley the ball around the triangle or square with the overhead volley.

Criteria for Success:

- High volleys
- Under the ball
- Toes to target

LEARNING EXPERIENCE: CONSECUTIVE VOLLEYS: TWO AND TWO

Divide students into groups of four, two on each side of the net. Play begins with a self-toss and volley to partner. Allow several minutes for students to explore volleying over the net, volleying to a partner, and receiving a volley from a partner and then volleying over the net.

- As groups become comfortable with the volleys of the game, establish the rule that each partner must volley the ball before it goes back over the net.
- Cooperative volleys score 1 point over the net.
- After three minutes, partners rotate to another set for a new Two and Two volley challenge.

Cues: *In position behind the ball. Toes to target, to the target player.*

Assessment

- Observe critical elements and evaluate readiness for dynamic challenges.
- Suggested station assessment: Toss by a skilled thrower to student, who volleys the ball back to the tosser over a 7-foot (210 cm) net with consistency and mature pattern.

Closure

- What was the focus of our lesson today?
- What new challenges did we add to the overhead volley in this lesson?
- How do you feel about the new challenges as you become more skilled in the overhand volley?

Reflection

- Can students perform the overhead volley using the mature pattern with accuracy to a target or partner?
- Are they ready for more dynamic experiences? Are they ready for competitive experiences?

STRIKING WITH SHORT IMPLEMENTS (UNDERHAND)

Force

Grades K-2

The physically literate individual demonstrates competency in a variety of motor skills and movement patterns.

Grade-Level Outcomes

- Strikes a lightweight object with a paddle or short-handled racket (S1.E24.K)
- Strikes a ball with a short-handled implement, sending it upward (S1.E24.1)
- Strikes an object upward with a short-handled implement, using consecutive hits (S1.E24.2)

Critical Elements for Striking With Short Implements

- Racket back in preparation for striking.
- Step on opposite foot as contact is made.
- Swing racket or paddle low to high.
- Coil and uncoil the trunk for preparation and execution of the striking action.
- Follow through for completion of the striking action.

Lesson Objectives

The learner will:

- Strike a balloon with a paddle or racket, sending it upward
- Strike a ball with a paddle or racket, sending it upward
- Strike an object upward in self-space with consecutive hits (grade 2)

Safety Concerns

- Ensure that space is sufficient for striking with paddles or rackets.
- Ensure that students have spatial awareness as they are visually tracking vertical fight of object and swinging rackets or paddles.

Materials and Equipment

- Inflated round balloons, one per student
- Lollipop paddles, one per student
- Small high-density foam balls, one per student
- Selection of short-handled rackets, Plexiglas or table tennis paddles, beaver-tail paddles (see note at end of lesson plan for construction)
- Shuttlecocks, 8 to 10

Introduction

Earlier in the year, you were introduced to the skill of volleying. In that lesson, you practiced striking a balloon upward with a flat, open palm. Today, you will learn to strike an object (balloon, ball, shuttlecock) with a racket or paddle and send it upward. The racket becomes an extension of your arm; the flat surface for striking is still important. The skills are similar, and so are the critical elements for success. As you are working today, you will hear some of the same cues you heard for the volley (opposite foot forward, flat surface, follow through upward). You will also learn some new ones, just for the paddle or racket (swing of racket, low to high). Oh, yes, always watch the ball!

Rackets have strings; paddles are solid.

LEARNING EXPERIENCE: STRIKING UPWARD

Students are scattered throughout general space, each with a lollipop or beaver-tail paddle and a balloon. Holding the paddle in the preferred hand and the balloon in the nonpreferred hand, they strike the balloon to send it upward and catch the balloon after each contact. Allow several minutes for exploration of striking the balloon so that it travels upward, not forward.

Problem Solving

What determines the pathway of the balloon? A kick, a volley? Right, directly behind, directly under.

Cue: *Under the balloon.*

- Students strike the balloon upward, using single hits, while remaining in self-space.

Cue: *Flat surface.*

Introduce the critical element of swinging the hand in a low-to-high striking action, emphasizing the action of the swing, not force. Demonstrate poor technique with rebound hits and floppy wrist action, followed by an example of proper technique, with low-to-high striking motion with firm wrist.

Note: The task appears simple, but correct performance is complex for beginning learners. Introduce a single cue and provide practice and feedback; introduce another cue only when you observe readiness of students.

Correct Grip

From the early stages of students' exploration of short and long implements for striking, learning the proper grip (bat, hockey stick, tennis racket, and so on) is important. Developing a skill with the proper grip is much easier than practicing with an incorrect grip only to face relearning later. Teach young students the correct grip to use with the implement. For example, introduce the shake hands and palms-up grip for the lollipop paddle before beginning the following task.

- Students are scattered throughout general space, each with a lollipop paddle and a foam ball. They strike the ball to send it upward and catch and collect the ball after each single hit. They continue to practice, emphasizing the correct shake-hands and palms-up grip for the paddle.

Cues: *Control of force. Swing low to high (to the chin). Flat surface.*

Safety Concern

Ensure that students are aware of others with balls, movement of paddles or rackets, and students attempting single hits.

- Students perform single hits, remaining in self-space.
- Challenge students to perform five single hits without moving from self-space (grades 1, 2).

Cue: *Flat surface. Firm wrist.*

Grade 2

Students strike the ball upward for two consecutive hits while remaining in personal space (no more than one step in either direction from self-space).

Cues: *Ball above head. Flat surface. Low to high swing (to the chin). Watch the ball contact the paddle.*

- Students perform consecutive hits upward without moving from self-space.
- Challenge students to achieve their personal best number of consecutive hits. If ball touches floor or student moves from self-space, he or she starts anew.

Shuttlecocks

If your program has a short racket and shuttlecock for each student, introduce striking an object with a racket with the task progression explained earlier. If you do not have a racket and shuttlecock available for every student, introduce striking an object in the station format that follows.

LEARNING EXPERIENCE: STATIONS FOR PRACTICE

Four stations are designed to provide maximum practice and adequate space for striking with paddles or rackets. The task is the same at all stations: striking upward (with control of paddle or racket, object, and body). Students rotate to all four stations, three to four minutes per station.

- Station 1: volleying a balloon upward for consecutive hits with focus on flat surface
- Station 2: striking a balloon upward with a beaver-tail paddle for consecutive hits with focus on watching the ball hit the paddle
- Station 3: striking a ball upward with a lollipop paddle for single hits in self-space; grade 2: consecutive hits in self-space with focus on correct grip
- Station 4: striking a shuttlecock with a short racket (for single hits) with focus on flat surface and low to high swing

Cues: *Watch the birdie. Swing low to high.*

These four stations lead to an excellent class discussion focused on easy and more difficult stations and reasons for decisions.

Closure

- What was the focus of our lesson today? What new skill was introduced?
- How do you know the correct grip for the racket? Show your neighbor the correct way to hold the racket.
- Which was easier: balloons, balls, shuttlecocks? Why?

Reflection

- Are students successful at striking with paddles and rackets?
- Do they have functional understanding (cognitive and performance) of the critical elements of striking with short implements?
- Can students strike the ball or shuttlecock with sufficient control of direction and force to remain in personal space?
- Can they maintain critical elements (flat surface, correct grip) when performing consecutive hits (grade 2)?

A beaver-tail paddle is made by stretching a knee-high hose over a wire coat hanger, pulling the hanger into the elongated shape of a beaver's tail, and tying the hose around the handle of the hanger. Thick tape around the "handles" protects the "grip." These paddles are lightweight and easy for young students to grip and swing correctly for striking balloons. Kindergarten children said they look like a beaver's tail—thus the name!

FOCUS▶ STRIKING WITH SHORT IMPLEMENTS (SIDEARM PATTERN)

Subfocus▶ Force, Space Awareness

Grades 3-5

<table>
<tr><td>Standard 1</td><td>The physically literate individual demonstrates competency in a variety of motor skills and movement patterns.</td></tr>
</table>

Grade-Level Outcomes

- Strikes an object with a short-handled implement, sending it forward over a low net or to a wall (S1.E24.3a)
- Strikes an object with a short-handled implement while demonstrating three of the five critical elements of a mature pattern (S1.E24.3b)
- Strikes an object with a short-handled implement while demonstrating a mature pattern (S1.E24.4a)

Readiness for the Following:

- Strikes an object with a short-handled implement, alternating hits with a partner over a low net or against a wall (S1.E24.4b)
- Strikes an object consecutively, using a short-handled implement, alternating hits with a partner over a net or against a wall in either a competitive or cooperative game environment (S1.E24.5)

Critical Elements for Striking With Short Implements

- Racket back in preparation for striking.
- Step on opposite foot as contact is made.
- Swing racket or paddle low to high.
- Coil and uncoil the trunk for preparation and execution of the striking action.
- Follow through for completion of the striking action.

Lesson Objectives

The learner will:

- Strike a ball with a racket using a side-arm striking pattern, sending the ball forward to a wall
- Strike a ball with a racket with selected critical elements
- Strike a ball with a racket, side-arm pattern, performing consecutive hits to the wall

Safety Concerns

- Ensure that students have spatial awareness for striking and retrieving balls.
- Ensure that wall space is adequate for sidearm striking.

Materials and Equipment

- Short-handled rackets, one per student
- Small high-density foam balls, one per student
- Low-compression tennis balls, one per student
- Tape line on wall, height of 3 to 4 feet (90 to 120 cm)
- Tape line on floor, approximately 10 feet (3 m) from wall, optional

Introduction

In previous lessons, you practiced volleying with emphasis on a flat surface for contact. You also practiced striking with paddles and rackets to send objects upward in self-space. Today, we will take those skills to a higher level—striking with a racket to send a ball forward to the wall and over a net. Personal space will become larger as you move to be always in position to strike the ball; challenges will increase as you attempt consecutive hits.

LEARNING EXPERIENCE: READINESS FOR STRIKING

The Grip

Students stand in a circle, and a racket is on the floor in front of each student.

When you first practiced striking with a racket, we discussed the importance of the correct grip. The grip will be very important today as you begin striking balls to the wall. Pick up your racket and do not move your hand from that position. Yes, it feels strange, but it will be correct when you begin sidearm striking to the wall.

Check students' grips. Remind them to recheck their grip anytime throughout the lesson by placing the racket face down on the floor, picking it up, and not moving the hand from that position.

Sidearm Striking (Foam Balls)

Position students around the perimeter of the work area, each facing the wall and 5 to 6 feet (150 to 180 cm) from the wall, with a racket and foam ball on the floor beside each student. Demonstrate as you introduce the striking skill.

In our previous work on striking with rackets, you practiced sending the ball upward; the striking pattern was back to front and up. Today, the striking pattern will be back to front, but in a side pattern. Ready position will be side to target.

- Students practice back to front swing of arm using underhand striking pattern two to three times; they practice back to front swing of arm, sidearm pattern, without rackets.

LEARNING EXPERIENCE: SIDEARM STRIKING TO THE WALL

You are now ready to strike the ball to the wall with the sidearm pattern.

After students pick up rackets and balls, position each in a ready position side to target with shoulder toward the wall.

Safety Check: Enhance safety by grouping right-handed students together and left-handed students together, as opposed to random placement.

- Students perform single hits to the wall: They drop, hit, bounce, retrieve, and wait for the signal. Allow several minutes of practice and exploration of sidearm striking for students to discover the importance of the grip for the angle of racket and the force needed for the ball to return to their personal space with one bounce.

Cues: *Side to target. Racket back. Sidearm swing. Control the force.*

   Note: These two components—correct grip and side to target—are critical to the sidearm striking pattern. Students at all grade levels need focused practice for mastering the critical elements of the striking pattern.

- Students strike the ball for contact just above the tape line on the wall, performing single hits on your signal.
- Students practice single hits independently. (Observe for class and individual remediation and reteaching.)
- Students continue striking with single hits, emphasizing correct grip and side to target in preparation. Introduce follow-through with arm extended toward target or wall.

Cue: *Extend the arm, extend to target.*

- Have students "freeze" the follow-through, checking to see whether they extend the striking arm toward the wall.

- Challenge students to choose a block or spot on the wall and aim just for that spot.

When you think you can do five perfect single hits (racket back in preparation, side to target, follow-through), ask your neighbor to observe your hits and give you feedback—positive comments and suggestions for improvement.

LEARNING EXPERIENCE: INCREASING THE DISTANCE

Students begin single sidearm hits at a distance of 5 to 6 feet (150 to 180 cm) from the wall.

Cues: Side to target. Racket back. Follow-through extension.

- When students can complete five single hits with the ball hitting the wall just above the tape line and bouncing one time in front of them on the rebound, have them take a giant step backward and repeat the practice of single hits. When they are again successful for five hits, they take another giant step backward. (No distance greater than 10 feet [3 m] from the wall.)

As distance increases, one new critical element becomes very important: swinging low to high.

Cue: Low to high.

Peer Assessment

Students choose distance for personal best and ask neighbor to observe the striking pattern—no closer than 5 feet (1.5 m), no greater than 10 feet (3 m).

Teacher Assessment

Observe striking pattern at distance selected by student. Focus on critical elements and do formative assessment for individual feedback.

LEARNING EXPERIENCE: CONSECUTIVE HITS

Students return to original positions, 5 feet (150 cm) from the wall. Striking the ball with the sidearm pattern, they attempt two consecutive hits: bounce, hit, bounce, hit, catch.

Cues: Side to target. Bounce, hit, bounce, hit.

Sidearm striking on preferred side only requires accuracy to the wall and moving feet to be in position for the striking action. Use quick feet and control force. Don't forget: opposite foot forward, watch the ball!

Grades 4, 5

- When successful with two consecutive hits, students can try for three, four, or five.
- Challenge students to set a personal best for consecutive hits. Ball must contact wall above tape line and bounce one time between hits.

LEARNING EXPERIENCE: READY, TURN (GRADES 4, 5)

Have students place balls on top of rackets, which are placed on floor beside work area. With all students facing the same direction, demonstrate the ready position of facing the target (wall) and turning to execute the striking motion. Have students practice several times without rackets.

Cue: Coil and uncoil (coil as racket arm extends backward, uncoil as racket arm swings and extends toward the target or wall).

- Return to challenge of performing two consecutive hits. Have students bounce and hit with side to target for the first striking action (uncoil), complete the striking action facing the wall, and immediately turn side to target in readiness for the second contact (coil). Increased distance from the wall will give students more time for the turning action.

Note: Sidearm striking pattern for third graders is complete with two consecutive hits and three of the five critical elements in performance. Students in grades 4 and 5 are ready for complexity of readiness with turn and greater number of consecutive hits. Developing a mature pattern for sidearm striking requires multiple opportunities for deliberate, focused practice.

LEARNING EXPERIENCE: SIDEARM STRIKING

If your school has an outside brick wall (no windows) with a concrete sidewalk or pathway adjacent to the wall, this work area is an ideal setting for students to practice the single and consecutive hits with tennis balls. Feedback about control of force is immediate because students want to practice striking rather than chasing balls.

Assessment

Conduct formative assessment of critical elements.

Closure

- What was the focus of our lesson today?
- What new skills did you practice?
- What is the same and what is different about underhand and sidearm striking?
- Model as you ask students to explain the critical elements of sidearm striking.

Reflection

- Do students have a functional understanding of the correct grip for sidearm striking?
- Are they making progress in mastery of the critical elements of the sidearm striking pattern?
- Can they control force to match distance for a bounce in front?
- Do students in grades 4 and 5 see the transfer of critical elements between skills, such as opposite foot forward, watching the ball, extension for follow-through, and so on?

STRIKING WITH SHORT IMPLEMENTS (SIDEARM PATTERN)

Force, Directions, Partner Relationships
Grades 4, 5

Standard 1 | The physically literate individual demonstrates competency in a variety of motor skills and movement patterns.

Grade-Level Outcomes

- Strikes an object with a short-handled implement while demonstrating a mature pattern (S1.E24.4a)
- Strikes an object with a short-handled implement, alternating hits with a partner over a low net or against a wall (S1.E24.4b)
- Strikes an object consecutively, with a partner, using a short-handled implement, over a net or against a wall, in either a competitive or cooperative game environment (S1.E24.5)

Critical Elements for Striking With Short Implements

- Racket back in preparation for striking.
- Step on opposite foot as contact is made.
- Swing racket or paddle low to high.
- Coil and uncoil the trunk for preparation and execution of the striking action.
- Follow through for completion of the striking action.

Lesson Objectives

The learner will:

- Strike a ball with a sidearm striking pattern, using a mature pattern in a nondynamic situation
- Strike a ball with a sidearm striking pattern, maintaining a mature pattern for two consecutive hits (grade 5)
- Strike a ball, alternating hits with partner over a low net
- Strike a ball, alternating hits in a 1v1 competitive game over a low net (grade 5)

Safety Concerns

- Ensure that space is sufficient for sidearm striking.
- Ensure that students are aware of others when striking and retrieving balls.

Materials and Equipment

- Short-handled rackets, one per student
- Small high-density foam balls, one per student
- Low-compression tennis balls, one per student
- Tape lines on wall at heights of 3 feet and 7 feet (90 cm and 210 cm)
- Tape line on floor at distance of 10 feet (3 m) from wall, optional
- Nets, stretch ropes, standards at height of 3 feet (90 cm), sufficient number and space to accommodate half of students per side with personal striking space

Introduction

In the previous lesson on sidearm striking, you practiced single and consecutive hits to the wall. Today, you will practice the skill of sidearm striking to send a ball over a net to a partner. (You will both cooperate and compete with a partner—grade 5). Personal space will become larger as you move to be always in position to strike the ball. Challenges will increase as you attempt consecutive hits while controlling force and being aware of your space and the space of your partner.

Let's review the critical components of the sidearm striking pattern. I will model the skill as you tell me the component that matches these cues: ready position, opposite foot, racket back, low to high, coil and uncoil, follow-through.

Face your neighbor and watch as he or she models the sidearm striking pattern (with pretend ball and pretend racket). Did your neighbor score a 5 with all the components?

LEARNING EXPERIENCE: REVIEW OF SIDEARM STRIKING

Position partners around the perimeter of the work area, each with a racket and foam ball. Standing approximately 5 feet (150 cm) from the wall, partner A assumes the ready position of side to target and performs five single hits; partner B observes one critical element per single hit (ready position, opposite foot forward, follow-through). After five single hits, partners switch positions.

- Grade 4: Determine a critical element for observation.
- Grade 5: Observer tells partner the critical element for observation.

Players perform consecutive hits at distance of 5, 7, or 10 feet (1.5, 2.1, or 3 m). Partner B begins consecutive hits; partner A counts the number of hits above the tape line. Partners switch positions when a mistake is made, such as ball not contacting wall above tape line, ball not bouncing in front of player striking, ball bouncing more than one time, or ball being missed completely. Allow several minutes for this practice as students engage cognitively and physically in practicing the striking skill.

LEARNING EXPERIENCE: STRIKING OVER A NET (INDOORS)

Partners face each other across the net at a distance of no more than 6 feet (180 cm) from the net and alternate hits with the partner so that the ball bounces in front of the partner.

Partner who starts the hits stands side to target for first contact.

Cues: *Control of force. Gentle hits. Quick feet to be in position.*

Safety Check: Ensure that students have spatial awareness as they strike, move to contact balls, and retrieve balls.

- Students alternate hits with partner for personal or partner best. Each time they begin anew, they attempt to match or better previous score.

Note: When students first engage in a game-like experience (hitting over a net), the skill level drops drastically. Stop the class every 30 seconds and provide a focus cue.

- When partners are successful for 10 consecutive hits (5 each without a mistake), they take a giant step backward and begin the consecutive challenge.

Cues: *Increased distance. Swing low to high.*

- Switch from foam balls to low-compression tennis balls and repeat task.
- Students try Cooperative Game With Partner (choice of foam or tennis ball).

At distance chosen by partners, they cooperate to see how many consecutive hits they can achieve with one bounce before hit. Note: Ball must bounce; sidearm striking only.

LEARNING EXPERIENCE: COMPETITIVE GAME WITH PARTNER (GRADE 5)

Partners choose either foam ball or tennis ball.

The cooperative game you just played with a partner now becomes a competition with your partner for striking over the net. The rules are the same as those used for the cooperative game: one bounce before hit, ball must bounce, sidearm striking only, players are within boundaries. Players try to avoid making the first mistake.

- Students use changes in force to make the ball travel to the back of the opponent's space or to the front of the opponent's space.
- They use changes in directions to send the ball to the right or left of the opponent.

Note: Fifth graders greatly benefit from practice of skills in a dynamic environment with 1v1 situations. Students not only enhance their skills but also, as partners, establish boundaries, determine rules of the game, score, and settle any disagreements within the context of the game (Standard 4). Refer to Handball Challenges for appropriate competitive challenges for fifth graders.

LEARNING EXPERIENCE: SIDEARM STRIKING (OUTDOORS)

- Low-compression tennis balls, one per set of partners
- Grades 4 and 5: Cooperative hits with partners over a net

Cues: *Low-to-high swing. Control of force.*

Assessment

- Ongoing formative assessment of critical elements
- Authentic assessment with cooperative and competitive game environments
- Journal entry for self-evaluation of sidearm striking skills

Closure

- What new component did we add to our sidearm striking today?
- What is different about striking over a net compared with striking to the wall?
- Tell your neighbor which is easier for you—striking by yourself to the wall or striking with a partner over a net? Why?

Reflection

- Did students maintain the same skill level when striking over a net compared with striking to the wall?
- What critical elements still need attention for mastering the skill?
- Were there any issues of partners working cooperatively and competitively that need my attention?

STRIKING WITH LONG IMPLEMENTS (BATS)

Space Awareness

Grades 2, 3

The physically literate individual demonstrates competency in a variety of motor skills and movement patterns.

Grade-Level Outcomes

- Strikes a ball off a tee or cone with a bat using correct grip and side orientation/proper body orientation (S1.E25.2)
- Strikes a ball with a long-handled implement (e.g., hockey stick, bat, golf club), sending it forward, while using proper grip (S1.E25.3)

 Note: Use batting tee or ball tossed by teacher for batting.

Critical Elements for Striking With Long Implements (Sidearm Pattern)

- Bat up and back in preparation for the striking action.
- Step forward on opposite foot as contact is made.
- Coil and uncoil the trunk for preparation and execution of the striking action.
- Swing the bat on a horizontal plane.
- Wrist uncocks on follow-through for completion of the striking action.

Lesson Objectives

The learner will:

- Stand in readiness for striking, with side to target
- Strike a ball off a batting tee, sending it forward
- Strike a ball tossed by the teacher, sending it forward (grade 3)

Safety Concern

Ensure that outdoor space is adequate for striking and retrieving balls safely.

Materials and Equipment

- Batting tees or large marker cones
- Wiffle balls, many
- Large plastic bats
- Carpet squares or domes to match number of bats
- Wiffle balls suspended on strings, stretch ropes, standards
- Bases for Just Home Runs (grade 3)

Introduction

Earlier in the year, we worked on striking with rackets and paddles, which are short implements. I asked you to think of the paddle or racket as an extension of your arm. Now the extension is much longer—a bat. Keeping your eyes on the ball will be important when practicing this skill.

LEARNING EXPERIENCE: READINESS FOR STRIKING

Arrange batting tees outdoors with sufficient space for swinging; arrange students so everyone is batting in the same direction or in an outward-facing circle so that all balls travel away from the core.

Place a carpet square or dome beside each tee, to be moved from side to side depending on whether the student is left-handed or right-handed. Place a second carpet square 4 to 5 feet (120 to 150 cm) behind the tee where the second and third students in the group can wait safely.

The Grip

Standing on the carpet square beside the batting tee on the side opposite the writing hand, students hold the bat with the nonwriting hand near the end of the bat; the writing hand should be just above the nonwriting hand so that the hands almost touch.

Side-to-Target Stance

Demonstrate the correct grip and side-to-target stance in preparation for hitting the ball. Have all students hold a pretend bat and assume a ready stance for striking a ball, emphasizing side-to-target body position. Observe students for correct grip and side-to-target position based on left- or right-handedness.

- On your signal, student 1 hits the ball off the tee, sending it across the field. After the first hit, another ball is placed on the tee and hit in response to your signal. After all three balls have been hit, each student in the group retrieves a ball and batter 2 is ready for the signal to strike the ball.

Cue: *Side to target.*

Bat Up and Back

After the first hit for each student, introduce the position of the bat in readiness for striking action; model while giving the cue "bat up and back." Continue practice of batting from the tee and give reminders of preparation cues: grip, stance, bat.

Cue: *What is the cue that never goes away? Watch the ball.*

- Challenge students to strike the ball so that it travels a distance from the tee.

Cue: *Swing through.*

Demonstrate the difference in a level swing and a chopping, downward action, matching each with distance (cognitive engagement).

When you practiced striking with paddles or rackets, we talked about shifting your weight from the back foot to the front foot for extra force. If you want the ball to travel really far, shift your weight as you contact the ball.

Cue: *Extra muscle, extra force, extra distance.*

- Students continue practicing batting from tee, emphasizing the transfer of weight from back foot to front foot.

LEARNING EXPERIENCE: SUSPENDED BALLS

Use a station format or divide the class into two groups, depending on equipment, space, and students' acceptance of responsibility for safety. Use Wiffle balls suspended from stretch ropes with sturdy yarn or string or stretch ropes anchored to standards, trees, or basketball poles at height of batting tees. Standing beside the suspended ball, student hits the ball, sending it forward.

Cue: *Watch the ball.*

- Provide several minutes of practice, observing for proper stance, readiness of bat, and level swing. Students get three hits each, attempting to achieve a perfect batting average. (Stop the ball after each hit; check body and bat readiness, swing.)

LEARNING EXPERIENCE: COMBINING LOCOMOTORS AND BATTING

Students select a partner and return to the batting tees. Partner A stands on the carpet square at the batting tee as before. Partner B stands on a carpet square 12 to 15 feet (3.5 to 4.5 m) from the batter.

This activity combines batting, running, and retrieving; we will call it Hit and Run.

Partner A, the batter, strikes the ball off the tee, sending it as far as possible. Partner A immediately runs to the carpet square and back to the batting tee. As soon as the ball is hit, partner B retrieves it and runs to replace it on the tee. Partners then switch positions.

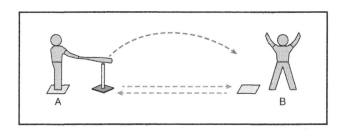

Cue: *Side to target. Bat way back. Level swing, no chop.*

Safety Check: Ensure that batters drop the bat before they run; they must not throw it. Both partners are running, so students must be careful.

Grade 3

After students have performed successful striking off the tee, demonstrated awareness of safety concerns, and are positioned with adequate spacing, introduce them to striking a tossed ball. With you as the pitcher, the batter hits the ball for maximum distance and then immediately runs the bases for a home run. Students positioned in the field retrieve and throw the ball to you—no outs, just home runs. The runner continues to run the bases regardless of the force of the hit or the activity in the field. We call the activity Just Home Runs!

Cue: *Watch the ball.*

Assessment

Observe critical elements of striking.

Closure

- What new skill did we introduce in our lesson today?
- Model as students explain readiness for batting: body position, correct grip, readiness of bat, swing action.
- How will the ball travel if the swing is level? Where will the ball travel if the swing is a chop?

Reflection

- Do the students display the correct grip and side orientation for batting?
- Are they successful in contacting the ball off the tee?

STRIKING WITH LONG IMPLEMENTS (BATS)

Space Awareness, Weight Transfer
Grades 4, 5

Standard 1 The physically literate individual demonstrates competency in a variety of motor skills and movement patterns.

Grade-Level Outcomes

- Strikes an object with a long-handled implement (e.g., hockey stick, bat, golf club, tennis or badminton racket), while demonstrating three of the five critical elements of a mature pattern for the implement (grip, stance, body orientation, swing plane and follow-through) (S1.E25.4)
- Strikes a pitched ball with a bat using a mature pattern (S1.E25.5a)
- Combines striking with a long implement (e.g., bat, hockey stick) with receiving and traveling skills in a small-sided game (S1.E25.5b)

Critical Elements for Striking With Long Implements (Sidearm Pattern)

- Bat up and back in preparation for the striking action.
- Step forward on opposite foot as contact is made.
- Coil and uncoil the trunk for preparation and execution of the striking action.
- Swing the bat on a horizontal plane.
- Wrist uncocks on follow-through for completion of the striking action.

Lesson Objectives

The learner will:

- Strike a ball with force
- Strike a ball with intent of direction

Safety Concern

Ensure that outdoor space is adequate for striking and retrieving balls safely.

Materials and Equipment

- Batting tees or large marker cones
- Wiffle balls, one per student
- Large plastic bats, one for each group of three students
- Carpet squares or domes, five for each group of three students

Introduction

As second and third graders, you learned the basics of striking with a bat. Pretend you have a bat and show me the proper grip. (Observe for proper hand position and spacing.) Turn to a neighbor and share two critical elements you learned about batting (bat up and back, side to the field, watch the ball, level swing). Today, we are going to focus on how to use the body to hit the ball really far and how to direct the placement of the hits.

LEARNING EXPERIENCE: REVIEW OF BATTING

Arrange batting tees outdoors with sufficient space for swinging; arrange students so that everyone is batting in the same direction or in an outward-facing circle so that all balls travel away from the core. Place students in groups of three.

- On your signal, student 1 hits the ball off the tee, sending it across the field. After the first hit, another ball is placed on the tee and hit in response to your signal. After all three balls have been hit, each student in the group retrieves a ball and batter 2 is ready for the signal to strike the ball. Repeat with batter 3. (Observe critical elements: bat position up and back, side to target or field, watching the ball, and level swing.)
- Students continue practice with emphasis on hitting the ball as far as possible. Demonstrate the rotation (coil and uncoil) and have students practice. Demonstrate the transfer of weight to front foot and have students continue to practice.

Cues: *Rotate, coil, and uncoil. Transfer weight to front foot for extra muscle, extra force.*

When older students complain about striking off a tee, remind them that professional baseball players use a tee to revisit their swings. Hitting off a tee is the best way to establish proper batting form.

LEARNING EXPERIENCE: PLACING THE HIT

Students are in groups of three. Place three bases in diamond formation and one at the shortstop position. See illustration.

Student C stands at the shortstop position. Student A hits three balls, purposely hitting them toward student C. Student B (catcher) places the next ball on the tee. After three hits, students rotate positions: The catcher becomes the batter, the batter moves to the field, and the fielder becomes the catcher.

Cues: *Transfer weight toward target. Front foot steps toward target.*

- Repeat the activity with fielder between second and third base.

LEARNING EXPERIENCE: COMBINING BATTING, RUNNING, THROWING, AND CATCHING

Now you will attempt to direct the ball away from the shortstop, to the open spaces (to the left, to the right). We call this activity Hit, Run, Throw. You will not only be directing the hit to open spaces but also adding three more skills to batting: running, throwing, and catching.

Partner A, standing at the batting tee as before, hits the ball really hard away from partner C and then run the bases for a home run. The batter runs all the bases and doesn't stop.

Cues: *Open spaces. Run as fast as you can. Remember to step on all the bases.*

Safety Concerns

- Batters must drop the bat before running; they must not throw it.
- Two players are running, so students must be careful.

Partner C collects or catches the ball and then throws it to home base, where partner B is waiting to catch it. Partner C must stand behind the midfield carpet square until the ball is hit. As soon as partner B collects or catches the ball, he or she places it on the batting tee.

- Even if the fielder catches the ball, the action is the same: The fielder throws the ball home, and the batter runs all the bases.

Batter, for every base you touch before the ball is on the tee, give yourself a point. For a home run, you get a bonus point for a total of 5.

- After each play, the catcher becomes the batter, the batter moves to the field, and the fielder comes to the safety square (home base) behind the tee.

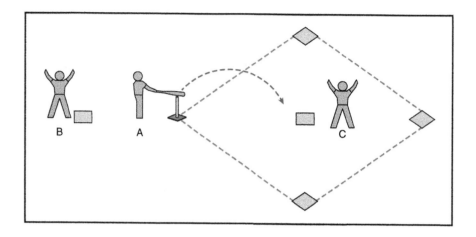

Assessment

- Observe critical elements of striking.
- Students self-assess ability to place the ball, hit with intent, and so on.

Closure

- What new batting challenge was introduced in the lesson today?
- What did you learn today that will help you hit the ball really far?
- How will you position the front foot for hitting to right field? Left field?

Reflection

- Do the students transfer weight from back foot to front foot by coiling and uncoiling the body?
- Are they successful in placing the ball?

Grade 5

Students in grade 5 are typically ready to be challenged with other batting experiences as well as more game-like opportunities. Following achievement of mastery of the critical components in the previous activities, the following are appropriate challenges:

- Batting a self-tossed ball.
- Batting a pitched ball. Encourage students in the role of pitcher to use "friendly" pitches, either underhand or overhand, that allow batter to be successful.
- Playing 3v3 softball with own team pitching (or using the tee). Defense: catcher, two fielders. Offense: pitcher, two batters. Teams rotate after five minutes regardless of "outs" recorded. Modify rules to promote success (e.g., after three pitches, switch to the tee or give students choice of pitch or tee).

STRIKING WITH LONG IMPLEMENTS (HOCKEY, BADMINTON, TENNIS)

Space Awareness

Hockey: Grades 3-5; Badminton, Tennis: Grades 4, 5

Standard 1 The physically literate individual demonstrates competency in a variety of motor skills and movement patterns.

Grade-Level Outcomes

- Strikes an object with a long-handled implement (e.g., hockey stick, bat, golf club, tennis or badminton racket), while demonstrating three of the five critical elements of a mature pattern for the implement (grip, stance, body orientation, swing plane and follow-through) (S1.E25.4)
- Combines traveling with the manipulative skills of dribbling, throwing, catching and striking in teacher- and/or student-designed small-sided practice-task environments (S1.E26.4)
- Combines striking with a long implement (e.g., bat, hockey stick) with receiving and traveling skills in a small-sided game (S1.E25.5b)
- Combines manipulative skills and traveling for execution to a target (e.g., scoring in soccer, hockey and basketball) (S1.E26.5)

The manipulative skills of striking with hockey sticks, badminton rackets, and tennis rackets each have unique skill components and direct links to previously learned skills. The critical elements for each focus on grip, stance, body orientation, swing, and follow-through. The skills of striking for each will be presented in the next sections with a suggested outline for addressing the Grade-Level Outcomes.

FLOOR HOCKEY

Critical Elements for Striking With Long Implements (Hockey Stick)

- Grip the hockey stick with hands 3 to 4 inches (8 to 10 cm) apart, preferred hand on the bottom, and thumbs down.
- Stance is forward–backward.
- Body orientation is side to target.
- Swing is a tap/dribble for traveling, passing and increased force for shooting for a goal.
- Follow-through is low to middle level to target.

Lesson Objectives for the Series

The learner will:

- Dribble a puck in general space with control of puck, stick, and body
- Dribble in different pathways and directions
- Dribble with changes in speed
- Combine dribbling with shooting for a goal
- Dribble a hockey puck, sending and receiving passes from a partner
- Control puck and body in small-sided practice tasks or game environment

Materials and Equipment

- Hockey sticks and pucks, one each per student
- Hockey balls, optional
- Marker cones (the more cones, the more goals for practice)

Introduction

Who can remember the skill you learned in first grade that used a tap dribble? The skill was soccer. The skill for today is floor hockey; the tap dribble will be with a hockey stick.

Safety Concerns

- Ensure that students have spatial awareness for striking with hockey sticks.
- Hockey sticks must be kept below shoulder height at all times.

Task Progression

Follow the task progression for soccer:

- Using proper grip, tap dribbling in self-space without pucks
- Tap dribbling in general space with control of puck, stick, and body
- Gaining control by checking the forward travel of the puck
- Shooting for a goal with increased force and swing
- Combined dribbling in general space and shooting for a goal
- Changes in direction, pathways, speed
- Passing and receiving
- Dribbling and shooting for a goal against defense (1v1, 2v1)

   Note: High sticks is a rule violation in all forms of hockey and a safety concern for all participants. Students must be taught the correct form of striking for the dribble and for increased force so that they can maintain sticks below shoulder height.

Assessment

- Observe critical elements.
- Authentic assessment can be done in small-sided practice tasks and games.

Closure

- What new skill did you learn today?
- What components of the skill were the same as those used in soccer? Did the similarity make learning the skill easier or more difficult?
- Discuss with the class the entertainment component of ice hockey versus the sport.
- Why is high sticks a violation that cannot be ignored?

Reflection

- Are students developing the skills and critical elements for floor hockey?
- Are they able to dribble with control of body, stick, and puck?
- Do they accept differences in skill levels for small-sided practice and play (Standard 4)?

BADMINTON

Critical Elements for Striking Upward With Long Implements (Badminton Racket)

- Opposite foot forward.
- Shake-hands grip with palm up and firm wrist.
- Flat surface for contact.
- Swing racket or paddle from low to high.
- Follow through to target.

Lesson Objectives for the Series

The learner will:

- Strike a shuttlecock with a badminton racket sending it upward and forward over a net
- Strike a shuttlecock with a racket over a net, to and from a partner, cooperatively
- Strike a shuttlecock with a racket sending it over a net, to and from an opponent, competitively
- Strike a shuttlecock with changes in force and direction as strategies in a dynamic game

Materials and Equipment

- Badminton rackets, one per student
- Shuttlecocks, one per student
- Hoops and tape lines on floor for targets
- Nets suspended at height of 6 to 7 feet (180 to 210 cm)
- Tape lines on wall at height of 7 feet (210 cm)

Introduction

Earlier in the year, we worked on striking with short implements. You practiced hitting balloons, foam balls, and shuttlecocks. We talked about the racket as an extension of your arm. Today, you will be striking shuttlecocks with badminton rackets, so the extension of the arms is much longer today. The focus will be on striking the shuttlecock so that it travels forward in an arch, like a rainbow.

Safety Concern

Ensure that students have spatial awareness for striking with long implements.

Learning Experiences

Many of the tasks for striking with a badminton racket relate directly to striking with a short implement to send an object forward. The critical elements for striking upward with short and long implements are the same.

- Review of proper grip, flat surface, low to high and forward and backward swing in self-space without shuttlecocks
- Drop, not toss, of shuttlecock and sending it forward to the wall with your observation of critical elements
- Single hits of shuttlecock for accuracy to hoops on floor
- Single hits of shuttlecock for distance to hoops or tape lines
- Cooperative hits over a net to a partner
- Competitive hits over a net with a partner (opponent)
- Changes in force and direction for strategy against opponent
- Student-designed cooperative or competitive 1v1 games

Assessment

- Observe critical elements.
- Perform authentic assessment in dynamic situations.

Closure

- What new skill did you learn today?
- How is striking with the badminton racket different from striking the shuttlecock with the short racket?
- Tell your neighbor whether you prefer cooperative or competitive games. Why?

Reflection

- Are students developing the skills and critical elements for badminton?
- Do they accept differences in skill levels for small-sided games when partners are switched and new ones are assigned (Standard 4)?

TENNIS

Critical Elements for Striking With Long Implements (Tennis Racket)

- Racket back in preparation for striking.
- Step on opposite foot when contact is made.
- Swing racket from low to high.
- Coil and uncoil the trunk for preparation and execution of the striking action.
- Follow through for completion of the striking action.

Lesson Objectives for the Series

The learner will:

- Strike a ball using sidearm striking pattern and demonstrating a mature pattern
- Strike a ball using sidearm striking pattern to send the ball to a wall for consecutive hits
- Strike a ball using sidearm pattern to send the ball over a low net to a partner
- Strike a ball using sidearm pattern to send and receive the ball over a low net with a partner
- Strike a ball using sidearm pattern to send the ball over a low net with a partner, cooperatively
- Strike a ball using sidearm pattern to send the ball over a low net with a partner (opponent), competitively
- Strike a ball using sidearm pattern with changes in direction and force as strategies in a dynamic situation

Materials and Equipment

- Tennis rackets, combination of junior and regular, one per student
- High-density foam balls, one per student
- Low-compression tennis balls, one per student
- Nets at height of 3 feet (90 cm), indoors and outdoors
- Tape lines on wall at height of 3 feet (90 cm)

Safety Check: Spatial awareness is critical with sidearm striking.

Learning Experiences

Follow the task progression for sidearm striking with short rackets or paddles. This task progression provides instruction for the forehand in tennis.

- Review of grip and sidearm striking pattern without balls
- Single hits to the wall, increasing distance with success, with your observation of critical elements (side to target, racket back)
- Consecutive hits to the wall with emphasis on coiling and uncoiling
- Outdoors: Single hits to partner with bounce, hit, catch. Consecutive hits or cooperative game with partner over a low net

Note: We recommend that you contact the United States Tennis Association (USTA) for in-service and tennis instruction beyond the basic striking skills of the forehand. The USTA Tennis in Schools program provides tennis rackets as well as professional development for teachers.

Assessment

- Conduct formative assessment by observing critical elements; provide individual feedback and challenge as needed.
- Have students make journal entries about their favorite skill or sport in physical education and the reasons they like it. Have them identify the most difficult skill and explain why it is difficult.

Closure

- What new skill did we begin to learn today?
- Let's look at all the striking skills you have learned this year (list on whiteboard). (Class discussion of favorites, most challenging, most likely to play after school with friends.)
- Why do you think we study many different skills in physical education?

Reflection

- Are students mastering the skill beyond hitting to the wall?
- Are they developing control of the ball and the racket to direct the ball to the target or partner (distance, force, direction, height)?
- Which students need extra assistance? Which students need challenge?

JUMPING ROPE

Grades K-2

Standard 1	The physically literate individual demonstrates competency in a variety of motor skills and movement patterns.

Grade-Level Outcomes

Short Rope

- Executes a single jump with self-turned rope (S1.E27.Ka)
- Jumps forward or backward consecutively using a self-turned rope (S1.E27.1a)
- Jumps forward and backward consecutively using a self-turned rope, while using a mature pattern (S1.E27.2a)

Long Rope

- Jumps a long rope with teacher-assisted turning (S1.E27.Kb)
- Jumps a long rope up to five times consecutively with teacher-assisted turning (S1.E27.1b)
- Jumps a long rope five times consecutively with student turner (S1.E27.2b)

LEARNING EXPERIENCE: SHORT-ROPE JUMPING

- Kindergarten students begin with exploratory practice.
- Your instruction includes how to grip the handles, turn the rope, and time the jumps. Guided practice allows students to progress from their first single jump in kindergarten to consecutive jumps in grade 1.
- With instruction and practice, students in grade 2 achieve a mature pattern with a smooth rhythmical jump; they are ready to be introduced to simple jump rope tricks.

LEARNING EXPERIENCE: LONG-ROPE JUMPING

- In kindergarten and grade 1, you are the turner. If a second teacher or volunteer is not available, a pole or volleyball standard serves well as your turning partner.
- Use spoken cues (jump, jump) to inform the new learner when to jump.
- Stations are recommended in kindergarten and grade 1, thereby minimizing waiting time for students.
- In grade 2, teach students to turn the rope.

Jump ropes made available for recess provide quality physical activity and practice as well as an opportunity for students to show off their skills.

JUMPING ROPE

Grades 3-5

The physically literate individual demonstrates competency in a variety of motor skills and movement patterns.

Grade-Level Outcomes

- Performs intermediate jump-rope skills (e.g., a variety of tricks, running in and out of long rope) for both long and short ropes (S1.E27.3)
- Creates a jump-rope routine with either a short or long rope (S1.E27.4)
- Creates a jump-rope routine with a partner, using either a short or long rope (S1.E27.5)

Students in grade 3 who have mastered the skill of short-rope jumping are ready for the challenge of basic and intermediate-level tricks (e.g., bell, skier, side-straddle, heel-toe, and crisscross). Jump rope tricks can be taught by teacher instruction, digital recordings, or posters and pictures. In grades 4 and 5, the challenge escalates with opportunities to create routines with music.

Long-rope jumping remains an enjoyable experience that offers new challenges of running in and out of the rope, playing rope-jumping games, creating new jump rope rhymes, and exploring long-rope tricks (e.g., hot pepper, egg beater, and double-dutch). Solo or partner routines are an added skill welcomed in grades 4 and 5.

The American Heart Association provides excellent charts and progression of tricks for both short and long ropes.

Appendix A

Scope & Sequence for K-12 Physical Education

This appendix serves as a quick reference for practitioners when planning and implementing lessons leading to student attainment of the Grade-Level Outcomes. The chart specifies the knowledge and skills expected at each grade level and illustrates how learning progresses across those grade levels. The arrows indicate the grade levels in which the knowledge and skills should be a focus of instruction; shaded cells indicate the grade levels in which the knowledge and skills need not be a focus of instruction. Skills and knowledge are coded for introduction and practice (emerging), demonstration of critical elements (maturing) and application in different contexts (applying). The following terms are used throughout the table:

E = **Emerging.** Students participate in deliberate practice tasks that will lead to skill and knowledge acquisition.

M = **Maturing.** Students can demonstrate the critical elements of the motor skills and knowledge components of the Grade-Level Outcomes, which will continue to be refined with practice.

A = **Applying.** Students can demonstrate the critical elements of the motor skills and knowledge components of the Grade-Level Outcomes in a variety of physical activity environments.

Standard 1. Motor skills & movement patterns

	Kindergarten	Grade 1	Grade 2	Grade 3	Grade 4	Grade 5	Grade 6	Grade 7	Grade 8	High School
Hopping	E	M	A	→						→
Galloping	E	M	A	→						→
Running	E	→	M	A	→					→
Sliding	E	M	A	→						→
Skipping	E	→	M	A	→					→
Leaping		E	→	M	A	→				→
Jumping & landing	E	→	→	M	A	→				→
• Spring & step					E	M	A	→		→
• Jump stop							E	M	A	→
• Jump rope	E	→	→	M	A	→	i	i	i	i
Balance	E	→	→	M	→	A	→			→
Weight transfer			E	M	→		A	→		→
Rolling	E	→	→	→	M	A	→			→
Curling & stretching	E	→	M	→	→	A	→			→
Twisting & bending		E	M	→	→	A	→			→
Throwing										
• Underhand	E	→	M	→	→	→	A			→
• Overhand	E	→	→	→	→	M	A	→		→
Catching	E	→	→	→	M	A	→			→
Dribbling/ball control										
• Hands	E	→	→	→	M	A	→			→
• Feet		E	→	→	→	M	A	→		→
• With implement				E	→	M	A	→		→
Kicking	E	→	→	→	M	→	A	→		→
Volleying										
• Underhand	E	→	→	→	M	A	→			→
• Overhead					E	→	ii	ii	ii	ii
• Set								E	→	M
Striking—with short implement	E	→	→	→	M	A	→			→
• Fore/backhand							E	→	M	A
Striking—with long implement			E	→	→	M	A	→		→
• Fore/backhand								E	→	M
Combining locomotors & manipulatives					E	→	M	→	A	→
Combining jumping, landing, locomotors & manipulatives						E	M	A	→	→
Combining balance & weight transfers			E	→	→	→	M	→	A	→

iJump rope becomes a fitness activity after grade 5 and is absorbed into Standard 3. Engages in fitness activities.

iiOverhead volley becomes a specialized skill for volleyball—setting—that begins being taught in middle school.

	Kindergarten	Grade 1	Grade 2	Grade 3	Grade 4	Grade 5	Grade 6	Grade 7	Grade 8	High School
Serving										
• Underhand							E	M	A	→
• Overhand							E	→	→	M
Shooting on goal						E	→	→	M	*
Passing & receiving										
• Hands						E	→	M	→	*
• Feet					E	→	→	→	M	*
• With implement							E	→	M	*
• Forearm pass							E	→	M	A
• Lead pass						E	→	M	→	*
• Give & go							E	M	→	*
Offensive skills										
• Pivots							E	M	A	*
• Fakes							E	→	M	*
• Jab step							E	→	M	*
• Screen									E	*
Defensive skills										
• Drop step							E	→	M	*
• Defensive or athletic stance							E	→	M	*

*Teaching team sports skills is not recommended at the high school level. See chapter 5 for rationale.

Standard 2. Concepts & strategies

	Kindergarten	Grade 1	Grade 2	Grade 3	Grade 4	Grade 5	Grade 6	Grade 7	Grade 8	High School
Movement concepts, principles & knowledge	E	→			M	→	A	→		→
Strategies & tactics				E	→		M	→	A	→
Communication (games)							E	→	M	A
Creating space (invasion)										
• Varying pathways, speed, direction							E	M	A	*
• Varying type of pass							E	M	A	*
• Selecting appropriate offensive tactics with object							E	→	M	*
• Selecting appropriate offensive tactics without object							E	→	M	*
• Using width & length of the field/court							E	→	M	*
• Playing with one player up (e.g., 2v1)							E	→	M	*
Reducing space (invasion)										
• Changing size & shape of the defender's body							E	M	A	*
• Changing angle to gain competitive advantage							E	→	M	*
• Denying the pass/player progress							E	→		*
• Playing with one player down (e.g., 1v2)							E	→		*
Transition (invasion)							E	M	A	*
Creating space (net/wall)										
• Varying force, angle and/or direction to gain competitive advantage							E	→	M	A
• Using offensive tactic/shot to move opponent out of position							E	→		M
Reducing space (net/wall)										
• Returning to home position							E	→	M	A
• Shifting to reduce angle for return							E	→		M
Target										
• Selecting appropriate shot/club							E	→	M	A
• Applying blocking strategy							E	→		M
• Varying speed & trajectory							E	→	M	A
Fielding/striking										
• Applying offensive strategies								E	→	*
• Reducing open spaces							E	→	M	*

*Teaching team sports skills is not recommended at the high school level. See chapter 5 for rationale.

Standard 3. Health-enhancing level of fitness & physical activity

	Kindergarten	Grade 1	Grade 2	Grade 3	Grade 4	Grade 5	Grade 6	Grade 7	Grade 8	High School
Physical activity knowledge	E	→				M	→		A	→
Engages in physical activity	E	→				M	→			A
Fitness knowledge	E	→				M	→			A
Assessment & program planning				E	→	M	→		A	→
Nutrition	E	→					M	→		A
Stress management							E	→		M

Standard 4. Responsible personal & social behavior

	Kindergarten	Grade 1	Grade 2	Grade 3	Grade 4	Grade 5	Grade 6	Grade 7	Grade 8	High School
Demonstrating personal responsibility	E	→		M	→		A	→		→
Accepting feedback	E	→		M	→		A	→		→
Working with others	E	→		M	→		A	→		→
Following rules & etiquette			E	→		M	→	A	→	→
Safety	E	→	M	→		A	→			→

Standard 5. Recognizes the value of physical activity

	Kindergarten	Grade 1	Grade 2	Grade 3	Grade 4	Grade 5	Grade 6	Grade 7	Grade 8	High School
For health			E	→			M	→		A
For challenge			E	→			M	→		A
For self-expression/enjoyment	E	→				M	→			A
For social interaction				E	→		M	→		A

Appendix B

Sample Yearlong Lesson-Planning Schedules

GRADES K-2

This sample yearlong lesson-planning schedule is based on a physical education program that meets two days each week during a 36-week school year, with grades K–2 meeting for 30-minute class periods. You can adapt this plan to other day or time program schedules. Additional adaptations might be needed based on your philosophy, your students' experience, and other factors. The sample plan addresses Standards 1 and 2 only; you need to embed content related to Standards 3, 4, and 5 within the lessons.

Note: Teaching to the fundamental motor pattern outcomes requires revisiting content at various points in the school year (distributed practice). Revisited skills are in **bold** print.

Week	Grade K	Grade 1	Grade 2
1	Establishing the Learning Environment Self-Space	Establishing the Learning Environment Self-Space and General Space	Establishing the Learning Environment Self-Space and General Space
2	Self-Space and General Space Locomotors	Self-Space and General Space Directions Locomotors	Self-Space and General Space Directions Locomotors
3	Directions and Pathways Locomotors	Directions, Pathways, and Levels Locomotors	Directions, Pathways, and Levels Locomotors
4	Pathways and Levels Creative Dance	Pathways and Levels Creative Dance	Pathways and Levels Creative Dance
5	Kicking	Kicking	Kicking
6	Dribbling With Feet	Dribbling With Feet	Dribbling With Feet
7	Throwing Underhand	Throwing Underhand	Throwing Underhand
8	Catching	Catching	Catching
9	Jumping and Landing	Jumping and Landing	Jumping and Landing
10	Body Shapes Time and Force	Body Shapes Time, Force, and Flow	Time, Force, and Flow
11	Balance	Balance	Balance
12	Balance **Locomotors**	Balance Weight Transfer: Rolling	Balance Inverted Balance Weight Transfer: Rolling
13	Curling, Stretching and Twisting Actions Weight Transfer: Rolling	Curling, Stretching, and Twisting Actions Weight Transfer: Rolling	Curling, Stretching, and Twisting Actions Weight Transfer: Rolling
14	Balance Curling, Stretching, and Twisting Actions Weight Transfer: Rolling	Weight Transfer: Weight on Hands	Weight Transfer: Weight on Hands

(continued)

(continued)

Week	Grade K	Grade 1	Grade 2
15	Levels and Force (Review) Dribbling With Hands	Levels, Force, Directions, and Pathways (Review) Dribbling With Hands	Levels, Force, Directions, and Pathways (Review) Dribbling With Hands
16	**Jumping and Landing**	**Jumping and Landing**	**Jumping and Landing**
17	Jumping Rope	Jumping Rope	Jumping Rope
18	Jumping Rope	Jumping Rope	Jumping Rope Throwing Overhand
19	**Throwing Underhand**	**Throwing Underhand** Throwing Overhand	**Throwing Underhand** Throwing Overhand
20	**Catching**	**Catching**	**Catching**
21	Volleying Underhand **Locomotors**	Volleying Underhand	Volleying Underhand
22	Striking With Short-Handled Implements	Striking With Short-Handled Implements	Striking With Short-Handled Implements
23	Levels and Pathways (Review) **Locomotors** Dance and Rhythms	Levels, Time, and Flow (Review) Locomotors Dance and Rhythms	Levels, Time, and Flow (Review) **Locomotors** Dance and Rhythms
24	**Balance and Weight Transfer:** **Rolling**	**Balance and Weight Transfer:** **Rolling**	**Balance and Weight Transfer:** **Rolling**
25	**Balance and Weight Transfer:** **Rolling** **Curling, Stretching, and Twisting** **Actions**	**Balance and Weight Transfer:** **Rolling** **Curling, Stretching, and Twisting** **Actions**	**Balance and Weight Transfer:** **Rolling** **Curling, Stretching, and Twisting** **Actions**
26	**Locomotors, Balance and Weight** **Transfer: Rolling**	**Locomotors, Balance and Weight** **Transfer: Rolling**	**Locomotors, Balance and Weight** **Transfer: Rolling**
27	**Dribbling With Hands**	**Dribbling With Hands**	**Dribbling With Hands**
28	**Jumping Rope**	**Jumping Rope**	**Jumping Rope**
29	**Jumping Rope**	**Jumping Rope**	**Jumping Rope**
30	**Volleying Underhand**	**Volleying Underhand**	**Volleying Underhand**
31	**Striking With Short Implements**	**Striking With Short Implements**	**Striking With Short Implements**
32	**Throwing and Catching**	**Throwing and Catching**	Striking With Bats
33	**Dance and Rhythms**	**Dance and Rhythms**	**Dance and Rhythms**
34	**Kicking**	**Kicking**	**Kicking**
35	**Dribbling With Feet**	**Dribbling With Feet**	**Dribbling With Feet**
36	Field Day	Field Day	Field Day

GRADES 3-5

This sample yearlong lesson-planning schedule is based on a physical education program that meets two days each week during a 36-week school year, with grades 3–5 meeting for 30- to 45-minute class periods. You can adapt this plan to other day or time program schedules. Additional adaptations might be needed based on your philosophy, your students' experience, and other factors. The plan addresses Standards 1 and 2 and the assessment of fitness for Standard 3 only; you need to embed content related to Standards 3, 4, and 5 within the lessons.

You should do health-related fitness testing in the fall and spring, although you should embed the fitness concepts and self-assessment opportunities within lessons throughout the year.

Note: Teaching to attain the fundamental motor pattern outcomes requires revisiting content at various points in the school year (distributed practice) Revisited skills are in **bold** print.

Week	Grade 3	Grade 4	Grade 5
1	Establishing the Learning Environment Review of Movement Concepts	Establishing the Learning Environment Dribbling With Hands	Establishing the Learning Environment Dribbling With Hands
2	Dribbling With Hands	Dribbling With Hands	Dribbling With Hands
3	Concepts of Fitness Throwing Overhand	Concepts of Fitness Throwing Overhand	Concepts of Fitness Throwing Overhand
4	Cardiorespiratory Fitness Introduction to Health-Related Fitness Assessment Protocols	Cardiorespiratory Fitness Health-Related Fitness Assessment	Cardiorespiratory Fitness Health-Related Fitness Assessment
5	Locomotors (Leaping) Striking With Bats	Health-Related Fitness Assessment	Health-Related Fitness Assessment
6	Kicking Dribbling With Feet	Kicking Dribbling With Feet	Kicking Dribbling With Feet
7	Kicking Dribbling With Feet	Kicking Dribbling With Feet	Kicking
8	Throwing and Catching	Passing and Catching	Passing and Catching
9	Jumping and Landing **Locomotors (Leaping)**	Passing and Catching	Passing and Catching
10	Concept of Flow Dance and Rhythms	Dance and Rhythms	Dance and Rhythms
11	Balance Weight Transfer: Rolling	Balance Weight Transfer	Balance Weight Transfer
12	Balance Weight Transfer: Weight on Hands	Balance Weight Transfer	Balance Weight Transfer
13	Weight Transfer: Curling, Stretching, and Twisting Actions Building a Gymnastics Sequence	Building a Gymnastics Sequence	Building a Gymnastics Sequence
14	Volleying Underhand	Volleying Underhand Volleying Overhand	Volleying Overhand
15	Striking With Short Implements	Striking With Short Implements	Striking With Short Implements
16	Dance and Rhythms	Dance and Rhythms	Dance and Rhythms

(continued)

(continued)

Week	Grade 3	Grade 4	Grade 5
17	Jumping Rope	Jumping Rope	Jumping Rope
18	Jumping Rope	Jumping Rope	Jumping Rope
19	**Dribbling With Hands**	**Dribbling With Hands**	**Dribbling With Hands**
20	**Throwing Underhand** **Throwing Overhand**	**Throwing Underhand** **Throwing Overhand**	**Throwing Underhand** **Throwing Overhand**
21	**Catching**	**Catching** **Passing and Catching**	**Catching** **Passing and Catching**
22	Striking With Hockey Sticks	Striking With Hockey Sticks	Striking With Hockey Sticks
23	Dance and Rhythms	Striking With Racquets	Striking With Racquets
24	Dance and Rhythms	Dance and Rhythms	Dance and Rhythms
25	**Balance** Weight Transfer on Low Equipment	**Balance** Weight Transfer on Low Equipment	**Balance** Weight Transfer on Low Equipment
26	Weight Transfer on Apparatuses Building a Gymnastics Sequence	Weight Transfer on Apparatuses Building a Gymnastics Sequence	Weight Transfer on Apparatuses Building a Gymnastics Sequence
27	**Dribbling With Hands**	**Dribbling With Hands**	**Dribbling With Hands**
28	**Jumping Rope**	*Health-Related Fitness Assessment*	*Health-Related Fitness Assessment*
29	**Jumping Rope**	*Health-Related Fitness Assessment*	*Health-Related Fitness Assessment*
30	**Volleying Underhand**	**Volleying Underhand** **Volleying Overhand**	**Volleying Overhand**
31	**Striking With Short-Handled Implements**	**Striking With Short-Handled Implements**	**Striking With Short-Handled Implements**
32	**Striking With Bats**	**Striking With Racquets**	**Striking With Racquets**
33	**Striking With Hockey Sticks**	**Striking With Hockey Sticks**	**Striking With Hockey Sticks**
34	**Kicking** **Dribbling With Feet**	**Kicking** **Dribbling With Feet**	**Kicking**
35	**Throwing Overhand**	**Throwing Overhand**	**Throwing Overhand**
36	Field Day	Field Day	Field Day

Glossary

affective domain—The domain in which the focus is on personal and social development, attitudes, values, feelings, motivations, and emotions.

applying—Learners can demonstrate the critical elements of the motor skills or knowledge components of the Grade-Level Outcomes in a variety of physical activity environments.

assessment—The gathering of evidence about student learning and making inferences on student progress and growth based on that evidence (adapted from SHAPE America, 2014).

cognitive domain—The domain in which the focus is on knowledge and information (facts and concepts), with an emphasis on the understanding and application of knowledge and information through higher-order thinking skills.

critical elements—The key components of a motor skill that can be observed, the sum of which result in movement efficiency.

cues—Short phrases or words that focus the learner on the critical elements of the skill to be practiced (Graham, Holt/Hale, and Parker, 2013, p. 118).

curriculum mapping—The process of curriculum planning within the grade level (horizontal mapping) and across the grade levels, K–5 (vertical mapping). Curriculum mapping requires a commitment to when a skill will be taught.

dance and rhythmic activities—Activities that focus on dance or rhythms. Rhythmic activities for early elementary students focus on recognizing and moving to rhythm, progressing to creative dance, partner and group, for upper elementary students.

dance stems—An idea from which a dance grows, such as a study of the elements of movement, emotions, words, ideas, ad stories.

deliberate practice—A highly structured activity, the explicit goal of which is to improve performance. Tasks are invented to overcome the learner's weaknesses, and performance is monitored carefully to provide cues for ways to improve further (Ericsson et al., 1993, p. 368).

differentiated instruction—Instruction that is varied to address the needs of students and their various levels of skill or knowledge.

dynamic environment (open skills)—Skills performed in an environment that is dynamic, unpredictable, and in motion (Schmidt and Wrisberg, 2008, p. 9).

educational gymnastics—Gymnastics that focuses on children challenging themselves to maneuver their bodies effectively against the force of gravity (Graham et al., 2013). Educational gymnastics centers on challenges appropriate for each student and his or her skill level, as contrasted with Olympic gymnastics, which centers on defined stunts performed the same way by all students.

embedded objectives—Secondary objectives placed in the supporting learning experiences of the primary objective.

emerging—Learners in the beginning stages of acquiring motor skills and knowledge. Mastery of the skills and knowledge is emerging through deliberate practice tasks, and, at this stage, learners are developing competency.

formative—Assessments that are ongoing during instruction, allowing teachers to track student progress and adapt instruction (SHAPE America, 2014, p. 90).

foundational skills—The skills of elementary physical education (psychomotor, cognitive, affective), the composite of which serves as the foundation for the application of skills for middle school physical education and the pursuit of personal choice physical activities in high school and beyond.

functional fitness—The ability to perform common movements at home, at school, or in sports safely and without undue fatigue (adapted from Mayo Clinic, 2013; Corbin and Le Masurier, 2014).

fundamental motor skills—The locomotor, nonlocomotor/stability, and manipulative skills that provide the foundation for the more complex movement patterns of games and sports, gymnastics, and dance.

inverted position—Balances and transfers of weight in educational gymnastics in which the head is lower than the hips.

locomotor skills—Skills that allow people to navigate through space or move the body from one point to another (Gallahue et al., 2012, p. 223). Locomotor skills include jogging, running, hopping, galloping, skipping, sliding, leaping, and jumping—in the horizontal plane.

manipulative skills—Skills that require controlling or manipulative objects, such as kicking, striking with short and long implements, throwing, catching, volleying, and dribbling.

mature pattern—Executing with efficiency the critical elements of the motor skills pattern in authentic environments.

maturing—Demonstrating the critical elements of the motor skills and knowledge components of the Grade-Level Outcomes, which will continue to be refined with practice. As the environment context changes, a maturing pattern may fluctuate, reflecting more maturity in familiar context and less maturing in unfamiliar or new contexts, thus the term *maturing*.

movement concepts—The application of knowledge and concepts related to skillful performance of movement and fitness activities. Movement concepts include spatial awareness, the effort qualities of time and speed, force, flow, relationships with partners and groups, strategies and principles related to movement efficiency, and health-enhancing fitness.

movement patterns—The more complex sport, gymnastics, and dance specific movements that are developed from the fundamental motor skills.

nondynamic environment (closed skills)—Skills performed in an environment that is constant, predictable, or stationary (Schmidt and Wrisberg, 2008, p. 9).

nonlocomotor, or stability, skills—Movement that focuses on gaining and maintaining equilibrium in relation to the force of gravity (Gallahue, et al., 2012, p. 49). Nonlocomotor movements include balance, weight transfer, and the actions of stretching, curling and twisting.

outcomes—Statements that specify what learners should know or be able to do as the result of a learning experience.

physical literacy—A physically literate person has learned the skills necessary to participate in a variety of physical activities, knows the implications and the benefits of involvement in various types of physical activities, participates regularly in physical activity, is physically fit, and values physical activity and its contributions to a healthy lifestyle.

psychomotor domain—The domain in which the focus is on motor skills.

summative—End-of-instruction evaluations that occur at the close of the instructional sequence, providing teachers with a comprehensive summary of each student's progress and growth (SHAPE America, 2014, p. 90).

References

Preface

SHAPE America. 2014. *National standards & grade-level outcomes for K–12 physical education.* Champaign, IL: Human Kinetics.

Chapter 1

Barnett, L.M., van Beurden, E., Morgan, P.J., Brooks, L.O., and Beard, J.R. 2008. Does childhood motor skill proficiency predict adolescent fitness? *Medicine & Science in Sports & Exercise,* 40, 2137–2144.

Bernstein, E., Phillips, S.R., and Silverman, S. 2011. Attitudes and perceptions of middle school students toward competitive activities in physical education. *Journal of Teaching in Physical Education,* 30, 69–83.

Bevans, K., Fitzpatrick, L., Sanchez, B., and Forest, C.B. 2010. Individual and instructional determinants of student engagement in physical education. *Journal of Teaching in Physical Education,* 29, 399–416.

Ennis, C. 2011. Physical education curriculum priorities: Evidence for education and skillfulness. *Quest,* 63, 5–18.

Ericsson, K.A. 2006. The influence of experience and deliberate practice on the development of superior expert performance. In *The Cambridge handbook of expertise and expert performance,* ed. K.A. Ericsson, N. Charness, P.J. Feltovich, and R.R. Hoffman, 685–705. Cambridge, UK: Cambridge University Press.

Ericsson, K., Krampe, R., and Tesch-Romer, C. 1993. The role of deliberate practice in the acquisition of expert performance. *Psychological Review,* 100(3), 363–406.

Gao, Z., Lee, A. M., Ping, X., and Kosam, M. 2011. Effect of learning activity on students' motivation, physical activity levels and effort/persistence. *ICHPER-SD Journal of Research in Health, Physical Education, Recreation, Sport & Dance,* 6(1), 27–33.

Kambas, A. Michalopoulou, M., Fatouros, I., Christoforidis, C., Manthou, E., Giannakidou, D., Venetsanou, F., Haberer, E., Chatzinikolaou, A., Gourgoulis, V., and Zimmer, R. 2012. The relationship between motor proficiency and pedometer-determined physical activity in young children. *Pediatric Exercise Science,* 24, 34–44.

Mandigo, J., Francis, J., Lodewyk, K. & Lopez, R. (2012). Physical literacy for educators. Physical Education and Health Journal, 75 (3), 27-30.

Patnode, C.D., Lytle, L.A., Erickson, D.J., Sirard, J.R., Barr-Anderson, D.J., and Story, M. 2011. Physical activity and sedentary activity patterns among children and adolescents: A latent class analysis approach. *Journal of Physical Activity and Health,* 8, 457–467.

Placek, J.H. 1983. Conceptions of success in teaching: Busy, happy, and good? In *Teaching in physical education,* ed. T. Templin and J. Olsen, 46–56. Champaign, IL: Human Kinetics.

Silverman, S. 2011. Teaching for student learning in physical education. *JOPERD,* 82, 29–34.

SHAPE America. 2014. *National standards & grade-level outcomes for K–12 physical education.* Champaign, IL: Human Kinetics.

Stodden, D., Langendorfer, S., and Roberton, M. 2009. The association between motor skill competence and physical fitness in young adults. *Research Quarterly for Exercise and Sport,* 80(2), 223–229.

Strong, W.B., Malina, R.M., Blimkie, C.J., Daniels, S.R., Dishman, R.K., Gutin, B., Hergenroeder, A.C., Must, A., Nixon, P., Pivarnik, J.M., Rowland, T., Trost, S., and Trudeau, F. 2005. Evidence based physical activity for school-age youth. *Journal of Pediatrics,* 146, 732–737.

Whitehead, M. (2001). The concept of physical literacy. European Journal of Physical Education, 6, 127-138.

Chapter 2

Ericsson, K., Krampe, R., and Tesch-Romer, C. 1993. The role of deliberate practice in the acquisition of expert performance. *Psychological Review,* 100(3), 363–406.

Ericsson, K.A. 2006. The influence of experience and deliberate practice on the development of superior expert performance. In *The Cambridge handbook of expertise and expert performance,* ed. K.A. Ericsson, N. Charness, P.J. Feltovich, and R.R. Hoffman, 685–705. Cambridge, UK: Cambridge University Press.

Placek, J.H. 1983. Conceptions of success in teaching: Busy, happy, and good? In *Teaching in physical education,* ed. T. Templin and J. Olsen, 46–56. Champaign, IL: Human Kinetics.

SHAPE America. 2010. *Opportunity to learn: Guidelines for elementary school physical education.* Reston, VA: Author.

SHAPE America. 2014. *National standards & grade-level outcomes for K–12 physical education.* Champaign, IL: Human Kinetics.

Chapter 3

Corbin, C.B. 2001. The "untracking" of sedentary living: A call for action. *Pediatric Exercise Science*, 13, 347–356.

Ennis, C.D. 2010. On their own: Preparing students for a lifetime. Alliance Scholar Lecture, AAHPERD National Convention, Indianapolis, IN.

SHAPE America. 2014. *National standards & grade-level outcomes for K–12 physical education.* Champaign, IL: Human Kinetics.

Silverman, S. 2011. Teaching for student learning in physical education. *JOPERD*, 82(6), 29–34.

Chapter 4

Ayers, S.F., and M.J. Sariscsany, Eds., 2011. Physical education for lifelong fitness. 3rd ed. Reston, VA: National Association for Sport and Physical Education).

Corbin, C.B., Welk, G.J., Richardson, C., Vowell, C., Lambdin, D., and Wikgren, S. 2014. Youth physical fitness: 10 key concepts. *JOPERD*, 85(2), 24–31.

Graham, G., Holt/Hale, S.A., and Parker, M. 2013. *Children moving: A reflective approach to teaching physical education.* 9th ed. New York: McGraw-Hill.

Chapter 6

Gallahue, D.L., Ozmun, J., and Goodway, J. 2012. *Understanding motor development: Infants, children, adolescents, adults.* New York: McGraw-Hill.

Chapter 8

SHAPE America. 2014. *National standards & grade-level outcomes for K–12 physical education.* Champaign, IL: Human Kinetics.

Glossary

Corbin and Le Masurier, 2014. Fitness for life. 6th ed. Champaign, IL: Human Kinetics.

Gallahue, D.L., Ozmun, J., and Goodway, J. 2012. *Understanding motor development: Infants, children, adolescents, adults.* New York: McGraw-Hill.

Graham, G., Holt/Hale, S.A., and Parker, M. 2013. *Children moving: A reflective approach to teaching physical education.* 9th ed. New York: McGraw-Hill.

Ericsson, K., Krampe, R., and Tesch-Romer, C. 1993. The role of deliberate practice in the acquisition of expert performance. *Psychological Review*, 100(3), 363–406.

Mayo Clinic. 2010. Functional fitness training: Is it right for you? Retrieved from http://www.mayoclinic.com/health/functional-fitness/MY01378.

Schmidt, R.A. & Wrisberg, C.A. 2008. Motor learning and performance: A situation-based learning approach. 4th ed. Champaign, IL: Human Kinetics.

About the Authors

Shirley Holt/Hale, PhD, is a retired physical educator from Linden Elementary School in Oak Ridge, Tennessee, where she taught physical education for 38 years. Dr. Holt/Hale is a former National Elementary Physical Education Teacher of the Year and has served as president of both the American Alliance for Health, Physical Education, Recreation and Dance (now SHAPE America) and the National Association for Sport and Physical Education. She is the coauthor of *Children Moving: A Reflective Approach to Teaching Physical Education* (in its ninth edition), and a contributing author for three other texts. She served as a member of the task force for the revision of the *National Standards & Greade-Level Outcomes for K-12 Physical Education.* Dr. Holt/Hale is a consultant in elementary physical education curriculum, assessment, and curriculum mapping throughout the United States.

Tina J. Hall, PhD, is an associate professor in the department of health and human performance at Middle Tennessee State University. She taught elementary and middle school physical education for 18 years and has been in physical education teacher education since 2003. Dr. Hall has conducted numerous curriculum and content workshops and in-services for physical education teachers across the nation. She is the coauthor of *Schoolwide Physical Activity: A Comprehensive Guide to Designing and Conducting Programs* and *Teaching Children Gymnastics.* Dr. Hall is also an author of several articles in refereed publications.

About SHAPE America

SHAPE America – Society of Health and Physical Educators – is committed to ensuring that all children have the opportunity to lead healthy, physically active lives. As the nation's largest membership organization of health and physical education professionals, SHAPE America works with

its 50 state affiliates and is a founding partner of national initiatives including the Presidential Youth Fitness Program, *Let's Move!* Active Schools and the Jump Rope for Heart and Hoops for Heart programs.

Since its founding in 1885, the organization has defined excellence in physical education, most recently creating *National Standards & Grade-Level Outcomes for K-12 Physical Education* (2014), *National Standards & Guidelines for Physical Education Teacher Education (2009),* and *National Standards for Sport Coaches* (2006), and participating as a member of the Joint Committee on National Health Education Standards, which published *National Health Education Standards, Second Edition: Achieving Excellence* (2007). Our programs, products and services provide the leadership, professional development and advocacy that support health and physical educators at every level, from preschool through university graduate programs.

Every spring, SHAPE America hosts its National Convention & Expo, the premier national professional-development event for health and physical educators.

Advocacy is an essential element in the fulfillment of our mission. By speaking out for the school health and physical education professions, SHAPE America strives to make an impact on the national policy landscape.

Our Vision: Healthy People—Physically Educated and Physically Active!

Our Mission: To advance professional practice and promote research related to health and physical education, physical activity, dance and sport.

Our Commitment: 50 Million Strong by 2029

Approximately 50 million students are currently enrolled in America's elementary and secondary schools (grades pre-K to 12). SHAPE America is leading the effort to ensure that by the time today's preschoolers graduate from high school in 2029, all of America's students will have developed the skills, knowledge and confidence to enjoy healthy, meaningful physical activity.

One step can start a national movement.

Membership does more than advance your career—it's also your first step in a national movement to help all children become healthy, physically educated adults.

Joining SHAPE America Is Your First Step Toward:

- **Improving your instructional practices.** Membership is your direct connection to the books and other classroom resources, webinars, workshops, and professional development you need. **Members save up to 30%!**

- **Staying current on trends in education.** We will deliver the news to you through our weekly e-newsletter *Et Cetera*, our quarterly member newsletter *Momentum*, and peer-reviewed journals like *Strategies: A Journal for Physical and Sport Educators*, the *American Journal of Health Education*, *Journal of Physical Education, Recreation & Dance*, and *Research Quarterly for Exercise and Sport*.

- **Earning recognition for you and your program.** Showcase your school's achievements and gain funding through grant and award opportunities.

- **Growing your professional network.** Whether it's a face-to-face event or online through the member-exclusive community—Exchange—you'll gain access to a diverse group of peers who can help you respond to daily challenges.

Join Today.   www.shapeamerica.org/membership